THE
Tropical Fishkeeper's
HANDBOOK

THE
Tropical Fishkeeper's
HANDBOOK

KEVIN M FOX

ARGUS BOOKS

Argus Books
Argus House
Boundary Way
Hemel Hempstead
Herts HP2 7ST
England

First published by Argus Books 1992

ISBN 1 85486 069 0

Phototypesetting by Photoprint, Torquay
Printed and bound in Great Britain by Clays Ltd., St Ives plc, Bungay

Contents

Acknowledgements & Thanks

My grateful thanks and sincere appreciation to the following, without whose help this book would not have been possible. To anyone I've missed: sorry and thanks.

Doctor Neville Carrington for bravely keeping up with the barrage of letters I fired at him, and for all the invaluable information he so kindly supplied. To The World Famous Cichlid Expert Mary Bailey, for scientifically validating the typescript as well as being a good friend to me when I needed one most. Tim Vincent, of Rolf C Hagen (UK) company, for his generous help and for showing me around the place. Mrs Janet Cruise of JMC Aquatics, for permission to photograph and to borrow various equipment from The International Aquatic Centre, Sheffield, and to the shop's manager, David Redfern, for putting up with me (his shop has the cleanest tank fronts in the world, I wonder if that was why I was so welcome?).

To Phillip, the owner of Superpets, Worksop Notts. For all his expertise, his interest in the book, and his unbelievable generosity to me personally. Thanks Phil (g'on, who's breeding the Guppies?). Thanks to Aquarian for their kind permission to reproduce one of their charts. Thanks also to: Interpet, Tetra, King British, Medcalf Brothers, Sera (UK), Hockney, NT Laboratories for generously supplying literature. Thanks to the guys at Rocon for sorting out my Digi-Stat (see, you never know who you're talking to on the telephone!), thanks also to Chris Clark of the Anabantoid Association Of Great Britain, for allowing me to share one of their meetings. Thanks to Steve Windsor, of *Practical Fishkeeping* magazine, for putting me in touch with Mary Bailey.

Finally, and much closer to home. My gratitude and thanks to Bob and Barry Sinclair, for printing-out the typescript, to Carlos – who did all the usual. Thanks to everyone at Rotherham District General Hospital, for allowing space for me to create this book. My sincere appreciation and gratitude to the following, for putting me back together yet again. Sisters Thompson, Lawson and Pepper, of wards A3, A4 and B2 respectively. Also to the incredibly skilful Doctor Bardhan and his capable team. Last but by no means least, my own family and Argus Books, for bearing with me. Bless you all.

Preface

It is not given to all of us to be successful sportsmen or women; few of us can afford to go flying or ocean racing; not everyone has the talent needed to paint or make music. But there is one hobby which is open to anyone and everyone: I refer, of course, to the subject of this book – fishkeeping.

In the course of many years as an 'aquatic agony aunt' I have heard from people in all walks of life; with an age range of a few years old right up to the occasional nonagenarian; from the fighting fit to the severely handicapped. The degree of involvement can range from an 18″ tank through to a palatial fish-house, from aesthetic pleasure to serious scientific study. There are relatively sane people with a single attractive aquascape in their living-room; and lunatics who devote every spare minute and most of their money to their fishes. But all these people have one thing in common – they are all aquarists, and they all share a tremendous enthusiasm for their hobby, at whatever level they have chosen to follow it.

It is also a very affordable pastime. Although it is possible to spend a small fortune on a large hi-tech set-up full of rare and expensive fishes, a very attractive aquarium can be established for a relatively small outlay on equipment and occupants. Running costs are normally rather less than those of the television, and many would rate the entertainment and educational value rather higher!

The beginner may, however, find himself rather daunted by the huge array of equipment and choice of fishes that confronts him as he takes his first tentative steps into this fascinating hobby. He will quickly realise that he has to get everything right at the first attempt in order to avoid causing harm and suffering to the little lives for which he will be responsible. This book, with its unique approach, will not only guide him safely through this initial confusion, but also act as a valuable work of reference for the years to come.

Mary Bailey

Foreword

Not many years ago, fishkeeping was considered to be a rather oddball hobby. Possibly a combination of factors has been responsible for changing this so that in the UK alone about 10 per cent of families now keep fish.

Fishkeeping is an appealing hobby for many reasons. Some people simply want to keep fish as an attractive form of live decoration in their home. An aquarium also acts as a focal point of interest in a waiting room, a hospital ward, etc. For those who wish to become more involved it is a hobby which can take as much or as little time as you wish. Aquarium keeping can embrace almost every field of science from biology to chemistry to chemical engineering and must have sparked off initial interest to very many individuals in these professions. Fishkeeping is an ideal hobby for the very young, for the family man or woman and for the retired besides being an invaluable and useful pastime for those lacking full mobility.

There are many other obvious advantages to keeping fish. For instance, you do not have to take them for walks every day and you can generally leave them without attention for one or two weeks while you go on holiday. There are lots of interesting aquariums all over the world and there is a worldwide camaraderie of fish clubs.

One of the factors which must have increased the popularity of the hobby in the last few years is the dramatic improvement in technology and the understanding of water chemistry. Both these subjects must be very confusing, particularly for the beginner, and Kevin must be congratulated in helping to clarify the subject in the unusual and practical approach adopted in this book.

Dr Neville Carrington Ph.D

THE
Tropical Fishkeeper's
HANDBOOK

Introduction

If you are interested in fish – if you want to know more about their lives, what they eat, how they sleep, hear, swim, smell, talk to each other, behave, and reproduce themselves – then that makes you an *Aquarist*, and this book was written just for you. It will take you stage-by-stage, with full explanations and pictorial guides along the way, through the complete process of setting up a display of tropical fishes. But it doesn't end there! Once you have created a suitable biosphere, the *Handbook* then continues with how to keep your fish healthy and contented, how to breed them, exhibit them at a fish show, and even where to go next.

Tropical fishkeeping is a peaceful, educational and stress-free hobby which cuts right through all artificially created barriers. It is a non-sexist, non-racist, completely classless pursuit where age and/or money are meaningless. Creating an artificial biosphere within your living room where fishes can live happily, and even reproduce themselves, seems to hold a delightful fascination for millions of people from all walks of life around the world. It really is amazing how just a few minutes spent watching your fishes enjoying a game of chase around the aquarium can ease away hours of daily stress! Housebound and disabled people can follow the hobby with the same enthusiasm and, often more importantly, the same level of success as their more able-bodied counterparts. Therefore, everyone is able to enjoy the hobby with complete equality!

Is Fishkeeping Cruel?

In a word: no. If it was, then I wouldn't have anything to do with it at all. As you will see later, in the *Conservation Debate*, there are specific matters to be discussed. However, there are certain 'groups' of severely misinformed people who maintain that to keep fish well fed, in practically 'perfect' water conditions, free from predation and disease, is somehow hurting them dreadfully.

Many aquarists spend a great deal of time and money in re-creating water which, at the very minimum, mimics that found in the fishes' natural environments. Often aquarists go much further and remove harmful toxins and bacteria from the water, ensure that their fishes get fed a well-balanced, nutritious diet, and that they are not subject to predation. In practice, this means that the average tropical fish's chances of survival to a ripe old age are lengthened enormously when looked after by an aquarist. In the wild their survival time is often measured in days!

I'd Like To Keep Tropical Fish But . . .

Many people have the mistaken idea that keeping tropical fishes means that you need Greek shipping connections to finance the hobby. Of course, what you spend depends on the depth of your pocket.

Assuming that you're going to be buying new materials throughout, then £100 will set you up very nicely indeed; including everything, even a few fishes. Of course you can economise and spend around £60. If you're good with your hands – and making your own all-glass aquarium is a very simple process – then the cost will drop even further, down to around £40. And then there's the second-hand market. In my local free newspaper, there are usually two, and often more, 90×30×30 cm (36×12×12 in) aquaria, usually offered complete with all accessories, for around £25–£45 each. However, buying second-hand aquaria needs special care: not everyone keeps fish in fish tanks!

But My Neighbour Started Keeping Fishes And They All Died!

But he didn't have the benefit of reading *The Tropical Fishkeeper's Handbook* first, did he? If he had, he would have realised why his fishes had died and would have been able to stop it. Many people enter the hobby purely because they want an upmarket, living, colourful room ornament. Such people want instant results. If you're of a like mind, then I have to tell you now that some of the aquaria illustrated within this book have taken months, often years, to get to this level. There are no short cuts – try them and the fishes die.

Becoming an aquarist – a person who's interested in the daily lives and behaviour of fishes – requires a certain level of commitment from you in terms of time. Although this time commitment is never onerous, and is often the most enjoyable part of the hobby, such as feeding the fish, it has to be done on a regular basis. You can never simply say: 'Oh, I don't feel like bothering today!' You have to bother, that day and every other day too. Becoming an aquarist means that you have accepted complete responsibility for the lives of living creatures. By your hand alone they will flourish and reproduce; or suffer horrendously and die a slow and often painful death. As with all creatures on earth, the level of care you give to them should be no less than you would demand and expect for yourself, be that creature an ant or your mother.

All The Latest News

This book contains the very latest information on all matters relating to tropical fishes. Indeed, its publication was specifically delayed so that changes to aquarium electrical equipment, as specified under new EEC regulations, could be included and the new equipment explained and reviewed. Unfortunately, the Common Market cannot reach common agreement, and no-one can standardise the standard! In any case, the implementation of the new safety regulations

Kissing gouramis. The kissing isn't thought to be affectionate, more a trial of strength, with the weaker fish 'giving ground' to the stronger fish.

has now been deferred until 1994! You will also find the latest situation regarding medicaments and chemicals withdrawn from open sale to aquarists, and the results and conclusions (if any) of any conservation policies affecting the keeping of freshwater fishes.

Value For Money?

I've attempted to do the impossible. Most beginner's books on setting up your first aquarium are excellent. The trouble is, once the tank is up and running, the book is no longer of any use to you. I wanted to write an up-to-date book, which included information on all of the new aquarium technology, the latest ideas and concepts, and also snatch a glimpse into the next century to see where fishkeeping will be in twenty years' time.

I've also tried to write a book which will grow along with you as your aquatic skills develop and mature, so that you won't have to throw it away and buy a more advanced book. All of the basic information the newcomer to the hobby needs to set up his or her first aquarium is here. But what then? A quick glance at the contents page will show you the ground covered by this book.

At first, much of the information contained within will seem unnecessary, even baffling, to the newcomer. But in every case, I've made a very clear distinction between what a newcomer must do immediately, and why it has to be done, and what may safely be left until more experience has been acquired, and why it can be left until later. For example, I've strongly advised the newcomer to avoid tampering with the chemical nature of the domestic water supply until more experience has been gained. (In actual fact, I've encouraged you to practise on a spare tank which holds no fishes.)

Changing just one aspect of the basic water chemistry has a knock-on effect on everything else in the water as well. Fairly soon, the newcomer becomes so confused that the pH in the aquarium is going up and down about as quickly as his blood pressure! But this information is necessary. You cannot change things without understanding the fundamental reasons why things are the way they are to begin with. You cannot use a map to find a route out of a forest if you've no clue as to your present position on the map. Once you know where you are, well . . . that's exactly what *The Tropical Fishkeeper's Handbook* is all about. It demonstrates where you are now and shows you many routes into the future.

Making A Start

Over the years, aquarists have made ready use of advanced technology to create more natural conditions for their fishes. However, the hobby of fishkeeping is such that it is possible to enter at many levels. It can be as simple – as easy as adding water to a bowl – or as complicated as you choose to make it. From a fairground goldfish (kept in a suitable container, of course) right up to a computer-controlled, bio-feedback adjustable, six foot aquascape containing a family of beautiful Discus fishes.

You may choose to buy one of the many and extremely popular *complete biosphere aquariums*, which have built-in heating, lighting, aeration and filter equipment, all hidden from view so there are no external boxes, switches or pipes to clutter up your display, and just a single electric plug. At the other end of the scale you can build your own tank, hood and stand, add your own filtration system and arrange whatever lighting suits you best. The average aquarist falls somewhere between these two extremes. What you most certainly do not need to be is a marine biologist!

The newcomer is encouraged to begin his/her aquatic career by starting with a Community Tank – that's an aquarium which is set up to cope with a variety of fishes from around the world. I know that beginners are *always* told to start with a community aquarium, and I make no apology for continuing this 'tradition'. There is a very good reason for this as there are numerous advantages to the community tank as opposed to the species tank.

A fish's-eye view of its aquatic world.

First and foremost, creating a community tank requires the water to be around neutral pH and average hardness, because many of the fishes intended to be kept come from a variety of different, natural water conditions, ranging from soft to hard, and acid to alkaline. Striking a mean level of both pH and hardness gives the fishes their best chance of adapting to your local water conditions. (Don't worry what these terms mean yet, they're all fully explained later on.) And that's the usual type of water which the majority of aquarists find coming out of their taps. So the first advantage of a community tank is that you can use your domestic water supply without having to make major adjustments to its chemical make-up. Other advantages include keeping a range of different species all of which act, feed, swim and generally behave in a distinctly different way to the other fishes kept in the community tank.

The Young Aquarist

Where young people are concerned, enthusiasm may outstrip their patience and knowledge level. Therefore, parents must ensure that children fully understand exactly what they're taking on, and be prepared to assume a background supervisory role; maybe even take over when the going gets tough! Within fishkeeping there is a huge educational potential for the young (and not so young!) mind to get to grips with. Firstly there is biology. What actually is a fish; why, where and how does it differ from other animals and how can it breathe underwater? Why do some mothers protect their

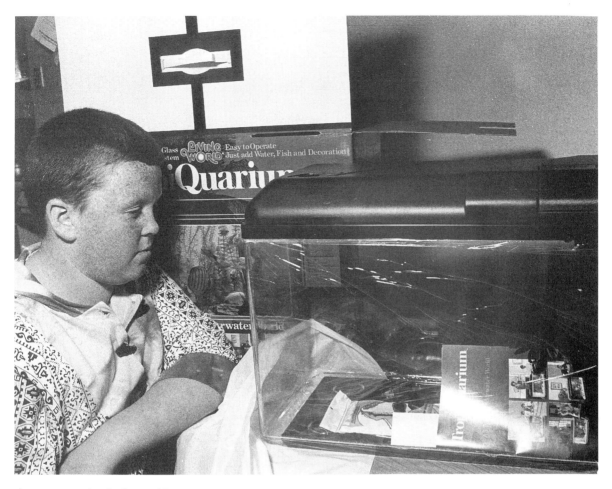

A young aquarist checks out his new purchases.

babies by scooping them up into their mouths when danger threatens, and spit them all clear again once the hazard has gone?

Then there's chemistry such as the aquarium water, technology in the shape of fishkeeping hardware, geography – where do fish come from? Botany – how can a plant grow underwater and how do you plant them? In short, fishkeeping is a most powerful learning tool: the children want to learn, they want to read and find out more because they become so fascinated and involved with their very own aquarium. Just as I taught my son to swim like a fish when he was two, he now thinks like one having just turned eleven!

Units Of Measurement

The UK's system of weights and measures is, at the moment, very confusing. We are going through a transitional stage, where my young son can't understand a yard, and I can't (or won't!) visualise a metre. In this book, litres and centimetres are used as the basic units of volume and size, with inches and gallons in parenthesis. The same for area calculations, cm^2 (inch^2). Temperatures are in degrees Celsius (with *no* Fahrenheit conversions!), but there are Celsius/Fahrenheit Fahrenheit/Celsius conversion formulae in Appendix 2. Wherever appropriate, US gallons have been given.

**An Angelfish. The one fish
all beginners seem to want.**

The only other metric measure used is milligrams per litre, (mg/l) which is exactly the same as saying Parts Per Million (ppm) – 50 mg/l is precisely the same as 50 ppm. Where various levels of substances in the aquarium water are mentioned as so many mg/l, I'll explain what levels are reasonable and what levels are toxic.

The Conservation Debate

In the UK, aquarist shops obtain their fishes from one or more of the following sources – direct imports from breeding farms, mostly in Asia and America, imported wild-caught fish, commercial breeders in the UK and Europe, and occasionally from amateur (you and me) fish breeders, mostly in Britain.

It has become apparent that certain species of fish are becoming quite rare in their natural habitat, mainly due to local pollution problems. Consequently there is a move towards severely restricting in some cases, and in others completely banning, their exportation. This won't affect a newcomer to the tropical fishkeeping hobby. In this book, all of the species discussed and recommended will almost certainly have either been bred in the UK or come from one of the specialist breeding farms, such as those in Florida and Singapore. In other words they won't have been captured live from their natural waters. By the way, many amateur aquarists are heavily involved with the breeding of rarer species so that they do not have to be captured and then imported from the wild.

And Finally

This book was written by an enthusiast for other enthusiasts, and not by a staff writer working for some publisher, who probably has no real interest in fishkeeping at all. What I've written is backed up by knowledge gained by three decades in the hobby. I've received no commission (in any shape or form – I only wish I had!), from any of the companies or manufacturers mentioned within the book. Neither am I connected with them professionally in any way. Therefore, my comments on various pieces of equipment used are entirely my own subjective opinions, based purely on usage.

None of the equipment borrowed or bought was put into a test-bed situation, just to see if the manufacturer's claims could be checked as being true. All I did was to simply do exactly what you would. I followed the instruction book closely, assembled the gear and then used it. It then either did its designed job or it didn't. If it didn't, then I have said so; and I don't care what anyone else says: if it didn't work for me, then it didn't work for me: end of story!

Similarly, no conclusions should be drawn just because a particular company hasn't been referred to within the book. Those companies and people which have been named in the book are those who actually answered my letters and in many cases have gone to a great deal of personal trouble on my behalf. Companies not mentioned are simply those who never answered my (often numerous) letters; so as I know nothing of them or their products, I can hardly tell you anything about them, can I?

Chapter 1
What Is A Fish?

Fishes are the most successful group of vertebrate animals on earth, with over thirty thousand different species already known and catalogued, and more being discovered each year. Such a large number of species indicates clearly that fishes must be highly adaptable, and indeed this is what we find. From a temporary rain-filled African puddle to the deepest ocean abyss, fish occupy almost every drop of water on the planet.

The Chinese have been breeeding fancy Goldfishes for centuries. It is often difficult to reconcile the fancy Goldfish with its progenitor, the common Goldfish.

An adult Dwarf gourami. Its brilliant, iridescent colours make it a firm favourite in the community tank.

The common Goldfish.

Protofish first appeared on earth around forty million years ago. Since then they have been evolving, and of course still continue to do so. For thousands of years their evolution has been modified somewhat by man's intentional tinkering with genetics at the breeding stage. Witness the current range of ornamental coldwater fishes. Apart from a similarity of colouring, it is very difficult to reconcile the fancy goldfishes with their progenitor, the common Goldfish (*Carassius auratus*), cultivated for more than a thousand years by the Chinese.

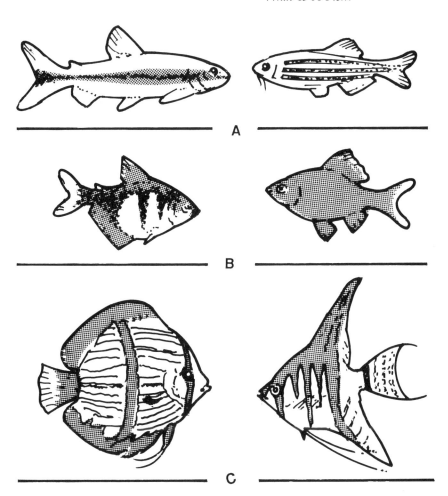

Figure 1.1 **The body shape of a fish tells us much about its natural habitat. The sleek, torpedo-shaped fishes, as in 'A', prefer fast-moving water and are fast swimmers. Fishes in the 'B' group are deeper bodied, more muscular and occupy the middle areas of slow, strong rivers. Fishes shown in 'C' are also deep bodied but narrow. They prefer very slow or still water, relying on their body markings to keep them safe from predators.**

Body Shape

Because fishes spend their lives in water, their biology and physiology have evolved to allow them to survive and flourish in this environment. You can actually tell much about a fish just from its body shape – things such as the main type of food it prefers and where it finds it, whether it likes fast or slow moving water, whether it's a quick or a slow swimmer.

Scales

Externally, most fishes are covered in bony plates called *scales*. These act as a form of chain-mail armour, to protect them from predation and parasitic attack. Sometimes the scales are so small that they can't be seen without a microscope – the fish looks like it's covered with actual skin tissue. Like the circles in a tree stump, fishes produce growth rings in their scales from which we can calculate their age. Some catfishes don't have scales as such. Instead they have large overlapping bony plates called *scutes*. Very few fishes have no scales at all.

Fish usually have a slimy mucus covering over their bodies. This is perfectly natural, and is not an intrinsic health problem. This slimy coating exists as a shield, protecting them from infection, and also helps the fishes 'slip' more easily through the water, reducing drag.

Some fishes don't have scales. This Catfish has overlapping bony plates known as 'Scutes' instead.

As much as possible you should avoid hand contact with fishes. They are exothermic – they acquire their body temperature from the heat of their surroundings i.e. warm water, warm blood, cold water, cool blood. By directly handling them you can accidentally cause quite a lot of pain just from the heat of your hand. You may also rub off some of their protective mucus, and leave a way open for parasitic or bacterial attack and infection.

Fins

To give them mobility, fish are equipped with various fins, which are just the same to them as arms and legs are to us. Some of the fins are paired, one each side of the body, such as the pectoral and pelvic fins. There are a number of important points concerning fins. As they vary so greatly between species, Ichthyologists –

1. Anterior dorsal fin
2. Posterior dorsal
3. Caudal
4. Anal
5. Pectoral (paired)
6. Pelvic / ventral (paired)
7. Caudal peduncle
8. Nostrils
9. Operculum
10. Lateral line

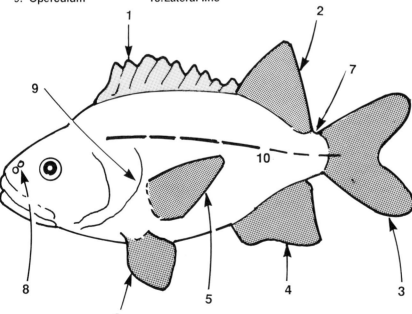

Figure 1.2 Position and names of fins.

scientists who study fish – use them to help decide to which family a fish belongs. Figure 1.2 shows where the fins are located on the body, and their special names.

Pectoral fins are used for fine position adjustment, much like the hydroplanes on a submarine. Using these fins, singly or in pairs, fish can move up and down in the water, turn right and left or even use them as brakes to stop instantly. Pelvic, sometimes called ventral fins, are again paired. As well as assisting the pectoral fins for changes in depth and position, they act together with the dorsal fin on the fish's back to provide stability as it swims through the water, stopping it from rolling over. If you consider the set of flights on a dart or an arrow, the pelvic fins act in the same way as horizontal flights, while the dorsal and anal fins are similar to the vertical flights of an arrow.

Much like the dorsal, the anal fin helps to stabilise the fish. It works like the keel of a ship, or the centreboard of a sailing dinghy. The adipose fin seems to be a remnant of evolution, much like the coccyx in a human spine. They both appear to serve no purpose.

The appendage which provides fishes with their main method of forward propulsion is the caudal (tail) fin. This is often very powerful, enabling high speeds to be achieved through water. The caudal fin is also used as a rudder for major changes in direction. Again, much information regarding the fish's habits may be

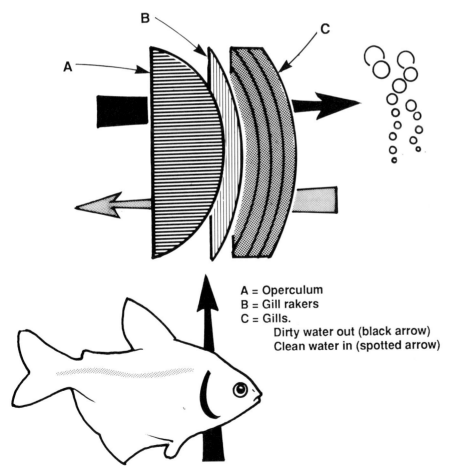

A = Operculum
B = Gill rakers
C = Gills.
Dirty water out (black arrow)
Clean water in (spotted arrow)

Figure 1.3   The gill system at work.

obtained from the shape and size of their various fins.

Fins come in a wide variety of colour, shape and size. Some of them have evolved into special purpose tools, like the pectoral fins of the Climbing Perch, which give it locomotion over land, or the hair-like pelvic fins of certain Anabantids, which contain touch, taste and smell receptor cells. Fins are often braced for strength with hard rays. For example, the dorsals of some fishes have hard, spiny rays at the front (anterior) part of the fin, and soft rays at the back (posterior). This helps them keep the fin erect and, in some species, also acts as insurance against being eaten. By erecting the anterior spined ray, the prey fish causes the predator to choke and regurgitate its intended meal.

Male Siamese fighting fish. So-called because, should two males meet, they will often fight to the point of utter exhaustion, when the weaker fish will die.

Breathing

All fish breathe. They do this mainly by absorbing oxygen dissolved in water through their gill system. On the fish's head, just behind the eyes, are two relatively large semicircular slits called the gill plates (*opercula*). Under these protective hard bony covers lie the actual gill mechanisms, which are further protected against floating debris by a system of fine bones, acting as mechanical filters, and called gill rakers. To breathe, the fish opens its mouth and sucks in water. On closing, water is pushed down the throat under pressure, and out through the gills, which works in much the same way for fishes as lungs do for humans. Gills give up gases such as carbon dioxide and ammonia, plus a little bodily fluid (see *Osmosis*, p34) to the water passing over them, and then absorb fresh oxygen. Of course, just like us, fishes don't have to think about breathing – it all happens automatically.

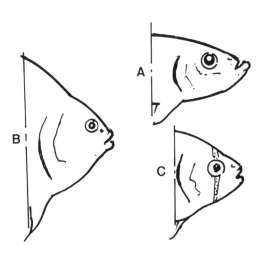

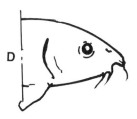

A = Superior – surface feeder
B/C = Terminal – all–level feeder
D = Inferior – bottom feeder

Figure 1.4   Mouth shape and meaning.

One litre of atmospheric air contains around 200 millilitres of oxygen. But one litre of water *saturated* with air, at a constant 10 degrees Celsius, contains only around 9–11 millilitres, and very much less in warm or dirty water. Fishes also have far less oxygen-carrying red blood cells in a given volume than have humans. Therefore, the gill system has to be very efficient if they're to extract enough oxygen to sustain life. Fortunately, the fishes' dissolved oxygen needs are slight, and nowhere near as great as some aquarists claim!

Auxiliary Breathing

With certain fishes, such as Anabantids (Gouramis etc.), their natural environment can, and often does, become very dirty and hot which leads to greatly depleted levels of dissolved oxygen, and certainly not nearly enough for them to continue breathing via their gills alone. These fishes have evolved a special feature which permits them to take some of their oxygen requirement directly from the atmosphere; this is called *aerobic* breathing.

Inside their body, behind the head, they have a curled tube called the *labyrinth organ*. The Anabantoid fish swims to the surface, takes a gulp of air and then passes the resulting bubble into the labyrinth organ, where the oxygen is then absorbed into the bloodstream.

The Swim Bladder

Within the abdominal cavity of a fish lies the swim bladder. Note that not all species have

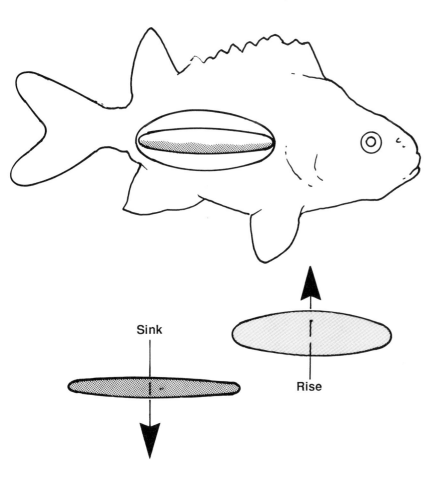

Sink

Rise

Figure 1.5 The swim bladder. When it fills with air, it causes the fish to rise, and when it empties, the fish sinks. Neutral bouyancy is the balance between air/size of the swim bladder.

one. The purpose of this organ is to regulate the buoyancy of the fish. The swim bladder is filled either from a gulp of air at the surface, passing it via an oesophagus-like connection into the swim bladder, or by gases accreting within it from the bloodstream. In both cases, the swim bladder contains an amount of oxygen and various other gases.

Some fishes have negative buoyancy – they're heavier than water. For them to remain still in a liquid environment, hovering at a fixed depth is very difficult. They have to use all their various fins and work quite hard just to stay still.

Fishes with a swim bladder have neutral buoyancy - they're neither heavier nor lighter than water. For such fishes to change depth, to move upwards or downwards, the swim bladder performs in a very similar way to the trim tanks of a submarine. To rise, the fish uses its fins to head in the desired direction. As it moves upwards, water pressure decreases and the volume of gases in the swim bladder is increased, automatically maintaining neutral buoyancy. The fish can now stop using its fins and still hold position. When the fish swims deeper, the reverse happens. As water pressure increases, gases are expelled from the swim bladder, again maintaining the fish's neutral buoyancy.

Fishes have no conscious control over activity

Just about every way imaginable is used by fishes to gather food. Here, a Butterfly fish lies at the surface, its mouth waiting for a passing insect.

of their swim bladders much as we humans don't really have to think about breathing (unless it becomes a problem, of course!). It works automatically, according to the pressure of the water acting upon the body. As the fish swims downwards or upwards, its body cavity expands and contracts forcing the gases in the swim bladder out or in, adjusting automatically to the current depth.

Illness which affects the swim bladder produces a characteristic behaviour pattern by the fishes. They adopt strange swimming postures such as tilts and lists, or even floating upside-down, although there is actually one fish which swims upside-down most of the time! I told you that fish exhibit varied and wonderful behaviour patterns!

Sex, Size And Colour

Apart from their fascinating behaviour, colour is probably the greatest attraction to the hobby fishkeeper. Colour in fishes is achieved by two main processes – pigmentation cells within the dermis, and/or a layer of guanin, an excretory waste product stored by some fishes under the surface of the epidermis, the outer skin layer. Pigmentation cells are genetically inherited, and are directly linked to the central nervous system. When stressed, colours may fade or darken, according to species. At breeding time, colour deepens and becomes much more striking, fulfilling its job of attracting mates.

Guanin, basically made up from urine, is a highly reflective silvery material which gives fish an iridescent, sparkling look. Under certain types of lighting, the guanin layer can give out a *moiré* pattern of multi-hued, rainbow-like reflections, which can often look quite stunning. There are some fish which have no colour at all, such as the so called Glass, or X-ray Catfishes, which should never be kept singly. Buy at least a shoal of four.

Many fishes use colour as a form of camouflage, for example the dark bars of the Angel and the Discus fishes, *Pterophyllum scalare*, and *Symphysodon discus* respectively. These

The female Guppy is much larger and less coloured than the male.

fishes' natural environment is reedy, still water. They swim in and out of the reed beds, where their dark vertical bars on their flanks perfectly match the upright patterns of light and shade between the tall stems of these types of plants. However, local pollution and other troubles have caused many fishes to move away from their traditional habitats into areas not usually associated with that species.

With schooling fishes, colour is a 'uniform' identifying a swimming partner as acceptable, 'one of the boys' and not to be feared. Colour also acts as a warning to others, telling them to keep well away.

Colour has yet another function for fishes, that associated with sex. Male fish are often far more highly coloured than females – see the differences between the male and female Guppy (*Poecilia reticulata*). Males use their brilliant hues to attract mates. During the spawning cycle, they make great efforts to show off their colours to good effect by erecting or opening all their finnage, causing the various hues and patterns to intensify greatly, and hopefully impress a female.

Fish size varies greatly. Sizes quoted in Chapter 10 *Database of Community Fishes* are maxima, reached under ideal conditions, which are, by the way, easily realisable in the 'perfect' setting of an aquarium, where the fish are much better

A = Eyesight   B = Nostrils (smell)   C = Mouth (taste)
D = Pressure / vibration (lateral line)   E = Smell distribution – anus / breathing (from)
F = Touch

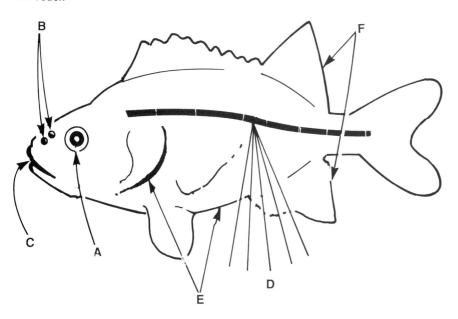

Figure 1.6 Fish sense receptors and locations.

protected than in the wild. A crowded aquarium will restrict the growth of all the fish within it, as will incorrect feeding, temperature and water quality.

Fishes do actually sleep, in the sense that there is a part of the day when all their bodily functions slow to the point of stillness. Their metabolic rate decreases as does the rhythmic opening and closing of the gill covers. They don't close their eyes, though, because they don't actually have eyelids.

Sense

Smell

Just like us, fishes can hear, see, smell, taste and touch, although these senses (plus others we don't have) are adapted for living in water. Fishes smell using their nostrils, two or four little holes on their forehead (snout) connected directly to that part of the brain dealing with the olfactory sense. Unlike ours, a fish's nostrils are not used for breathing. Although their sense of smell is in some species not generally highly developed, certain fishes have a very strong response to a specific odour, and can detect it from phenomenal distances. Both shark and piranha can go into an absolute feeding frenzy in the wild on detecting the smell of fresh blood in the water, especially if they're hungry!

Taste

Taste cells are grouped mainly around the mouth and tongue, although they can extend up onto the head for certain species. Some fish have their taste receptors on various appendages, such as on barbels (whiskers) around the mouths of catfishes, and at the end of the pelvic fins on gouramis. Taste sense, again, is mainly concerned with the suitability of a possible food supply. Humans use memory and smell for identification and classification of odours; fishes apparently don't, each smell is a new experience for them and classified as either good or bad to eat. I'm not aware of any current research which links a fish's olfactory sense with memory.

Eyesight

Fish eyes are similar to ours, in that they contain the same basic features of rods and cones for colour detection, cornea, iris and lens. However, due to their globular lens and flat cornea, they are very shortsighted and cannot see very far underwater. This isn't a problem because visibility in water is usually restricted anyway. Fish can see colours and are able to differentiate between them – ask any fisherman. But, they are able to perceive much further into the ultraviolet and near infra-red parts of the electromagnetic spectrum than humans. This extended colour response helps them locate food and avoid predators.

Human eyes offer stereoscopic vision – the sight from each eye overlaps, giving a three dimensional image. This makes the judging of distance and perspective a simple matter for us. However, due to their location on either side of the head, fishes' eyes give mainly monocular vision – the image from each eye remains a separate view. This type of eyesight confuses perspective and distorts distance, making it difficult to gauge just how far away that tasty morsel actually is. Fishes do have other senses which make up for this, and which often prove much more reliable for judging distance, and warning of danger, such as the already mentioned extended colour response to ultraviolet and infra-red light, as well as an ability to detect both changes in pressure and vibrations in their aquatic environment – see later.

Some fishes don't have eyes at all – the Blind Cave Characin, for example – and others have limited eyesight. Such fish don't find this a particular handicap as they have other senses which more than compensate for this. Obviously, if a fish has no eyes at all then they're not required in its natural habitat.

Hearing And Touch

Ears on fish perform much the same function as

in humans, ie. balance and detection of sound waves. The two ears are sited inside the skull, with no external openings. Sound travels much better through water than air, due to the former's greater density. Therefore, fish ears don't have to be as sensitive as ours. They can hear approximately the same range of audio frequencies as us, but they are much more attuned to specific frequencies and sounds, particularly those of their own species.

The hearing system in fishes is linked with their sense of touch. And particularly in fish with either no or poor eyesight, these two senses combine to provide all the necessary information regarding navigation and position. Scattered around their bodies, on barbels and various fins, are sensors which detect touch.

Yet another sense fishes have, which is like a combination of hearing and touch, is pressure, or vibration sensing. Around the body, but particularly along the flanks, are cells directly connected to the central nervous system which can detect differences in pressure caused by vibrations in the water. The lateral line, clearly marked in many species, is a row of sensor 'portholes' along the flanks of the fish. These cells can detect vibrations and changes of pressure in the water, caused by the swimming movements of other aquatic organisms.

By comparing the received 'signals' from sensors around its body, the fish can pinpoint the source, and gauge distance from the strength of the 'echoes'. It can then either swim away from or towards the source, depending on how it interprets the information. New research into fish sense, and how they navigate in often impossible situations, such as zero visibility, indicates that certain fishes emit a weak radar-like electro-magnetic field from their bodies and, from the pattern of received reflections, can successfully navigate, and remain aware of, any other aquatic neighbours.

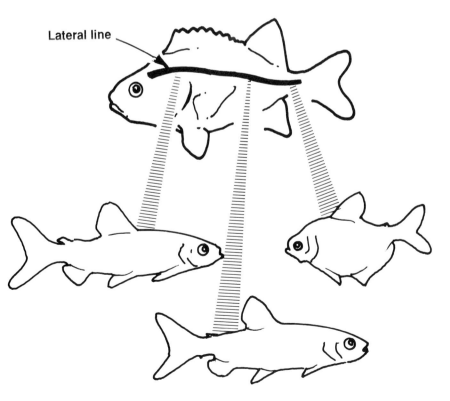

Lateral line

Figure 1.7 Lateral line 'radar' emissions. A fish uses its lateral line to sense changes in pressure, and detect vibrations and changes in the Earth's magnetic field. Some species even have a kind of 'radar' which emits an electro-magnetic field and receives the echoes. This provides information on its location and neighbours.

What Is A Happy Fish?

Later in this book you are going to create a community tank of tropical fishes. This means an aquarium stocked with examples of species from different countries around the world which, although they have their own unique requirements, do share enough common characteristics to enable them to live peaceably together. But it's not enough just to ensure that the fish won't actually kill each other: that's not what a community aquarium is about at all. The fishes must be able to live as natural a life as possible and to do this they must be happy fish, which invites the question: exactly what is a happy fish?

A fish will be happy if: a) it continues to live a safe and healthy life, b) it obtains enough food and c) is able to reproduce. Not much to ask is it? You now know quite a lot about basic fish biology and what conditions must exist for survival. In later chapters, you will also learn about the equipment needed, and the quality of water to provide, so by the time you are ready to set up your community tank you will know exactly what items you have to buy, why they're needed and their purpose. And you will have happy fish.

Fish Names

Most aquarists refer to their fishes by nicknames, such as Guppies, or Swordtails etc. The only problem is that often these nicknames vary from country to country, and even within the same country from shop to shop. Chapter 10 *Database of Community Fishes* lists the most common community fish with their full trinominal, latinised name as well as their usual familiar names. Even if you can't get your tongue around the name, at least you'll know what the fish looks like!

Chapter 2
Water

The most important factor in a fish's life is the water it lives in. Your success as an aquarist is entirely dependent on the quality of this liquid. However, water is usually one of the things most newcomers have the greatest difficulty with. The important thing is to recognise where problems may arise and be prepared to meet them.

Water Water Everywhere

Even though our awareness of water in the 1990s has been raised considerably by events such as the privatisation of water companies, drought, hosepipe bans and domestic supply pollution, there aren't too many who wonder how it arrives at our taps in the first place. As a keeper of fish, you have to delve a little deeper. After all, water means as much to fish as air does to you.

For success as an aquarist, you must get the aquatic environment of your aquarium right. Neither success nor progress will come your way at all until you do. Fish will not survive nor will plants grow if this is not so. I've tried to present a very complex subject in a non-technical manner, but there's much I've had to leave out due to restrictions on space. No one expects you to become a chemist simply by reading this book. Nevertheless, the more you understand, then the easier it will be for you to create and maintain the correct water conditions within your aquarium. And there's certainly enough information here to help you achieve this.

In my own opinion, it is now no longer safe to take water directly from your tap and use it to top-up or even fill your aquarium, without special treatment first. I have a letter from the Yorkshire Water Company, confirming this statement. To make direct use of tapwater is to take an avoidable risk with the lives of your fishes. Exactly why this is so, we'll discover later when I explain how your local water company collects, treats and distributes your domestic water supply. And no, it really isn't fair to blame them for this deplorable state of affairs. In fact we're all equally guilty at some level.

The Water Cycle

Most of this planet is covered with water, mainly salt. Only the minor part of earth's water is 'freshwater' ie, not salt. While the make-up and salinity level of sea water is much the same all over the world, and has been so for millions of years, ponds, lakes, streams and rivers of freshwater vary considerably in their basic make-up. What causes these vast differences?

Water circulates in a never-ending process of evaporation and precipitation. Surface water from oceans, lakes and rivers is heated by the sun, causing it to evaporate into the atmosphere, where it forms clouds. These white masses of minute water droplets then roam the earth releasing their liquid cargo when conditions permit, completing the cycle by returning water to the surface. On evaporation, water is distilled and relatively pure. It has few dissolved salts or contaminents, and is quite soft (has a low hardness - see later). But, as rain falls from clouds to the ground, it passes through various gases and particles in the troposphere, such as oxygen, nitrogen and carbon dioxide, plus various other elements, which it absorbs. From being 'pure', rainwater begins to acquire the various substances which help to sustain life for us all. Pure (distilled) water will not feed plants, will eventually kill fish and tastes absolutely foul to humans, due to its lack of mineral content. However, it does have a use in the aquarium as we shall see later.

Unfortunately, falling rainwater also acquires some additives which are not so good and which are often detrimental to life. Atmospheric dust and soot particles, such as those from volcanoes and forest/oil well fires, are washed out of the air, mixed with the rain and fall to the ground (usually on my car just when I've cleaned it!). Soot particles, from factory chimney and power station emissions containing sulphur dioxide, are often caught up and mixed with rainwater to form the infamous phenomenon of acid rain.

Types Of Water

Water is a tremendously powerful solvent. Given enough time, there's not very much it will not ultimately dissolve. Water may be described as 'acid' or 'alkaline'; and 'hard' or 'soft'. It is important for the newcomer to understand what these terms mean because

Figure 2.1   The water cycle – evaporation to precipitation. Heat from the sun evaporates water into the atmosphere as clouds. The clouds rise, cool, then precipitate the water vapour back to earth as rainwater.

some fishes prefer acid water, and cannot live in alkaline conditions. Others live in hard, alkaline waters, and will not tolerate soft, acid conditions. There are some fish who can manage to survive in either. The type of water also affects aquatic plants as we shall see later.

Water hardness refers to the amounts of dissolved mineral salts, such as those of calcium it contains. If it has a lot, then it will not make soap suds easily, and will be known as 'hard' water. Very little mineral content permits easy lathering, and is known as 'soft' water.

Whether the water is considered acid or alkaline depends on how much it contains of either substance. For example, water containing acids such as tannic, humic etc. is said to be 'acid' water because it contains few ions of hydrogen. If there are amounts of lime or calcium-type minerals present, then the water is said to be hard because there are more ions of hydrogen present. The pH (power (of) hydrogen – pH) scale is used to measure how acid or alkaline a solution is, and we'll be looking at that later.

Hard/alkaline, soft/acid are the two usual types of water you'll deal with as an aquarist, both of which do exist naturally in the wild. But of course, how hard and how alkaline, as well as how soft and how acid varies greatly from location to location.

On hitting the ground, further changes take place in the rainwater which directly affect its eventual make-up. Rain falling onto hard, granite-like rocks will dissolve hardly any of this material, and so will remain soft. Rainwater which falls onto chalk or limestone terrain dissolves varying amounts of these minerals which makes for hard water.

Similarly, where rainwater percolates down through the soil, it gathers further amounts of carbon dioxide and various traces of organic and inorganic substances, such as that from rotting vegetation, peat and any minerals, and may become naturally acid water, unless the soil has a high alkaline content, in which case the water will become naturally alkaline. Our initially 'pure' evaporated water vapour within the clouds has now become a very complex cocktail of dissolved gases, minerals, and various other compounds as it arrives on the ground. This is water as we know it.

Water Hardness

Water hardness is dependent on the amounts of various salts and minerals present – substances such as carbonates of calcium and magnesium as well as sulphates and bicarbonates of strontium, boron and barium. Hardness is broadly divided into two parts: temporary and permanent. The total hardness of water is temporary-plus-permanent hardness. Permanent hardness of a solution is permanent-minus-temporary hardness.

Temporary Hardness

Hard water often contains bicarbonate of calcium (amongst others) which causes temporary hardness. This can be liberated from the water by boiling it. The white fur inside kettles of people who live in hard water areas is proof that the system works. Once heated, this mineral is precipitated out and is no longer present. That's why it's called 'temporary' hardness. After removal, the remaining calcium and magnesium salts make up the permanent hardness of the water. Figure 2.3 shows how water hardness is measured, and a scale of soft-to-hard waters. Test kits to measure and methods of adjusting water hardness for the more advanced aquarist are discussed later.

Acidity And Alkalinity - pH

Another vital aspect of water, from the fishes' viewpoint at least, is how acid or alkaline it is. The pH scale is a way of measuring this. It runs from 0 through to 14, with 0 representing the strongest acid, 14 the strongest alkali (both of these extremes will burn you very badly indeed), and pH 7 as neutral; neither acid nor alkaline.

Obviously, for the good health of the fishes, the pH of the aquarium water should match as closely as possible that found in their natural

A = rain falling through vegetative, peaty soil lowers pH
B = rain falling through calciferous rock hardens and raises pH.

Figure 2.2   **Rainwater passing through various soil types.**

habitat. While a Neon tetra will survive and even spawn at a pH of 7 or even higher, the eggs will not be fertilised nor develop at all unless the pH matches that found in their home water (around pH 6). In the community tank you're going to create later we'll be aiming for a pH of around 7. Because you're going to keep

fishes which originally come from different locations around the world, with different pH levels in their natural habitats, a neutral pH gives them their best chance of survival. It will be a 'compromise' pH – but none the less workable for that.

Today, many of the most popular tropical fishes for sale in shops have been acclimatised over generations to live in water which is nothing like that found in their natural habitat. While they may appear to live and thrive, breeding them in such water is very difficult. For example, it is now possible to buy Discus fish which will live quite happily in medium-hard water at a neutral pH; whereas their natural water is soft and acid. Many beginners cannot understand why, when their Discus' swim happily around in medium-hard water at a pH

Mg/litre CaCO₃	⁰DH	Water Type ≋
0–45	3	Soft
45–100	3–6	Medium Soft
100–200	6–12	Slightly Hard
200–300	12–18	Medium Hard
Over 300	18–25	Hard Water

Figure 2.3   **Chart of water hardness.**

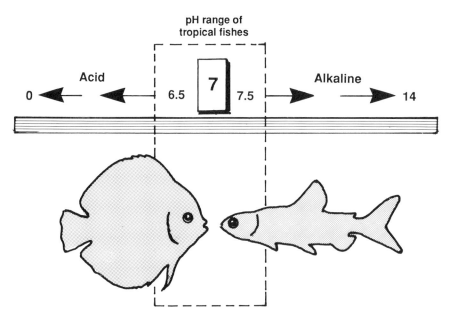

Figure 2.4   pH chart showing ranges for tropical fishes.

A family of beautiful Discus fish.

of 7.2, they cannot get them to breed. Or if they do happen to spawn, the eggs soon go mouldy.

Acclimatisation of fishes to alien water conditions has been going on for many years, both forced by man, and enforced upon the fishes by the destruction or pollution of their natural habitats. The problem is that, for millennia fishes have been used to spawning in specific water conditions, and, unless and until these conditions are recreated as closely as possible, breeding is going to be very difficult indeed. (See Chapter 8 *Breeding*.)

Natural Watercourses

To put water hardness and softness, and alkalinity and acidity into some kind of perspective, let's look at some of the places where tropical fishes live. On high ground, such as mountains and hills, streams and rivers usually have rocky beds and sparse vegetation. Water is fast-flowing and very well oxygenated. Because of the impervious rocky river beds, the water absorbs very little mineral content and stays moderately soft. In such conditions we find the sleek, torpedo-shaped danios.

As the mountain streams and rivers flow into the lowlands, rivers become deeper and more sluggish. Vegetation grows thickly and the water is less well oxygenated, sometimes becoming slightly acid due to the dense flora. The majority of tropical fishes kept by aquarists come from such locations, and include such species as the various barbs, catfishes, angelfish and tetras etc.

Rivers in Central America are often deep, slow-flowing with beds rich in calciferous rocks and iron-bearing substrates. The water is moderately hard and alkaline, perfect conditions for the livebearing species, such as guppies, mollies, swordtails and platys.

Another rich source of species – especially cichlids – for the hobby fishkeeper is the great lakes of Africa. These lakes have little flow in and out, but remain clean and well oxygenated by wind-driven wave action at, and just below, the surface levels. Calciferous rocky beds, little

aquatic plant life and high levels of evaporation – which leave behind the various calcium salts – keep these waters highly oxygenated, so species from these areas will need high levels of aeration in their tanks – hard and alkaline water.

So, from fast-flowing mountain streams to the hard, alkaline lakes of Africa, water conditions and species of fish vary widely. As a newcomer to the hobby, it is very much easier to keep a range of fish and plants which match the hardness and pH values of the water coming out of your tap. Otherwise, you'll be continually tinkering with water softeners/hardeners, and acidifiers etc. and trying to match water conditions to species, instead of the other way round. Initially, you'll have enough to be going on with when creating the basic community-tank biosphere. Save water modification until you've gained more experience as an aquarist and then, by all means, create water specifically for a particular species – that's the beauty and fascination of the fishkeeping hobby. But don't practise on your community tank!

Tap Water

Water companies have a legal duty to provide water which has to be 'Fit for human consumption.' And that's all they have to do! (Notice that there's no mention of fish?)

Collecting The Water

Rivers, brooks and streams flow into the various reservoirs, which act as 'warehouses' for the water companies. One of the difficult problems that these companies have to contend with is pollution of this water on its way to the reservoir, and over which they have little or no control. Intensive farming is very dependent on a range of growth-enhancing, pest-inhibiting chemicals to increase yield. Nitrogen-based fertilisers are often washed off fields and into rivers, as can be pesticides and herbicides.

Similarly, many factories and processing

plants often discharge waste material into the nearest watercourse. The more farmland and factories the water has to flow past on its way to the reservoir, then the worse this problem can become, each farm or factory adding their bit to the total and rapidly increasing effluent level. Of course there are laws preventing the unlawful discharge of toxic waste into rivers and canals, and even though some of the 'old' river authorities really did get their act together – witness the re-birth of the River Trent in Nottinghamshire, now one of the cleanest rivers in Europe and literally teeming with aquatic life of all forms – there just aren't enough inspectors to prevent these criminal acts by unscrupulous companies.

The water companies have a legal obligation to provide water fit for human consumption. They have no such requirement to provide water which is safe to keep fishes in. And often there is conflict between the needs of people and the needs of fishes. Many of the chemicals added by water companies (we'll see what these are in moment) are harmless to humans, but dangerous – often lethal – to fishes. Furthermore, water companies aren't going to spend large amounts of money on treating water to make it safe to keep fish in: that's not their job. So any pollutants in the reservoir which are judged to be 'harmless' to us, will be left in. To remove them would cost money, and who would stand for their water charges being doubled, or even tripled?

To make the water fit for human consumption, water companies are always going to choose the cheapest and quickest option; although this is frequently detrimental to the health of our fishes. Once we know what chemicals are added, and why they're put there in the first place, we can then adopt a policy of taking them out again, rendering tapwater safe to use in our aquaria.

Water Additives

The fastest and most economical way for a water company to render their product safe for human consumption is to disinfect it with varying amounts of chlorine gas. This kills bugs quickly and 'cleans' the water. Often when you first turn on a tap, you can actually smell the chlorine (the swimming-pool smell), as the flow from the tap mixes with air and causes some of the gas to leave the water.

Where the basic reservoir water has large amounts of organic/inorganic substances, such as that from peaty fell waters, algae or nitrate-laden run-off water from farmlands, the company may add a limited amount of ammonia as well as chlorine. Ammonia reacts with oxygen (O_2) and chlorine to form chloramines – chlorine byproducts, which are stronger and longer lasting in effect than chlorine gas. Consequently, they are much harder for the aquarist to get rid of, although it is still possible to do so. However, the situation is improving as more and more water companies are changing to using ozone and chlorine dioxides for disinfecting, which in the long run are much kinder to us and to fish.

An apparently increasing problem with tapwater is the amount of metal pollution it sometimes contains. Lead, iron and copper – even aluminium recently closely linked with the early onset of *Alzheimer's Disease* (senility) – have all been discovered in 'fresh' tapwater. While the individual levels of each metal may appear to be below those which cause damage to 'animals' (that includes us, by the way), metals are heavily synergistic. That is, the combined effect of all the metal pollution present in the water is much greater than any individual metal's effect. When water evaporates from the aquarium, these metals remain behind. Each top-up adds more and more of them (assuming that they're present in the first place, of course) and the concentrations may soon reach toxic levels.

Water companies try to supply drinking water to EEC standards (they don't always succeed). They will add enough hardness and try to hold a neutral-to-slight alkaline pH to protect their pipe work and machinery, and fulfil legal requirements for quality. They won't, however, spend a lot of money on treatment because we won't let them! They have no responsibility in law to protect your fishes, neither, if asked, will they test your aquarium water. They should however do a survey on your local domestic water supply if you request one.

Yorkshire Water Company

Water companies tend to take a lot of (often) unfair criticism over the quality of the water they supply. Yet they have no control over the creation of the source product! How many amateur photographers never bother to add neutralising chemicals to the (often highly toxic) processing solutions they use, before dumping them down the sink? How many people are over-spraying their gardens with commercial pesticides and fertilisers, which will be washed

Yorkshire Water Company Survey Report (Kiveton/Anston Sampling Zone, 1 Jan 1990 to 31 Dec 1990

Parameter	PCV*	Units	No. of samples	% samples failing PCV	Concentration or Value (all samples) Min†	Mean	Max‡
Colour (Filtered)	20.0	HAZEN	81		<1.0	2.57	7.9
Turbidity	4.0	ETU	88		<0.10	0.347	1.23
Odour	3.0	Dilution –	9		0.0	0.0	0.0
pH	9.5	pH value	88		6.1	7.57	9.2
Sulphate	250	mg/SO4/l	2		71.5	80.80	90.1
Magnesium	50.0	mg/Mg/l	2		6.3	7.58	8.8
Sodium	150	mg/Na/l	2		15.2	19.15	22.6
Ammonium (ammonia + ammonium ions)	0.50	mg/NH4/l	12		<0.013	0.0138	<0.013
Nitrite	0.10	mg/NO2/l	12		<0.033	0.0361	0.067
Nitrate	50.0	mg/NO3/l	9		11.9	14.1	19.4
Total Organic Carbon	—	mg/C/l	2		2.5	3.75	5
Total Hardness	60	mg/Ca/l	2	50.0	58.4	60.60	62.8
Aluminium	200	mg/Al/l	89	2.2	<10.0	63.92	560.0
Iron	200	mg/Fe/l	89	13.5	10.0	105.6	910.0
Copper	3000	mg/Cu/l	5		<10.0	20.00	60.0
Zinc	5000	mg/Zn/l	5		<10.0	16.00	40.0
Fluoride	1400	mg/F/l	2		<9.2	53.67	98.0
Silver	10	mg/Ag/l	2		<1.0	1.00	<1.0
Arsenic	50	mg/As/l	2		<5.0	5.0	<5.0
Cadmium	5.0	mg/Cd/l	9		<0.50	0.500	<0.50
Cyanide (Total)	50.0	mg/CN/l	2		<3.0	3.00	<3.0
Chromium	50.0	mg/Cr/l	2		<5.0	5.00	<5.0
Mercury	1.0	mg/Hg/l	2		<0.10	0.100	<0.10
Nickel	50.0	mg/Ni/l	2		<5.0	5.00	<5.0
Lead	50.0	mg/Pb/l	23		<5.0	8.05	41.6
Antimony	10.0	mg/Sb/l	2		<1.0	1.00	<1.0
Selenium	10.0	mg/Se/l	2		<1.0	1.00	<1.0
DDT	0.10	ug/1	1		<0.010	0.0100	<0.010
Hexachlorobenzene	0.10	ug/1	1		<0.0010	0.0100	<0.0010
Polycylic Aromatic Hydrocarbons	0.20	ug/1	9		<0.040	0.0400	<0.040

* PCV=prescribed concentration or limit.
† Qualified values – taken at face value in all calculations.
‡ Total Coliforms – 95% of the samples should comply with PCV.

Figure 2.5   A selection of the 93 different measurements carried out on the fresh water supply in my area.

away into the drainage system? And, exactly what was that horrible brown stuff you flushed down the loo yesterday? But 'we' then complain bitterly about any plans to increase water charges. 'We' (me, you, farmers, factory owners etc.) add the muck in the first place, and then 'prevent' water companies from cleaning it up by refusing to pay for it!

During the writing of this book, I had a fairly regular correspondence with the Yorkshire Water Company. They were completely honest with me when answering my questions, which they did without hedging, or adding any 'buts' and 'ifs'. They sent me various analyses of my local water, provided me with much information specifically aimed at fishkeepers, and were always kind and considerate with their responses as well as extremely interested in the book itself. Their great assistance and interest is gratefully acknowledged.

Reservoir water can often contain high concentrations of nitrates, built up from fish and plant waste, and nitrogen-based fertilisers. In the closed environment of an aquarium, nitrate is always present, and can get out of hand. Evaporation, excessive feeding etc. will add to the problem. On top of all that, you may be introducing tapwater which has itself an excessive amount of nitrate too. Levels of around 150–200 mg/l (which is one heck of a lot, and will colour your water practically yellow!) can seriously damage or even kill fishes: EEC nitrate level recommendation for drinking water is 50 mg/l.

When we discuss the *Nitrogen Reduction Chain* (p. 69), the end product produced by *aerobic aerobic bacteria* is nitrate. To further remove nitrate (NO_3), most aquarists rely on partial water changes to dilute the NO_3 levels. However, there are other methods too, such as denitrifying filters which use *anaerobic bacteria* (see Chapter 5 *Aquarium Hardware – Filters*).

I Never Knew That

So; chlorine, chloramines, metals, various dissolved gases, organic and inorganic substances, salts, sulphates, carbonates, bicarbonates and nitrates. Figure 2.5 shows the list of what's coming out of my tap. It seems so very complicated, doesn't it? Remember, this book was designed to grow in parallel with your skill as an aquarist. As you develop, then more of this book will become accessible to you. To begin with, dechlorination of freshly drawn tapwater is all you need to ensure, so don't worry about anything else at the moment. The rest of the information about changing your basic water chemistry is here for completeness and for your future knowledge; here as and when you need it. If you feel that you can make use of this information then please feel free to try. But do remember: lives are at stake!

Water Tests

Before you attempt to modify the nature of your tapwater, you have to know what its existing condition is, otherwise how will you know which way to go? You can achieve this by two methods. You may obtain a survey for your area from the local water authority, and simply take their word for it; or you can directly test the water yourself.

There are numerous kits available from various manufacturers which can be used to check hardness and pH, as well as nitrate/nitrite, CO_2 and ammonia concentrations, (more of which in Chapter 5). Most of these test kits rely on adding chemicals to a sample of water (either tap or aquarium), and then comparing the resulting colour of the mixture against a comparator chart, which provides you with the results of the test.

Testing For Hardness

Chemical indicator type, water-hardness kits can test for both temporary and permanent hardness. Most are quite simple to use, and accurate enough for the amateur aquarist. However, as with *all* chemical-based test kits

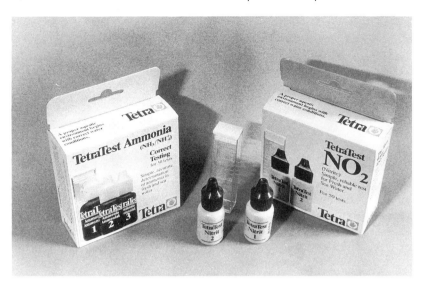

The minimum water test kits an aquarist will use – one for ammonia and one for nitrite.

used in fishkeeping, the manufacturer's instructions must be followed exactly.

There are available some electronic test meters, which measure the electrical conductivity of water. The harder the water, then the more electricity it will allow to flow, ideal for those of us who're colour blind. But do note that there are other things which affect water conductivity, too, without affecting hardness. Digital conductivity meters measure only the total hardness – they cannot distinguish between temporary and permanent – so to use one, lose the temporary hardness first.

Testing For Acidity/Alkalinity (pH)

There are a number of ways to test the pH of your aquarium/tapwater. Perhaps the simplest is litmus papers. To test, you tear off a strip from the packet, immerse in the aquarium for a while, and then compare the colour of the test strip with a chart which tells you the measured pH. Another method relies on adding a chemical dye to a sample of water, and then comparing the result, again with a comparator chart, or a graduated wheel in a *Colorimeter*.

Normally, pH test kits come in particular ranges. For example, kits for marine aquaria usually cover the range pH 7.5–9 because the normal pH of such water (unless there's something drastically wrong!) will always be somewhere within this range. Freshwater pH test kits typically cover from pH 4–9. It is possible to get a kit to cover the whole pH range from 0–14, but this is going 'over the top' for tropical fishkeepers and, in any case, won't have the same level of accuracy as a limited range test kit.

Testing Everything Else!

As well as hardness and pH test kits, you can obtain chemical type tests for aluminium, ammonium, various acids, cobalt and copper,

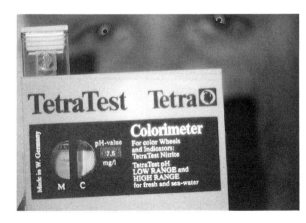

Colour comparitor wheel for various chemical tests.

various forms of iron, nitrate, nitrite, potassium, silver, tin and total hardness. Also, some companies produce multi-tests on a single strip, such as the combined pH/hardness testing of Aquarian's Watertest. Your local aquarist shop will usually carry a range of such kits, and will explain their use to you.

Levels Of Competence

What follows is a set of fairly advanced aquarist's techniques and methods with which you may not yet feel comfortable. It's a wise person indeed who knows their limitations! With the community aquarium you're going to create later, the only water treatment you'll have to become involved with is dechlorination – done simply and quickly by adding a chemical to freshly drawn tapwater, and maybe the addition of a tapwater conditioner – although these two separate products are often combined into a single bottle.

You can practise the following techniques on a small aquarium which doesn't have any fishes in it. This will give you the confidence to do it 'for real' when the need or the situation arises. In your practice tank, try moving the pH up or down and, more importantly, *keeping* it there. Change the water hardness, or set up an undergravel filter and monitor the progress of the biological filter bed (see Chapter 5 *Aquarium*

A young aquarist performing a chemical nitrite test.

Hardware – Filters). At first, you'll almost certainly get things wrong but, as I used to tell my college students, you'll learn far more by getting things wrong than you ever would by 'fluking' a correct result the first time. In any case, this won't matter because there won't be any fishes in your practice tank. But after a few attempts you'll soon see how easy it all suddenly becomes.

Ammonia Testing

When a biological filter ceases to work properly in an existing aquarium, or when a new tank is

Tinfoil barbs can grow very large indeed.

being set up which utilises undergravel filtration, in certain circumstances ammonia can become a highly toxic problem. Ammonia is toxic to fish, ammonium isn't. The percentage of ammonia to ammonium waste in the aquarium water is dependent on both temperature and pH. At high temperatures, greater than than about 27°C, and pH levels below 7.5, most of the waste will exist as relatively harmless ammonium. Below this temperature, with a pH greater than 8.5, ammonium easily transforms into deadly ammonia. Ammonium are salts of ammonia, by the way.

Both ammonium and ammonia represent the first stage in the Nitrogen Reduction Cycle, and are both further reduced by the action of *Nitrosomonas* aerobic bacteria into less toxic nitrite – NO_2. An ammonia test will alert you to any problems with the filter system, or to the fact that your water changes are not regular enough, or you're simply over-feeding the fishes. Whatever the reason, an inflated ammonia reading has to be dealt with immediately, or fishes may start to die. Action to take, both to avoid this situation arising and what to do in an emergency, are discussed later on in Chapter 5 *Aquarium Hardware – Filters*.

Cost Of Testing

If you're going to test your water's pH once a month (which is about average) then chemical test kits are your cheapest option. Assuming that the only thing you're doing to 'raw' tap-water is dechlorinating and conditioning it, and you are not tinkering with the actual pH or hardness, then a monthly check on ammonia and nitrite, to reassure yourself that nothing drastic is taking place, is all that needs to be done. However, should you suspect anything is going wrong, then for heaven's sake don't wait a month to check the ammonia/nitrite content of your aquarium water! Do it right away.

However, more advanced aquarists may need to make adjustments to the pH of their tap-water, raising or lowering it to a new level for a specific purpose (and not just because they're bored!). If such is the case, then you must keep a fairly close eye on what's happening to the tank water. At least a weekly pH test should be done – and preferably more often – until you've gained enough confidence in your technique and materials. At this level of testing, chemical kits begin to work out expensive. Therefore, consider the purchase of an electronic pH measuring device. After the initial purchase, the running costs will be much lower than chemical indicator types.

What Colour's That Red Fish?

Some people (I'm one of them) suffer from defective colour vision – what's commonly (and inaccurately) called *Colour Blindness*. Contrary to popular belief, we *do not* see colours as shades of grey! It's just that our names for the colours we can see, and distinguish between are rather . . . er . . . well, sort of different to yours. Unfortunately, and especially in my case, most of the colours which chemical test kits require you to match and distinguish between fall into those parts of the spectrum with which I have the greatest difficulty eg. red-to-yellow, and green-to-blue (doesn't leave much, does it?).

For fellow sufferers (you wouldn't believe the number of occupations from which defective colour vision bars you!), the only solution (pardon the pun) to chemical colour indicating water tests is to acquire electronic test equipment. You can buy a digital conductivity meter (for water hardness) from £56* plus the additional cost of a calibration solution (£5.20*), a digital pH meter for around £40* plus calibration buffers (set of three @ £14.95*). While we're spending money like water, we may as well treat ourselves to a digital thermometer, cost around £20*.

A digital *Redox* potential meter will set you back £56.50*. The concept of Redox is a very advanced subject. There is a combination digital test meter which measures pH, temperature and Redox, but the cost is £249* plus calibration solutions etc. Unfortunately, digital (or even analogue) electronic devices for measuring amounts of nitrite, nitrate, ammonia/ammonium content are way outside the pocket of the average aquarist. However, I gather that Tetra are about to introduce a chemically-based dissolved oxygen (O^2) test at a very competitive price. If you can't afford these exotic electronic measuring devices, then get someone with good colour vision to run these tests for you.

    * Prices taken from the *Spring '91* edition of the *Aquamail Catalogue*.

Testing: A Final Summary

One test does not a tragedy make! When you test you're not looking for the one exceptional result, you're looking for trends. Any single, oddball test result could be due to a variety of reasons, from tiredness on your part, to over-active bowels of the fish. Neither should you interpret test results in isolation from other factors. For example, a rising pH level could mean that relatively harmless ammonium in your aquarium water may be on the verge of transforming itself into toxic ammonia: and a problem which wasn't immediately important suddenly becomes vital. Get into the habit of thinking about water chemistry as a generic subject. Each change in the basic chemical nature of the water is going to have a knock-on effect on everything else within the aquarium, from the health of your fishes up to the salt deposits on cover glasses!.

    All changes to the basic chemical nature of your domestic water supply begin and end with testing. You test to see what needs to be done. Test again to ensure that whatever course you've adopted is actually having the desired effect; and then, when you've finished, you test yet again, to ensure that the end result is what you originally intended. Nobody ever killed their fishes by being too careful and testing too often. The reverse is, unfortunately, all too often true. The golden rule of water chemistry is never to change anything at all unless it absolutely *has* to be changed. And, if you have to, then make the changes slowly, so that the fishes may acclimatise to the changing chemical nature of their surrounding environment.

Removing The Unwanted

Now we know what goes into our tapwater, and how we can measure it, we can make plans to get it all out again! Do note that it is not our aim to provide completely sterile water. Some micro-organisms and bacteria are vital to life. In any case, nothing can live for very long in distilled (also known as de-ionised) water. What we want to remove are only those substances which are harmful to fishes; and then only enough to render the water safe for them.

Chlorine / Chloramines

These chemicals are harmful to fishes, even in very small quantities. Therefore, they have to be removed from fresh tapwater before adding it to the aquarium. Fortunately, this is now a very simple process, which takes only a minute or so. Chlorine products may be removed by agitation.

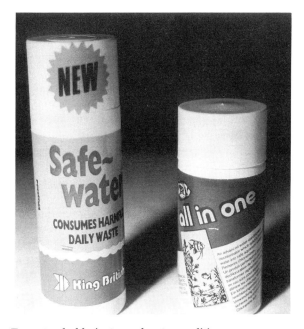

Tapwater dechlorinator and water conditioner.

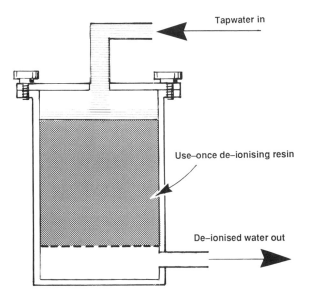

Figure 2.6   Water de-ioniser – resin type.

Leave a container of tapwater to stand for a few days, preferably with an airstone driven by an air pump in the bucket. The constant agitation from the bubbles of air will help liberate the chlorine gas from the water, but may still leave a residue.

Many of the specialist aquatic manufacturers supply dechlorinating agents. These are usually liquids which are added to tapwater, and neutralise any trace of chlorine or chloramine products. It's vital that you follow the maker's instructions regarding dilution very closely. With little aquaria, it's often difficult to measure the small amounts of dechlorination solution required. A five millilitre hypodermic syringe is ideal for this, and is what I use. Of course, you most definitely do not require the needle!

Some manufacturers combine dechlorinators within another product called a 'Tapwater Conditioner'. This is usually a liquid, again added to the tapwater, which not only removes chlorine/chloramine products, but also adds protective colloids which cushion fish from changes in the basic water chemistry. Also included in the Conditioner are artificial 'aging'

substances which are said to cut down on the time the aquarist has to wait before the water in a new aquarium becomes usable. I treat *all* tapwater with a dechlorinator and a conditioner, even when just 'topping up'.

Hardness

Unfortunately, there's no cheap and easy way to remove hardness from water. Boiling is perhaps the simplest way to remove temporary hardness, eg. calcium bicarbonate. But this is an expensive method too, especially if you want to fill a new aquarium from scratch! Boiling is best left to water which is used to make good evaporation losses. Dilution is a good, natural method, assuming that you have a supply of soft water, such as distilled or fresh rain. Using either of these two liquids, you can lower the hardness figure to whatever you need.

Collecting Rainwater

You would think that nothing could be simpler than collecting rainwater. After all, you only have to stick your arm out of the window, and

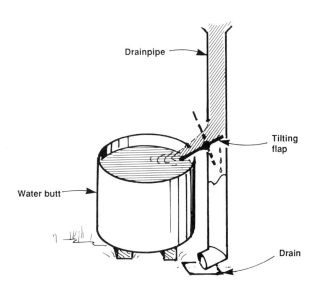

Figure 2.7   Collecting rainwater.

collect the falling rain in an old tin mug! Not so. As we've already seen, rainwater is often contaminated with chemicals, such as dust and soot particles from industrial areas. There's no doubt that clean rainwater is a cheap way to adjust the hardness of tapwater by dilution. A good way to collect it is shown in Figure 2.7. Allow the first ten minutes of rain to run to waste. By this time, much of the dirt and dust will have been washed out of the atmosphere, and off the roof etc. at the collecting site. The flap can be then be thrown over in the drainpipe, diverting the flow into a rain butt. But beware of 'creatures' making their home in your water butt, some of which can attack and destroy young fish fry.

Ion-Exchange Resins

The ion-exchange principle is basically quite simple. Ions of one type, the sort which cause hardness in water, are swapped with ions which don't. Ion-exchange water softeners often come in the form of a cartridge, where tapwater is squirted in at one end, and 'soft' water is extracted at the other, or as a loose resin which can be used in an external power filter. Typical of 'cartridge' systems is the Interpet *Water Guardian*, which consists of a length of hose connecting the ion-exchange cartridge to the water tap. The *Hobbyist Water Guardian Starter Kit* will process around 120 litres (30 gallons) of tapwater (depending on how hard it is) before the disposable cartridge has to be replaced.

Both cartridges and resins will eventually become depleted of the ions they're trading with your tapwater and (if they are of the right types) will have to be recharged. This is done simply by an overnight soaking in a strong salt (sodium chloride – NaCl) solution. The time between recharges will depend on how hard the water was to start with, and how much has been processed. There are some ion-exchange resins and complete cartridge arrangements (such as the one illustrated, sold by JMC Aquatics)

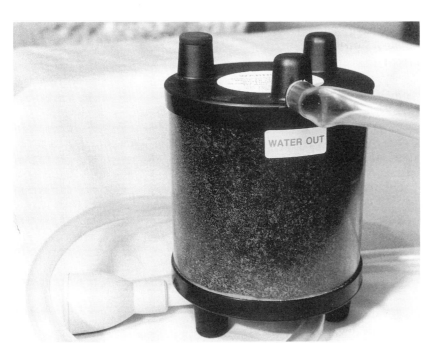

Tapwater de-ioniser, turning out distilled water.

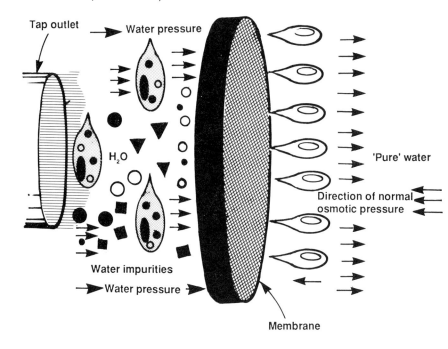

Figure 2.8   Reverse osmosis filter.

which are not rechargeable. Naturally, these are expensive to run, but usually much easier to operate.

Domestic water softeners, such as those on sale at your local DIY emporium, are *not* suitable for fishkeeping. They replace the calcium and magnesium ions with sodium, which is a highly toxic substance to fishes. The type of ion-exchange water softener to look for is one which uses hydrogen ions for replacement.

There are some resins and cartridge systems available which remove practically everything, and turn out almost completely de-ionised water. As we've already learned, we can't keep fishes in this. But we can dilute it, so don't write off de-ionisers from your list. They can be very useful indeed just as long as you realise that you can't utilise their output directly, without diluting it with 'ordinary' tapwater first. De-ionised water contains *no* dissolved oxygen, which is its main problem and why it can't support aquatic life for very long. Further, water de-ionising resins are not usually rechargeable.

To summarise then, use an ion-exchange resin which replaces the calcium and magnesium ions with hydrogen, and *not* sodium. Or if using a de-ionising resin, dilute the resulting output with (dechlorinated) tapwater.

Natural Methods

Filtering water through a peat medium will lower the pH and soften the water by trading ions with it. However, this is a slow process, and many aquarists don't appreciate the slight sepia colouring of the aquarium water which occurs when using this material. Peat also releases many helpful hormonal substances which both fish and plants find very beneficial. Similarly, filtering water over a bed of crushed coral or sea shells will add hardness to the water, allowing the pH to be raised more easily.

Certain plants, such as duckweed and water wisteria, absorb large amounts of calcium salts as part of their food intake, again removing them from the water and softening it. If these types of plants grow at an explosive rate in your tank (as they do in mine), then it's a safe bet that your water contains plenty of calcium salts. These natural methods are rather slow – but then *any* changes to the basic water chemistry *should* be done very slowly anyway. Of course, the bigger the peat filter, or the greater the number of these plants in your tank, then the quicker you'll get results.

The Ultimate Water Treatment?

Possibly the best method of treating 'raw' tap-water – and also the most expensive in terms of cash and water wastage – is to pass it through a reverse osmosis filter. Reverse osmosis filters will not only soften the water, they will also remove excess nitrate, metal pollution, and certain types of bacteria and waterborne parasites – a very handy gadget to have. The only trouble is a system such as I've just described will cost around £300–£400. Cheaper (smaller) versions are available, with a correspondingly lower throughput, but even these will still cost around £100. I think it would be a brilliant idea if the local aquarist shop bought a reverse osmosis filter, and then sold treated water to customers for a nominal sum. They would recoup the cost of the filter within six months, and would be on clear profit after that. I'd certainly buy some if the price was right (5p per litre?).

Adjusting The pH

The pH scale is a logarithmic one. Each point change represents an increase/decrease of TEN times! Therefore, to move the pH of your aquarium water from pH6 to 7 means the water has to become ten times more alkaline than it was before. Imagine the effect of such a dramatic change on a fish! A change of two points on the pH scale means an actual change of 100, while shifting the pH from 8 down to 5 means that the water is now ONE THOUSAND TIMES more acid – 10×10×10. That's why you should never attempt to change the pH of your aquarium water unless you're absolutely certain that you know what you're doing. As I have already said, the pH of your domestic water supply is more than likely to be around the figure needed for a community aquarium anyway, so you won't have to change it. (At least in most of the country.)

However, I accept that, in some areas of the UK, the water is 'odd', being hard/acid and even soft/alkaline. As you will read later, today's generation of the more common community species have been adapted to live in conditions greatly different to those of their natural habitat, so you can still get by without making major adjustments to the basic chemical nature of your tapwater. Do not mess with the pH unless you know a) why you have to move it, b) how to move AND hold it at the new level, and c) have the materials and the confidence to do it, and how to check that the new level is correct.

'Then why bother testing the pH if I'm not going to be changing it?'. A good question. Well, *you* may not be deliberately altering the pH but the living nature of the biosphere – plants, water and fishes – will be continuously modifying the chemical nature of the water via natural processes. And that's why you have to keep an eye on things. By all means read this section for your complete information, but be very careful if you decide to change the pH. Just one of the problems you have to overcome is holding the pH at its new level.

Adjustments to the pH value have to be handled with extreme caution. Hard, alkaline water has a natural resistance to being made more acid. The various dissolved salts act as a buffer, firmly denying change. Simply adding acid in any form is not a good idea because the buffer will resist the change. Testing will indicate no alteration of the pH, so in goes more 'acid'. No change. More acid. And then bang! The buffer suddenly breaks down and the pH swings violently and lethally to acid, killing the fishes.

To make hard, alkaline water more acid, the buffering effect has to be overcome first, by breaking down the hardness. Once the buffer is overcome, acidity is easily (and safely) achieved. The reverse, of course, also applies to making acid water more alkaline.

A Natural Approach

Any intended change of pH value, whether up (alkaline) or down (acid) has to be done very slowly, so that the fish may acclimatise to the new level. It is better to achieve the intended change by natural methods, rather than dumping chemicals into the tank. Both natural and chemical methods are discussed below.

Water which is alkaline (pH greater than 7) may be made more acid by the natural method of adding peat, either to a suitable filter or by burying peat mats underneath the substrate gravel. But *beware* of garden centre peat, which is often sprayed with fungicide or fertilisers. Read the pack carefully before buying. Garden centre peat is often less than half the price of what the aquatic dealers sell, so it is worth using, just as long as you read the pack carefully first.

There are some commercially-made liquids which, when added to aquarium water, will lower the pH, and, in the case of *Blackwater Extract*, also add some natural trace elements as well. Products such as Aquarian's *pH UP – pH Down* and *pH Maintain*, are an excellent and safe way of changing the water's pH, as they use natural constituents.

Dilution of the aquarium water (no more than 20% at any one time) with either de-ionised water, or rainwater, will naturally help overcome the buffering effect of hard water, and allow the photosynthesis/respiration of plants and fishes to effect a natural lowering of the pH – via the process CO_2 (carbon dioxide) + H_2O (water) = H_2CO_3 (carbonic acid) = acid water.

Acid water may be made more alkaline by diluting it (no more than 25% at a time) with hard (de-chlorinated) tapwater. Filtering through a crushed sea shell, coral sand or a marble chipping filter medium (see Chapter 5) will clean the water of particulate debris and make the water harder. But, if there's a layer of peat in the substrate or filter, then this will act as an acidity buffer, so remove the peat first. Adding sodium bicarbonate will increase alkalinity, but not the hardness.

Potential Problems

One potential hazard of tinkering with the pH value is that you may cause osmotic shock to your fishes. This phenomenon isn't easy to diagnose either, because it may not immediately affect your existing stock; only new additions to the aquarium. Simplified, osmosis is the balance between the fluids within a fish and those surrounding it.

Osmotic Shock

Providing the water absorbed by tropical fishes bears more than a passing resemblance to what it's used to, then there aren't too many problems. But, if the pH is messed about with, or through negligence and poor maintenance allowed to rise or fall from its usual level, then the water can become effectively toxic. This may happen so slowly that the existing stock in the aquarium acclimatise to the changes. However, as soon as any additions are made, they immediately die, due to the difference between the pH they were used to and that in their new home. This is osmotic shock.

Water – Summary

Firstly, establish the condition of your mains water supply. As a basic minimum, try to discover its hardness and pH. Smell it: can you detect any trace of chlorine? Your community aquarium will need water with a pH of around 7 (6.5–7.5 will be fine), slightly hard and with no chlorine present. Apart from removing the chlorine, this is what should be coming out of your tap, without any modification on your part. Of course there are exceptions to this, and *your* tapwater may be very soft or super-hard. At least you now know what to do about it! So initially, you won't have to get involved with ion-exchange resins, peat filters etc. That is, not unless you really want to, by practising on a fishless aquarium.

Chapter 3
Hygiene

I will be returning to the subject of water in Chapters 4 and 5 – *Aquatic Plants* and *Aquarium Hardware* respectively. After taking such care to provide the best quality water possible, you don't want to go and spoil it by accidentally introducing something nasty into the water. This chapter deals with the subject of aquarium hygiene.

With fishkeeping, if we can keep the number of variables down, then our chances of success are much improved. I've already dealt with the major variables, those associated with water, and explained how they can be adjusted, or at least made known to you. Having been so careful to ensure that the aquarium water is right, you don't want accidentally to introduce any contamination into the biosphere yourself.

How might undesirable substances be introduced into the aquarium? Well, gravel substrates can often contain the most surprising things, from shards of broken glass, to rusty nails, all of which I've discovered (sometimes very painfully!) in the past. Occasionally, synthetic rubber sleeving covering the mains wire of various electrical items can react with polystyrene packaging. This causes the sleeving to melt slightly, and give off toxic fumes. Although this hasn't happened to me for a long time now, I mention it just in case you come across it with older items of stock.

Aquatic plants are a well-documented source of various problems, from introducing strange insects, to harbouring infestations of snail eggs. They can also carry bacteria and parasites. Basically, anything which you bring into contact with the aquarium water has to be suspect. The most frequent intruders into the aquarium, and the one thing most people least suspect of introducing possible harmful substances, are your hands.

Avoiding Contamination

As your hands will obviously be used to create the complete aquascape, and will touch everything which goes into the aquarium at some stage, it is important that they remain clean. But don't use strongly scented soaps, or cleaning gels with bactericides in them; they can be toxic to fishes. If you've been handling paint, petrol, wood preservatives or any poisonous substances, then, as well as washing your hands, make sure the smell has gone too. Any cuts or abrasions on your hands should be well covered with waterproof plasters. This is for your protection as well as the fishes (see later).

Most animals have a unique, personal smell. Many animals use this smell to locate a mating partner, mark their home territory (cats and dogs) and even their supper! Humans produce this smell too, and this odour is passed into the aquarium water each time you put your hands into it, no matter how clean they may appear to you. The only real way to ensure that you are not passing anything dubious into the water is to wear rubber gloves, which you keep just for this purpose and nothing else. This will protect both you and the fishes. However, it has to be admitted that very few aquarists bother taking this precaution.

Cleaning The Substrate

Gravel, or whatever substrate you decide upon, must be thoroughly cleaned. Many aquatic books recommend that you simply dump *all* the gravel into a bucket, connect a hosepipe and, after inserting the nozzle into the bucket, leave the water on until the overspill runs clear; anything up to half an hour later. Apart from being very inefficient, this is a criminal waste of what is rapidly becoming a scarce (and expensive!) natural resource ie. water. It is much more efficient (and ecologically sensible) to wash a little of the total amount of gravel at a time within a bowl.

Conserving Water

Add the water, stir the gravel well and drain away the dirty water. It usually takes me three changes of water using an oblong plastic bowl, measuring 33x27x12 cm capacity = 9 litres (2 UK gallons). I had to repeat this procedure three times to wash enough gravel for the 60x30x30 cm (24x12x12 in) demonstration tank, which means a total water usage of a mere 27 litres (6 UK gallons). The true figure is actually lower than this because I haven't allowed for the volume in the bowl taken up by the gravel itself. Even so, a hosepipe would use 27 litres of water in a matter of minutes and, as the pipe is usually left running for around a half-hour, the water saved does add up to a large amount.

When you've finished washing the gravel (or whatever substrate you are using), wrap a magnet in a polythene bag and trawl through the washed substrate, searching for any stray pieces of iron. Inspect the gravel visually, using a strong, directional light. Watch for any glints as you stir the substrate with a wooden spoon (not your hands), and remove any bits of glass which show up with tweezers.

Rockwork, bogwood, heaters and thermostats, air tubing, power filters and pipework, undergravel filter plates and uplift tubes, artificial plants, even the thermometer, should all be

Don't wash gravel under running water – use a bowl.

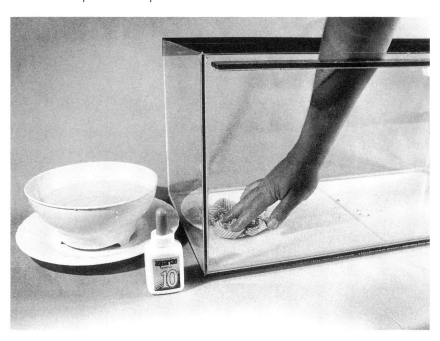

Using a proprietary aquatic disinfectant, clean everything which will go into the tank, including the aquarium itself.

washed in one of the commercial brands of aquarium disinfectants, such as *Aquarian No 10* which for some strange reason has now been discontinued. However, the occasional shop still has some left, so stock up while you can. An alternative to Aquarian's *Number 10* is Interpet's *Liquisil*. And don't forget to disinfect the tank and cover glasses too!

Disinfect all plants and inspect them closely and individually for stowaways. With containers such as those used to hold aquarium water, when performing some type of water check it is vital that these remain clean or you could get a disastrously misleading result.

Human Contraction Of Fish Disease

The bacterium *Mycobacterium marinum* is found in water around the world, and is a cause of fish tuberculosis (fish TB), which is a slow, painful, wasting disease of fishes, usually leading to their death anything up to a year after infection. Obviously, if you have a specimen showing symptoms of TB in your aquarium, and assuming that your diagnosis is correct, then the water

in the aquarium is likely to be contaminated as well. *Mycobacterium marinum* can be passed on to humans; the symptoms are painful red, swollen areas of hard skin on the fingers and backs of the hands, which may spread along the forearm.

The disease is *not* life-threatening to humans, and is very easily treated with complete success by a course of antibiotics. However, in this case, prevention is much better than cure. There are a few aquarists who always carefully don protective rubber gloves before immersing their hands into the aquarium water. But it's true to say that the majority don't. Neither do the majority contract fish TB either. In fact, the recorded numbers of fishtank-contracted *Mycobacterium marinum* in humans is very low indeed, especially when taken as a percentage of the worldwide population of aquarists.

Aquarium Position

Having thought of all the most obvious potential sources of contamination, it's now time to think of the not so obvious. Nicotine is a pretty poisonous substance to humans, so you might imagine what it will do to fishes. Try to position your aquarium in a room where no one will smoke. Better still banish the smokers! Smoke from pipes, cigars or cigarettes can be drawn into the intake of an air pump, and then injected straight into the heart of the aquarium.

Aquaria set up in kitchens can develop an oily scum on the surface, from cooking etc., which will inhibit the interchange of gases from the surface of the water. Furniture polish dispensed from (ozone friendly) aerosols can be sucked into the air pump inlet, or even settle directly onto the surface of the water. Of course, it makes good sense to ensure that your aquarium has a tight fitting hood and cover glasses, which will keep the fish in, and contamination out.

Topping-Up Water

Make sure that whatever container you use to carry top-up water to the aquarium is cleaned regularly. Better still, obtain a container and restrict its use to just that purpose. Some people are tempted to use water from 'the wild', such as a nearby stream, to make good evaporation losses, or even to fill the aquarium. The water may well look clean and sparkling, but bacteria and parasites cannot usually be seen with the naked eye and, as most streams or brooks carry thousands of different species of each, using such water is not a good idea. In fact, never use water from an unknown source – the risks are just too great.

Live Foods

Fishes just love live foods, such as *daphnia*, freshwater shrimp, bloodworm and whiteworms. Aquarist shops sell little bags of some of these creatures still alive. What troubles me is the water they are bagged with. What is it and where has it come from? You are expected to tip the contents of the bag – including the holding water – into your aquarium. Where possible, it is much better to strain the contents first, and then wash them with some fresh water, before feeding them to your fishes. This will go a long way to avoid the introduction of disease into your much-prized aquarium.

Summary

Most hygiene is simply a matter of common sense and a little thought by the fishkeeper. There are enough variables to worry about in the normal course of events. To add more by a poor hygiene routine is to invite disaster. After all, you wash your hands before handling your own food, so why not before handling the fish food as well?

I've left the single most important cause of poor aquarium hygiene until last deliberately, to emphasise its importance. Over-feeding has, and still does, kill more fish than any other form of aquarium pollution. I'll be returning to the subject of feeding in much greater detail later. As a newcomer you'll have no idea yet of what correct feeding actually is – neither is it something you can learn from books. We can only guide, the exact details you'll have to discover for yourself. But don't worry, it won't take you long.

I recently had a spell in hospital and left my wife – who understands the dangers of over-feeding – in charge of my various aquaria. I left her what I thought were very precise instructions regarding feeding, times and amounts. However, once I'd returned from hospital there was barely a single plant left with a leaf on it! This proves yet again that one person's idea of 'a pinch' is most definitely *not* quite the same as someone else's! At least none of the fishes died, although my aquascape looks a little like the after effects of a nuclear war zone!

Chapter 4
Aquatic Plants

Aquatic plants are much more than pretty aquarium decorations. They are a vital part of most fishes' ecosystem, performing a crucial role in the maintenance of water conditions. I must confess and say that, for me, these wonderful miniature processing factories rate at least equal in importance with fishes in my own aquarist activities.

The Green Guide

If you have no interest in aquatic plants – perhaps you plan to keep Rift Valley cichlids – then this section may safely be skipped. What follows is an explanation and description of aquatic plants, what they are, how they live and reproduce themselves, and the important work they do in the aquarium. I assume that you want to make maximum use of plants within your tank, giving them equal rating to the fishes. If this is not so, then you'll have to pick and choose the information relevant or important to you.

Plants

True aquatic plants live most of their lives submerged. They obtain nutrients from the surrounding water, absorbing them through roots, stem and stomata (pores) on leaves. They reproduce themselves in a variety of ways (see *Propagation* later on in this chapter). Aquatic plants come in a wide variety of shapes, sizes and colours, and most of them are quite easy to grow. Thanks to pioneering work by British, German and especially Dutch aquarists, the art of luxurious plant growth in aquaria is no longer a mystery.

For the new aquarist, obtaining the right type of plants can be a problem, as some shops and garden centres are not above offering bog plants, and even house plants, for sale as true aquatic species. In nature, bog plants live with their roots submerged, and their foliage clear of the water (emerse). They are accustomed to occasional complete submersion, such as when rivers or lakes flood, but they don't like to be kept permanently under water, and will usually wither and die if they are. House plants will survive for only a short time submerged before they too die. In this book, the plants listed in Chapter 11, *Database of Aquatic Plants* are nearly all true aquatic species, known and grown by generations of fishkeepers the world over.

The Role Of Plants

Aquatic plants have many roles in the tropical aquarium. They look natural, as if they really do belong there. They provide areas of shade and light which mimic that found in the fishes' natural habitats, offer shelter and protection for shy or very young fishes, supply food for herbivores and serve as spawning sites for many species. But by far their single most important attribute is the vital contribution they make in establishing a balanced biosphere, which helps to maintain good water quality. Indeed, plants are so good at 'cleaning' the water that the best filtration system available to the aquarist is actually to have none at all!

Although it seems strange to say, but none

A good aquatic shop will keep their plants in running water rather than just a simple bucket or tray.

the less true for all that, ideal water conditions for plants don't always coincide with the needs of the fishes. Naturally, compromises have to be made, and balances struck. Many fishes expect to find plants in their aquaria, and can become very stressed if they're not present. Conversely, some species would be very puzzled indeed to find plants within their aquatic environment.

How Plants Live Underwater

Just like species which grow on land, aquatic plants photosynthesise, which generates the energy for them to live, and which also provides a very useful service to the aquarium water as an integral byproduct of this process.

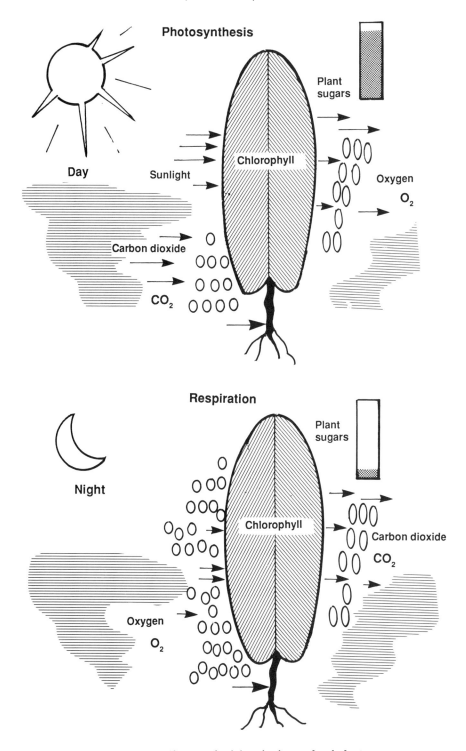

Figure 4.1   Photosynthesis/respiration cycle of plants.

Photosynthesis

Photosynthesis is the process whereby chlorophyll in the plant (the green colouring), carbon dioxide and water all chemically interact in the presence of light, to produce glucose-type sugars within the plant. As a natural byproduct of photosynthesis, oxygen is generated and 'exhaled' into the surrounding water. That's why aquatic plants are often described as oxygenators. Further processing by the plant during darkness, using various enzymes, turns the sugars into starches, and ultimately amino-acids.

Respiration

At night photosynthesis ceases, due to the absence of light. The plant begins its respiration cycle, which is basically the reverse of its daytime activity of photosynthesis. Sugars and starches, built up throughout the day, are consumed during respiration. Oxygen is now *absorbed* from the water, to aid the reduction of sugars, which produces energy for the plant mainly in the form of heat. Just as oxygen is a byproduct of photosynthesis, carbon dioxide (CO_2) is produced during the respiration stage, and is 'exhaled' into the surrounding water.

Remember from Chapter 2 that CO_2 can lower the pH of the water by producing carbonic acid (H_2CO_3). When testing the pH, avoid taking a sample in the early morning. The CO_2 level will have been increasing throughout the night, due to respiration. Make your test around midday, or early afternoon. For those aquarists who ignore stocking levels, and who keep large numbers of fishes in small, heavily planted aquaria, their fishes are at their greatest risk during the night, when oxygen levels are lowest, and CO_2 content is highest. Plants generally produce more O_2 during the day than they do CO_2 throughout the night.

Chlorophyll Production

A plant generates its chlorophyll from nutrients such as nitrates, sulphates and phosphates, which are present in the aquarium water. Plants also require many trace elements for successful growth. Amongst the more important are iron, copper, zinc, and manganese. Although nitrates, phosphates and sulphates are normally in plentiful supply, thanks to the super-efficient filtration systems used by many of today's aquarists, the aquarium water may become deficient in trace elements which have been 'snatched' by the filtration system. Many manufacturers make a range of fertilisers and substrate additives designed to rectify this.

Sometimes, again purely due to over-efficient aquarium filters, even the basic nitrate level may be well below what the plants require, low though this value is, and will naturally restrict their development. Again, various aquatic companies offer nitrogen-based fertilisers for sale. But do stop and think long and hard before adding such a product to your water. Excess nitrate in aquarium water is often an explanation for poor plant growth! The only way to be sure how much nitrate is in your tank is to measure it directly.

If you don't have a nitrate deficiency problem – there are many other reasons why plants won't grow – then, by adding more, in the form of a fertiliser, you could be killing your fishes by building up a toxic amount of nitrate. Adding a nitrogenous substance to an aquarium already rich in nitrates will cause problems. Levels above 150/200 mg/l will kill your fishes. Levels around 100 mg/l will inhibit good growth of plants.

A Balanced Biosphere

In the wild, a natural balance is established between the waste products of aquatic animals and plants and their surrounding biosphere. Providing there is no additional loading on this system, such as pollution from whatever source, rivers and lakes are quite able to maintain the naturally good quality of their water. In nature (as in the aquarium), the balance is always between the amount of fish and other waste products produced, and the effluent which the biosphere can dispose of without artificial aid.

An aquarium with a large amount of aquatic plant growth and few fishes will not need any additional filtration at all to maintain the water quality. Both plants and fishes will grow and thrive, and there are many aquarists around the world who firmly believe in this homoeostasis principle, even though they were laughed at during the late 1970s and 1980s! This *does not* mean that a *naturally* balanced aquarium may be safely left to its own devices once homoeostasis has been achieved! Balanced biospheres still require attention, but not as much as one set up with an artificial filtration system.

This densely planted aquarium still allows the fishes plenty of free swimming space at the front of the tank.

Obviously, in the aquarium the number of fishes which may be safely kept in an amount of water will be many times lower than in the wild, due to the smaller volume of water and its static nature. It is only when the production of waste products exceeds the biosphere's ability to break down the effluent, and utilise the results as plant food etc., that the balance is broken, and you have to introduce artificial filtration methods to cope with the extra loading and to maintain good water quality. (See *Filters*, p69.)

Keeping more fishes than is recommended for that particular size of tank, over-feeding or poor maintenance routine are the usual methods by which the natural balance of an ecosystem is broken. But there aren't that many aquarists who're prepared to keep just six, 75 cm (3 in) size fishes in a 90×45×30 cm (36× 18×12 in) aquarium!

No Grow Area

Having established that aquatic plants in an aquarium are highly desirable, many aquarists seem to have nothing but trouble trying to cultivate them.

There is no simple answer to the question 'Why can't I grow plants?'. What we can do is examine some of the situations which will prevent vigorous growth, and then go on to discuss what we can do to promote healthy, flourishing plants – and ultimately, reproduction – within the water available for our use.

Starting with the more obvious first; the basic life-process of a plant is photosynthesis. Therefore, anything which interferes with this is going to either restrict growth or prevent it completely. The essentials of photosynthesis are carbon dioxide (CO_2), water (H_2O), chlorophyll and light. Problems in any of these areas will affect the health of plants.

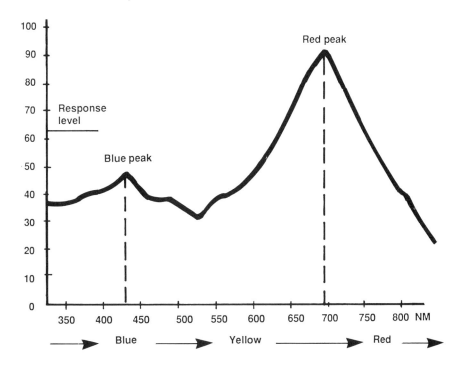

Figure 4.2 Photosynthesis response of plants to light. Violet-blue/orange-red spectral peaks on photosynth.

Light

For millions of years, plants have been photosynthesising using the light from the sun, and even today it cannot be bettered for promoting healthy plant growth. However, we have little control over sunlight – it varies from day to day and season to season – and is often too much or not enough. Aquarists mostly prefer controllable forms of lighting, and mainly use artificial methods, such as incandescent bulbs or fluorescent tubes.

Plants' photosynthesis response to light peaks at two different parts of the spectrum: at the violet/blue end, and also in the orange/red. In simple terms, plants respond best to orange/red and violet/blue lighting. Therefore, any artificial illumination we supply for our aquaria should have a healthy output in these areas of the spectrum. If it doesn't, then the plants' photosynthetic process will not be as efficient as it could be.

Furthermore, the intensity and duration of the light is very important. If there is an insufficient light level, then the photosynthesis process cannot work properly. It is not simply a case where you may leave a weak light on for a longer time; it doesn't work like that. There has to be a certain minimum level of light for the process to start working in the first place.

Incandescent light bulbs give most of their output in the red end of the spectrum, with little at the blue, so they aren't very efficient for photosynthesis purposes. Many manufacturers produce scientifically-researched fluorescent tubes which have spectral outputs carefully tailored for the needs of aquatic plants. More details of these and lighting in general will be found in Chapter 5 *Aquarium Hardware*.

Carbon Dioxide / Water

As I said earlier, purely from the viewpoint of providing Utopian conditions for plant growth, there is often conflict between the needs of fishes and plants. The photosynthesis process requires fairly large amounts of CO_2 gas dissolved in the aquarium water (assuming that there are a lot of plants, of course). Most beginner-type fishkeeping books advocate aeration to remove as much CO_2 from the water as possible! The trouble with many hobby aquarists is that their tank water is usually too clean! Chemical, mechanical and biological methods of filtration may further remove large quantities of CO_2 from the water, depriving the plants. Insufficient CO_2 will restrict aquatic plant growth, and is the most usual cause of poor growth in an aquarium.

Similarly, fishkeepers often have quite violent aeration running, which, apart from liberating large amounts of the necessary carbon dioxide gas at the water surface/air interface, also increases the amount of dissolved oxygen present in the water. Normally we would say that this is a very good thing from the fishes viewpoint. Unfortunately, high levels of dissolved oxygen will oxidise some of the vital trace elements plants need to aid chlorophyll production. Oxidation turns certain trace elements into a form which is unusable by the plants. If these trace elements cannot be removed by the plants, then they stay in the water and will eventually become a problem. So, apart from possible CO_2 deficiencies, the plants may also be suffering from nutriment deprivation as well. Don't worry yet about answers – I still haven't finished with the problem!

Undergravel Filters

Many aquarists claim that they cannot grow plants when using undergravel filters. The standard explanation for this is that they (the plants, not the aquarists!) don't like moving water around their root systems. I've had tanks with undergravel filters and healthy, even luxurious plant growth. I've also had other tanks with an undergravel (U/G) filter where plant growth has

been abysmal. Again, I've also succeeded and failed in growing good plants in aquaria without U/G filters too. So you see, it's not quite as simple as saying that you can't grow good plants if you use undergravel filtration.

There almost certainly is a link between U/G filters and poor plant growth, because so many aquarists have reported this problem over the years. And, as the only connection between all the complainants is the U/G filter system (water quality varies, even with two tanks on the same stand), then this obviously must be at the heart of the problem. In truth, I don't know what causes this strange effect when using U/G filters. It may be that the flow of water past the roots is taking nutrients and trace elements away from the plant before it has time to absorb them. Maybe there are high levels of dissolved oxygen in the substrate which is oxidising trace elements and depriving the plant. Only more research will answer the question. Whatever the cause, take it from me, that you *can* grow perfectly healthy aquatic plants in the aquarium when using undergravel filters. Especially if you follow the advice in this book, and are prepared to take a little trouble.

Growth Industry

CO_2

To promote vigorous growth we have to ensure that we're giving the plants what they want, and that they receive adequate amounts of light, nutriment, trace elements and dissolved gases. It's easier for the newcomer to ensure that less CO_2 is removed in the first place than to try and add extra amounts into the aquarium afterwards – it's much cheaper as well. Injecting additional amounts of CO_2 into the aquarium water is an advanced aquarist technique, and requires very careful attention, otherwise fishes may suffer or even die. Also, the extra equipment needed to inject CO_2 into the aquarium is expensive. I am presently running an experiment to add CO_2 into the aquarium, but which doesn't cost a fortune, nor requires expensive electronic test equipment – more of this later.

I said earlier that compromises have to be made between the needs of the fishes and those of the plants, so start compromising with the airstone first. Try not to have violent aeration, with masses of bubbles causing mini maelstroms on the surface. This will help retain CO_2 in the water. After all, the amount of dissolved oxygen required by fish is usually grossly overstated anyway. If you stick to the stocking formula, as detailed in Chapter 5 – which has been carefully calculated on the assumption that *no* additional aeration will be used anyway – then you will not require that airstone in the first place.

On the other hand, fishes which don't usually have much plant growth in their biosphere, and which also require a higher dissolved oxygen content, such as Rift Valley cichlids, *will require* strong aeration. However, here we are discussing Utopian plant conditions, and not fishes.

Filters

If it wasn't for the amount of food dumped into the aquarium by the aquarist in the first place, tanks wouldn't need filters at all! Many filter systems in home aquaria, and often in complete biosphere tropical aquaria as well, are just too efficient, practically turning out drinking water. As well as those substances which should be removed, useful organic, and inorganic trace elements are often taken out by chemical, mechanical and biological filter systems. Again, a balance has to be struck – you have to accept that, although conditions are not perfect, they're the best you can provide given what you're trying to achieve. If you must have a powerful filter, that's OK, but remember that you might have to add supplements to the plants' diet to replace trace elements snatched by the filtration system. Products such as *FloraPride*, by the Tetra company, or *Flora Boost*, from Interpet are designed for this purpose.

Lighting

For an aquarium 60×38×30 cm (24×15×12 inches) long, deep and wide, the recommended lighting is 30 watts of fluorescent tubing – usually provided by 2 tubes of 15 watts each. One of the so-called secrets of lush plant growth (apart from injecting extra CO_2) is to boost the light level by adding extra fluorescent light tubes. I use a similar size tank to keep gouramis and, in the last one I set up, it had

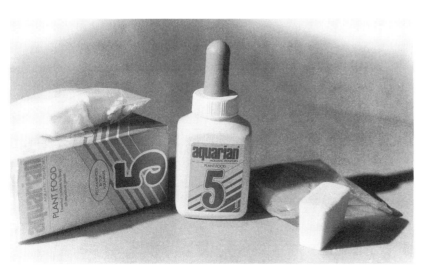

Plant fertilisers come in tablet and liquid forms.

three 15 watt tubes crowded in. You don't have to have this extra lighting on all the time. Over-bright illumination can cause stress in the fishes, and may damage their eyes after a while. I used two tubes as the normal lighting (one *Grolux* and one *Northlight*), and switched in another *Northlight* tube for an extra four hours a day. The plants grew.

Sometimes with extra lighting, whether deliberately introduced or by unavoidable exposure to sunlight through a window, the ever-present algae can run riot. Glass, electrical equipment, plants and decorations can be plastered in the stuff. The higher your tank temperature, then the worse the algae problem. Adding an *Algicide*, such as *Alg Away*, from Interpet, will help clear

An algae-eating Catfish going eagerly to work on the glass front of an aquarium, rasping away the algae with its specially shaped mouth.

the tank, as will a UV sterilising system. But, as always, I prefer natural methods. If I get an explosion of green algae (which is quite rare, but it does happen), I first check conditions. Is it a one-off situation, or will it recur? Adding extra plants to utilise more of the light, nitrate and CO_2 present in the water will keep the algae down. Just keep on adding more plants until the algae problem stops.

Keeping algae-eating species of fishes, such as *Hypostomus sp.*, in the tank can help too, but not as much as people often claim. Only reduce the level of illumination as a last resort if the problem still exists after taking all these steps.

Substrates

A not unreasonable question for a new aquarist would be: 'Why do we need a substrate at all?'

Once you understand the need for some form of substrate, then providing one of the right sort is a simple matter. Firstly, we are keeping fish in a glass container, which is in itself unusual from the fishes' viewpoint. Without a substrate covering the bottom glass, they can become very stressed. *We* understand what a reflection is – the fishes have no idea. We also need something for the aquatic plants to root into, so that they may grow well and so we can arrange them in an attractive display.

In some types of filter, the whole of the substrate is utilised as a huge biological filter bed, housing colonies of millions of aerobic bacteria, which help convert toxic gases and chemicals into other, safer substances. The substrate also forms an important buffer for the water chemistry, helping to maintain its composition. There are species of fish which have evolved to feed on and in the river or lake bed, such as the various catfishes. A gravel or sand substrate neatly imitates conditions such species expect to find in their immediate aquatic environment. Finally, certain fishes lay their eggs and bury them in the substrate. If there isn't one then they will not, *cannot*, breed at all.

Substrate Types

Non-calciferous river gravel is the substrate preferred by tropical aquarists – actually getting it is another thing entirely! Practically all gravel sold by aquatic dealers contains some (often a lot!) calciferous content. Pick a fairly dark colour with a 2mm particle size, which permits easy passage for plant roots, as well as good stem support. Fishes can get very nervous swimming over light-coloured substrates, although what they make of the current trend for using yellow, pink, purple, scarlet and blue dyed gravels is anybody's guess! As light-coloured substrates reflect a fair amount of the aquarium illumination back up through the water, it can 'bleach out' the colours of the fish, and sometimes

Plate 1   Male Siamese Fighting Fish – *Betta splendens*.

Plate 2   Female Siamese Fighting Fish – *Betta splendens*.

Plate 3   Suckermouth Catfish – *Hypostomus* sp.

Plate 4   Male Dwarf Gourami – *Colisa sota (lalia)*.

Plate 5   Lace (Pearl) Gourami – *Trichogaster leeri*.

Plate 6   Three-spot Gourami – *Trichogaster trichopterus*.

Plate 7   Opaline Gourami – *Trichogaster sumatranus*.

Plate 8   Corydorus Catfish – *Corydorus paleatus*.

Plate 9   Beacon Fish – *Hemigrammus ocellifer*.

Plate 10   Male Guppy – *Poecilia reticulata*.

Plate 11 Black Molly – *Poecilia sphenops (mexicanus)*.

Plate 14 – Swordtail (male) – *Xiphophorus helleri*.

Plate 12 Sailfin Molly – *Poecilia velifera*.

Plate 15 White Cloud Mountain Minnow – *Tanichthys albonubes*.

Plate 13 Platy – *Xiphophorus maculatus*.

Plate 16 Zebra Danio – *Brachydanio rerio*.

Plate 17   Black Widow – *Gymnocorymbus ternezti.*

Plate 18   Silver Dollar – *Mylossoma argenteum* (*Metynnis rossevelti*).

Plate 19   Bleeding Heart Tetra – *Hyphessobrycon* sp.

Plate 20   Neon Tetra – *Parachirodon innesi.*

Plate 21   Angelfish – *Pterophyllum scalare.*

Plate 22   Tiger Barb – *Barbus tetrazona.*

Plate 23   Japanese Rush – *Acorus gramineus*.

Plate 24   Aponogeton – *Aponogeton crispus*.

Plate 25   Bacopa – *Bacopa caroliniana*.

Plate 26   Cabomba – *Cabomba caroliniana*.

Plate 27   Water Wisteria – *Hygrophila difformis (Synema triflorum)*.

Plate 28   Canadian Pondweed – *Elodea densa*.

Plate 29   Water Milfoil – *Myriophyllum*.

Plate 30   Hairgrass – *Eleocharis acicularis*.

Plate 31   Ambulia – *Limnophila aquatica*.

Plate 32   Ludwigia – *Ludwigia natans*.

Plate 33   Amazon Sword – *Echindodorus* sp.

Plate 34   Pygmy Chain Sword – *Echinodorus tenellus*.

Plate 35   Sagittaria – *Sagittaria*.

Plate 36   Vallis – *Vallisneria tortifolia*.

Plate 37   Twisted Vallis – *Vallisneria spiralis*.

Plate 38   Java Moss – *Vesicularia dubyana*.

Plate 39   Pennywort – *Hydrocotyle vulgaris*.

Plate 40   Cascade waterfall aquatic plant display.

Substrate additives, to give your plants a flying start.

causes their intrinsic colours to lighten, to match with the ambient light level, making them look faded and somehow 'odd'.

Enriched Substrates

There's no doubt that some form of additional substrate planting medium, whether it be *Laterite* clay, or a simple hydroculture plant pot, is a good idea for enhanced plant growth. However, some of the additives and mixtures now discussed make it either impossible to use the undergravel filter system, or reduce its effectiveness by so much as to make it virtually useless. Where this is the case I have given a warning.

Laterite Clay (Everite Number 1)

This iron-enriched powder is mixed with water into a paste and then spread evenly across the glass bottom of the aquarium, on top of which will go the gravel substrate. Of course, this makes the use of undergravel filters impossible. Many aquarists seeking perfection in their substrates like to add Everite No.1 to *Aquasoil* – a product sold by water gardens for potting up water lilies etc. Add enough *Aquasoil* to form a 12mm layer (.5 in) at the bottom of the tank, sprinkle on both sachets of *Everite No.1*, and then add just enough water to make a thick paste. Spread out the *Everite No.1/Aquasoil* mixture and then leave it for a couple of days to 'harden' off.

Finally, add 75 cm (3 in) of gravel on top to finish off the 'perfect' plant substrate. The

An Aquasoil/gravel substrate. Using undergravel filters is impracticable when laying this type of substrate.

whole idea is that the clay/soil/gravel mixture releases trace elements slowly, over a period of time, up into the plant's roots.

Aquasoil – Aqualit

A very useful planting medium can be made from an *Aquasoil*/gravel, *Aqualit* (which is a granular mixture of peat and enriched clay) and gravel; or *Aqualit*/*Aquasoil* and gravel mixtures. Lay the *Aquasoil* or the *Aqualit* first, if using them separately, and the gravel on top; or put the *Aqualit* on top of the *Aquasoil* if combining both these products, creating a layer around 25mm (1 in) and place 5 cm (2 in) of gravel on top. This will severely restrict the effectiveness of any undergravel filtration system being used. Changing to powerheads as the U/G driving force isn't the answer either, as the increased water flow tends to start circulating the *Aquasoil* or the *Aqualit*.

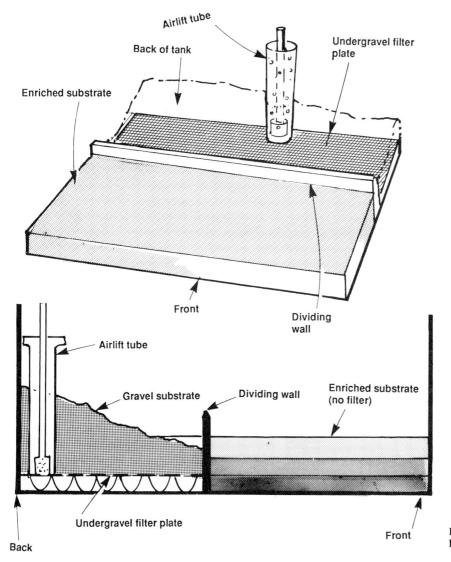

Figure 4.3   Half enriched/half U/G filtered aquarium.

Peat

Peat planting mats can be buried underneath a gravel substrate, and will add various hormones and nutrients to the aquarium water, as well as acidifying it (lowering the pH). I must admit that peat is one of my favourite substrate additives, but there are one or two slight problems associated with its use. First, be careful when using peat sold by garden centres. This may contain growth-enhancing hormones and pesticides, which can be lethal to fishes. It is quite true, though, that many experienced aquarists prefer to buy and use peat from garden centres.

Secondly, some aquarists in the interest of economy add loose peat to the substrate, as an additive. Now, this is fine, just as long as you don't put it directly on top of undergravel filter plates. If you do, you'll find that you have particles of peat endlessly circulating around the aquarium! The specially-prepared peat planting mats are compressed, which prevents

this happening, although they do restrict the flow of an undergravel filter system. Remember that peat does 'wear out' eventually, and will need replacing.

Hybrid Systems

You may want the best of all possible methods and decide that you want to use Laterite clay, *Aquasoil, Aqualit*; and yet *still* use undergravel filters! Well, all things are possible, given enough time and motivation. What you could do is give over half the aquarium space to an enriched substrate (which won't have any U/G undergravel) filtration), such as the back half of the aquarium, and put undergravel filter plates your U/G system is only half as good as it could be, so you will have to make up the difference somehow, such as by adding an internal power filter arrangement.

This may sound like a filter conflict, with the U/G filter etc. removing nitrite from the

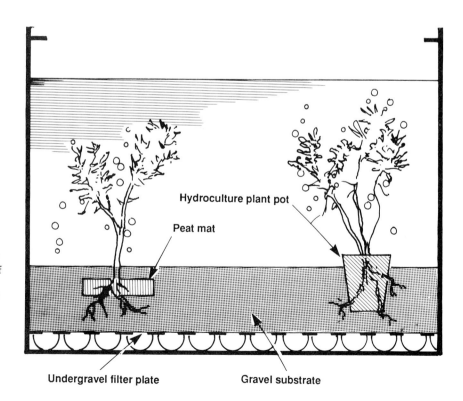

Figure 4.4 Peat planting mats. Placing small pieces of peat just below the surface of the substrate and then rooting your plant into it can give the plant a good start when using the undergravel filter system. Alternatively, you can use the special hydroculture plant pots which are designed for this purpose.

Hydroculture plant pot

Peat mat

Undergravel filter plate

Gravel substrate

enriched substrate. But remember why we're enriching the substrate in the first place – to allow a steady release of trace elements. There will usually be no shortage of nitrite, not with the average amount of food dumped into the tank each day!

Established Substrates

All this is fine for those aquarists who are about to set up for the first time. But what about the aquarium which has been established for some time, yet still experiences poor plant growth? I've already mentioned liquid/tablet aquatic fertilisers. There is also *Everite Number 2*, which has the same constitution as *Everite 1* but comes in a pelleted form, so that it can be added to an existing substrate. Finally, the more care and pre-planning (and reading, of course) that you do *before* starting to construct your aquascape, then the more pleasing and cheaper will be the final result. Imagine constructing your complete aquarium and then reading this section of the book!

As an aside I just can't resist, the famous aquarist Mary Bailey tells me that she 'knew' someone who used to place a guinea-pig dropping next to an *Echinodorus sp.* (Amazon sword plant), which made the plant grow very well indeed!

Potty Plants

If you've no particular interest in involving yourself with the often messy business of creating an enriched substrate, and in any case prefer to use undergravel filters, there is still much that you can do. One way of avoiding water passing around the roots of plants in aquariums utilising undergravel filters, is to plant them over a mat. (See Figure 4.4.) Although this does cut down the efficiency of the U/G filter plates, this is no bad thing. However, a more elegant solution is to locate the plants in specially made hydroculture plant pots. These pots can be loaded with either rock wool, *Aquasoil* or sphagnum moss. Fertiliser, in tablet form, can also be added to the substrate in the pot. The container, complete with the plant may now be buried in the gravel.

Hydroculture planting kit. Pots, rockwool and tablet fertilisers.

Plant Care

Why some aquarists believe that, once planted, aquatic plants may safely be left to their own devices, is beyond me! What state would your front garden be in if the grass was never cut, flowers and shrubs never pruned back, or borders left to grow wild? In Chapter 6, *Creating A Community Aquarium*, I've covered the subject of designing and building your basic aquascape (ie. the way you set out your tank decorations and plants).

When you create your aquascape – exactly like a landscape gardener – you're *not* creating a finished product. What you are doing is arranging things so that they will grow into the

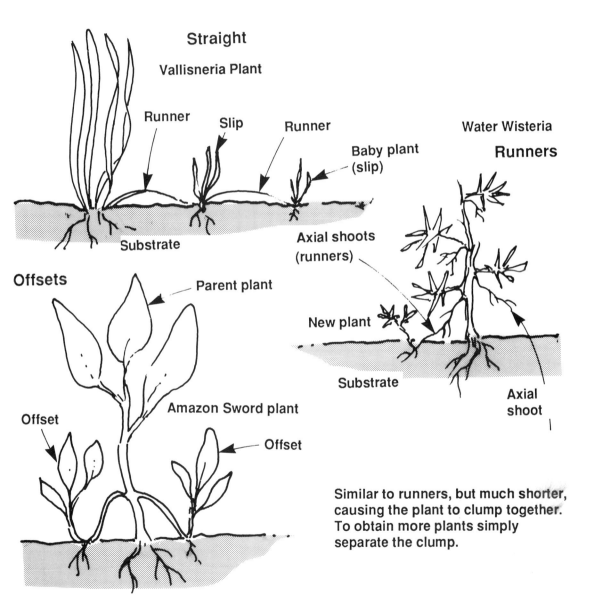

Figure 4.5 Asexual plant propagation.

final product. Room has to be left for plants to grow, for gaps to fill-in, and the various sections allowed to reach their maximum heights. After a while, and if all is well, *now* you should see that aquascape you originally planned. And now is the time to start working to keep it this way. This may mean re-planting, pruning, cutting back, even thinning out. Whatever it takes, you must work at it to keep your tank looking the way you originally envisaged.

Adventitious shoots

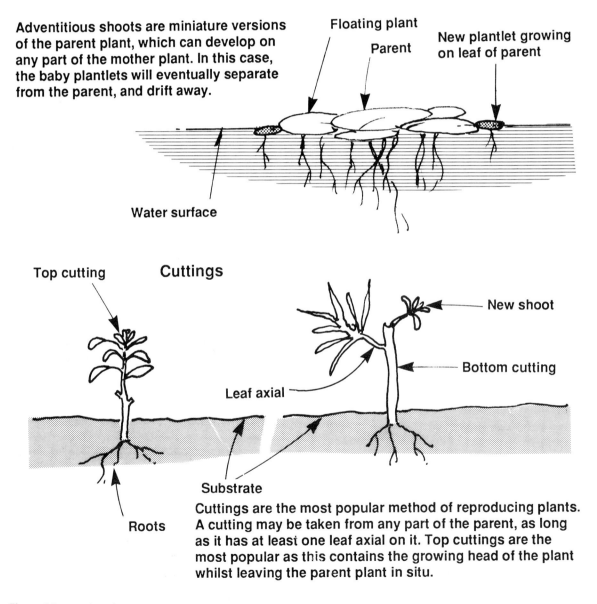

Adventitious shoots are miniature versions of the parent plant, which can develop on any part of the mother plant. In this case, the baby plantlets will eventually separate from the parent, and drift away.

Floating plant

Parent

New plantlet growing on leaf of parent

Water surface

Cuttings

Top cutting

New shoot

Bottom cutting

Leaf axial

Substrate

Roots

Cuttings are the most popular method of reproducing plants. A cutting may be taken from any part of the parent, as long as it has at least one leaf axial on it. Top cuttings are the most popular as this contains the growing head of the plant whilst leaving the parent plant in situ.

Figure 4.5 *continued.*

Propagation

A Blooming Business

Having taken such care to ensure that our plants have everything they need for a healthy life, and having established and watched them grow, it's time to start thinking about increasing their numbers. An aquarist who's good with plants will always have lots of friends. I must have equipped every aquarium in the city of Nottingham during the 1970s, with *Hygrophila difformis*, which grew at such an explosive rate in my tanks!

Species listed in Chapter 11, *Database of Aquatic Plants* mostly reproduce themselves asexually - they don't go through the flower/ pollination and seed stages. Asexual propaation may be by runners, offsets, rhizome splitting or cuttings. Figure 4.5 demonstrates how each method is used.

A Rubber Plant?

There is one species of plant which even the most ham-fisted aquarist cannot kill, which doesn't need any special substrate, has no pre-ferred pH, lighting, temperature or water hardness requirements, and which the fishes can't eat – an artificial one. In the past, these items were little more than fun tank decorations. However, today's artificial creations are often quite stunning in their realism. Some even sway gently underwater, exactly like the real thing. Often you simply cannot tell fake from real. The *Plantastic* range, distributed by the Interpet company, are about the best I've seen.

Although a tank full of these 'plants' isn't going to do a thing for your water quality directly, they will still look good, provide areas of light, shade and protection, and give spawning fish somewhere to put their eggs. When they've been in the aquarium for a while, artificial plants acquire a coating of nitrifying bacteria which will assist with maintaining water quality – but not all that much! Even though an aquarium full of artificial plants such as the *Plantastic* range would look as good as their real counterparts, this is not the best way to utilise them. And it would cost a fortune too.

When aquascaping, blend artificial with real plants. I've seen some really stunning aquascapes using this method, completely unaware that some of the display were plastic and not cellu-

Plantastics **artificial plant range distributed by Interpet. (*Reproduced by kind permission of Willinger Bros., Inc. Oakland, New Jersey, USA*)**

lose based! Use the easily grown species as your real plants, and artificial for the exotic (which are often costly) or hard to grow specimens.

Choosing Aquatic Plants

The *Database of Aquatic Plants* in Chapter 11 lists a range of suitable species for the newcomer, together with their growing height, main characteristics, temperature range, water conditions, pH and lighting requirements. The *Database* also explains where the plant should be located in the aquarium. Because a plant is

not listed, that doesn't mean you can't grow it. The *Database* is purely my own opinion on what is easy to grow.

Many of the specialist aquatic nurseries offer special selections of plants at very advantageous prices, such as a forty-plant selection for a 60cm (24 in) tank for around £6. This is a much cheaper option than buying the same forty plants individually which, at an average cost of .45p each, would add up to a whopping great £18! As aquatic nurseries, such as *Ocean Aquatics* and *The Tropical Plantation* (addresses in Appendix 3) survive on their good reputation for supplying

Making up a bottle of aquarium water and injecting it with CO_2 from a Soda Stream machine. The idea is to increase the amount of CO_2 in the aquarium.

quality plants, you can be reassured that your forty-plant tank selection won't consist of rejects!

When buying plants – whether in bulk or singly – look first at the root system. If there are lots of clean, healthy-looking white or green shoots, then the plant is a good specimen, even though it may have hardly any leaves showing. Plants with soggy, brown/black roots should be rejected immediately, even though they may have a luxuriant growth of foliage. If the basic root system is dead or dying, the rest of the plant will shortly follow suit.

The CO_2 Experiment

As intimated earlier, I am at the moment experimenting with adding extra amounts of CO_2 into my aquarium water. Now, I'm no millionaire, so the system has to be cheap, use everyday articles and not require a doctorate in water biology to operate. This is what I've been doing.

My son (the 'model' in most of the photographs) is rather fond of fizzy drinks, so we bought a carbonising outfit called a *Sodastream*. You fill the special bottles with ordinary water and place the bottle into the machine. You then press a button which squirts CO_2 gas into the bottle, making it fizzy and then add a flavouring.

After giving this a deal of thought, I filled a Sodastream bottle (which I keep just for this purpose) with water from my test aquarium, and added some CO_2 gas; then emptied the bottle back into the aquarium. It's too early yet to report anything significant. What will be interesting is that I'm presently looking after a pair of Silver Dollars, which are eating every piece of Amazon sword and water wisteria in the tank! It will be interesting to see what effect the extra carbon dioxide has on these 'empty' plant stalks, as well as my other plants.

Lead Weights

Finally, many aquarists prefer to anchor their plants into the substrate with lead weights. What concerns me – apart from the concentration and build-up of lead particles in the water – is the sheer number of plants I've seen which have died below the level where the lead weight has been attached, proving that it was put on far too tightly in the first place, strangling the plant. Specimens with good roots don't need lead weights. As long as the root system is spread out and anchored purely by the gravel substrate, then you don't need lead weights anyway. But if you must use them, then attach them to the plant loosely.

Correct planting is also important. Ensure that the plant isn't pushed too deeply into the gravel, burying the crown (the part where the stalks start to split away from the roots), which will kill the plant. Planting them slightly higher than the crown is a better idea because as the roots begin to grow they will 'pull' the plant down to its correct position.

Chapter 5
Aquarium Hardware

Plant life in the aquarium is totally dependent on water conditions, which are maintained by the aeration, lighting, heating and filtration apparatus. This chapter explains what this equipment is, what it does, how to use it and what it will cost you. I merely explain what the stuff is, its average cost and what it all does – *you* have to make the choice as to what you actually buy.

Tanks

Fish tanks are usually bought with a specific purpose, number or breed of fish in mind – for example, as community, hospital, breeding or hydroculture aquaria, as growing-on tanks for fry, as a room-corner filling ornament or as a single-species biosphere. Try to decide which species you're going to be keeping, and in what numbers *before* laying out money on a tank. If only I had a few pennies for every aquarist who's ever said to me in the past: 'I wish I'd bought a bigger tank!'

Assuming you don't yet know which species you are going to be keeping, then fall back on plan B – always buy the biggest tank you can afford. This keeps all your options open for the future. An under-populated aquarium hurts nobody. Over population results in rapid death for the fishes. Additionally, the bigger the volume of water you have available then the easier it is to maintain. Things tend to happen much more slowly in large aquaria. For example, in a power failure the water temperature of a 90 litre (20 gallon) aquarium will fall more slowly than a 45 litre (10 gallon) tank – and not just twice as slowly either!

Tank Construction

Today's tanks are usually of all-glass construction, with no supporting metal framework of angle-iron. Each glass wall is bonded to its neighbour with silicone sealant adhesive. This is a tremendously strong, watertight glue which is 'tougher' than the actual glass itself. I once dropped a 30×30×30cm (12×12×12in) exhibition tank, which shattered. All, that is, except for the joints, which were still firmly stuck together!

Some of the newer all-glass tanks (as well as the older *GEM* tanks) have a decorative plastic trim around the top and the bottom. At the top, this trim prevents the hood from scratching, or chipping the glass. At the bottom, it helps with levelling the aquarium. Even so, many aquarists still prefer to stand their plastic trimmed aquaria on polystyrene tiles.

The advantages of all-glass construction are many. For the marine aquarist there's no angle-iron to rust and poison the water. Because of the adhesive – which is completely inert and impervious to saltwater – leaks are most unlikely. Special tank sizes or shapes are easily built and, because of their simplicity, all-glass aquaria represent remarkable value for money, as well as looking very stylish and modern.

All-glass isn't the only way tanks are made today. Aquarists who are planning to have a tank built into a wall of their home may use a GRP (Glass Reinforced Plastic) moulded shell for the bottom, back and two ends, which will be hidden in the walls, and a sheet of high quality glass for the front.

Small aquaria, up to around 50cm (20 inches) in length, can be made from a one-piece injection moulding of acrylic plastic. They are cheap and fairly hard wearing, although the plastic is said to scratch easily. The Interpet and Rolf C Hagen companies (amongst others) make a range of such plastic aquaria – usually aimed at junior fishkeepers. They also make good 'hospital' or breeding tanks for adult aquarists as well, so don't write them off just because they're made from plastic.

However, there is one acrylic tank available which has impressed me greatly. I know it sounds silly, but the transparency of the plastic material, from which the tank is made, seems to be somehow much clearer, brighter and sharper than glass itself! It is a self-contained *Biosphere* tank, and these are discussed later.

Tank Size

Fish tanks come in a range of standard sizes, or can be custom-made to any dimensions. Almost all the standard sizes are based on the 'double' or 'triple' cube principle, eg. 60×30×30cm (24×12×12 inches), and 90×30×30 cm (36×12× 12 inches) – twice, or three times as long as they are wide. There is good reason for this. Not only

A typical all-glass aquarium.

must the tank hold everything (gravel, plants, fishes and water), but it also has to afford the fishes space in which to swim, and have as large a water surface area as possible to facilitate the exchange of gases with the surrounding air. The double or triple cubes are the best ratio compromise to achieve this. It is the surface area of the water in the tank which dictates just how many fishes it is safe to keep, *not* just the dimensions of the tank themselves. This may take some explaining, so keep reading.

Stocking Level

Consider two tanks: tank A is 30cm long by 90cm deep and 30cm wide (12×36×12in). (*All tank dimensions in this book are given as length, depth and width respectively*.) Tank B is 90×30×30cm (36×12×12in). Both tanks hold exactly the same amount of water, 80 litres (17 gallons). Yet we can keep *three* times as many fish in tank B than we can in A. Working out the surface area of tank A we find that it is $900cm_2$. But the surface area of tank B is a whacking $2700cm_2$!

One of the widely available range of acrylic plastic aquaria.

Tank Size		Volume			Heating	Lighting	Substrate		Stock level		Volume - 10% for medication		
cm	in	ltrs	UK gall	US gall			kg	lb	cm	in	ltrs	UK gall	US gall
30x30x30	12x12x12	27	6	7	50/100w	15w	15	35	30	12	24	5	6
45x30x30	18x12x12	40	9	10	50/100w	20w	23	52	45	18	36	8	9
60x30x30	24x12x12	54	12	14	100/150w	30w	31	70	60	24	48	10	12
60x38x30	24x15x12	68	15	18	100/150w	30w	31	70	60	24	61	13	16
75x30x30	30x12x12	67	15	18	100/150w	40w	40	87	75	30	60	13	16
75x38x30	30x15x12	82	19	22	150/200w	40w	47	105	75	30	73	17	19
90x30x30	36x12x12	81	17	21	150/200w	45w	47	105	90	36	72	15	18
90x38x30	36x15x12	102	22	27	150/250w	45w	47	105	90	36	91	20	24
120x30x30	48x12x12	108	23	28	200/250w	60w	63	140	120	48	97	21	25
120x38x30	48x15x12	136	30	36	250/300w	60w	63	140	120	48	122	26	32
120x45x30	48x18x12	162	35	42	300/350w	60w	63	140	120	48	145	32	38
160x45x30	62x18x12	216	47	56	350/450w	75w	79	175	160	62	194	42	51

Figure 5.1 Vital statistics of various sized tanks.

The much smaller surface area of tank A restricts the water's ability to give up CO_2 and other gases, and absorb O_2, and, of course, this means that the number of fishes must also be restricted, or the aquarium's ability to support life will be exceeded.

Stocking Formula

Surface area is calculated simply by multiplying the aquarium length by its width, and the answer will be in the square of whatever units were used to measure (inches or centimetres). For tropical fishes – which are the *only* type of fishes discussed in this book – allow 2.5cm (1in) of fish length (excluding the tail fin) for every $75cm^2$ ($12in^2$) of surface area. Once again, this formula only applies to tropical fishes. For cold-water or marine species, a different stocking formula is used, as these fish require more 'space' than tropicals.

If we take an aquarium of 60×25×30cm (24× 10×12in), then the surface area is $1800cm^2$ ($288in^2$), and the volume is 45 litres (10 gallons).

Volume = length × width × depth (in centimetres) divided by 1000, answer in litres. Multiply litres by 0.22 for UK gallons: multiply UK gallons by 1.2 for US gallons. So our tank will hold $1800cm^2$ surface area divided by $75cm^2$ (tropical stocking factor), answer = 24 inches of fish. In an aquarium measuring 60×25×30cm (24×10× 12in) we can keep 24 fishes, as long as they're all exactly 2.5cm (1in) long. Or 12 fishes, 5cm (2in) long, 6 fishes 10cm (4in) long, etc. What we most certainly cannot do is keep one fish 60cm (24in) long in a 60cm (24in) aquarium! The figures have to be interpreted with common sense. I'd never even think of keeping 24 fishes 25mm (1in) long in such a small tank as this.

Tank Shape

Although the majority of tank shapes are rectangular, based on the double or triple cube, this is by no means the only style available to aquarists. In fact, just about any shape which can be imagined can also be built. However, there are a few configurations which do not lend themselves naturally for keeping fishes, such as a deep cube or any form of upright triangle! Hexagonal tanks are very popular, as are 'flat' triangles, which are designed to fit into corners.

An unusual (but practicable) aquarium shape can and does lend an extra dimension to fish-keeping. However, as almost all accessories are designed for rectangular aquaria, you may experience difficulty when fitting certain types of lighting, or the pipework of a power filter, for example. The undergravel filter plates made by the Rolf C Hagen (UK) company (amongst others) are so designed that unusual-shaped tank bottoms can easily be accommodated.

An unusually-shaped aquarium can often add something extra to the combined beauty of the finished biosphere and fishes.

Buying an unusually-shaped aquarium may mean you adapting existing technology to fit the shape of your tank, so the decision whether to buy an unusual-shaped tank is not one you can take lightly, or on a whim!

Buying A Tank

Having decided on what size aquarium you need, and travelled to the shop to get it, pick out your tank and begin your pre-purchase inspection. Examine the glass closely – you're looking for minute cracks or chips, especially at the corners. Check the flow of silicone sealant along the seams – is it smooth and well finished? If fitted, check the cover glass shelves running the length of the front and back. Are they firmly attached? Are all the bracing struts (strips of glass running across the top of the tank, bracing the front and back glasses) present and secured?

Inspect the bottom of the tank thoroughly, too, especially if buying second-hand. Are there any worn areas which indicate that the tank hasn't been stood on a mat of some form, which could lead to a stress fracture in the future? If buying a second-hand tank, stick your head inside and smell. It should have a 'warm' watery odour. Any trace of sourness, be suspicious: not everyone keeps fishes in fish tanks!

Assuming that you're happy and have bought the tank, you have to transport it home. Don't pick it up using the cover glass rests or bracing struts. If it's small enough for one person to move, carry it with both your arms tucked underneath the bottom, like you would a baby. Try not to have it inside the car with you. Should anything happen, you really don't want that amount of glass laid unsecured on the back seat. If it will fit, stow it in the boot, wrapped in a blanket or travelling rug. If it must travel inside the car, then secure it on the back seat with rear seatbelts.

Cover Glasses And Hoods

You'd be amazed how many people forget

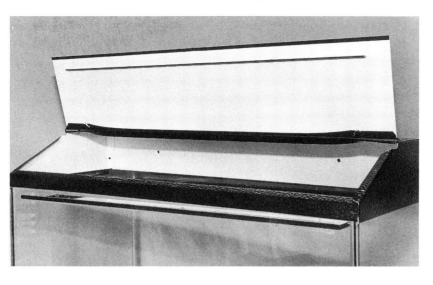

A fairly conventional and cheap aquarium hood showing fitting holes for the fluorescent lighting tube.

about hoods and cover glasses when buying a tank. Luckily, the shop owner will know what you should have, and drop a useful hint or two. Cover glasses are thin sheets of glass or plastic, sometimes referred to as 'condensation' covers, which seal off the surface of the aquarium, keeping condensation (and the fishes) in, and pollution out. The hood is simply somewhere to hide the chokes and tubes of fluorescent lighting systems and, increasingly, the place where a trickle biological filter may be located.

The best types of hood are those which fit the aquarium tightly, and have a hinged flap allowing access to the water, while leaving the main part of the hood, with its heavy lighting/filtration equipment, *in situ*. The light will have to pass through the cover glasses on its journey into the tank, so keep these very clean or you could find that your plants are losing around forty percent of the available light.

Cabinets

A growing trend today is fish tanks built into custom-made wooden display cabinets. These are often very practical, as well as beautiful, because they contain cupboards for storage, as well as hiding places for the necessary fish-keeping hardware, such as power filters, air pumps etc. But the thing I most like about them is that they can often swing a decision about whether or not you may be allowed to keep fish in your favour. Cabinet aquaria are very attractive, and form a very acceptable centrepiece in any living room or office environment.

Heavy Water

No matter what type of tank you acquire, it has to be located with a little thought – 4.56 litres (1 gallon) of water weighs approximately 4.53Kg (10lb). Using our example tank of 60×25×30cm which holds 45 litres (10 gallons). The weight of this fully set-up tank will be something like 45Kg (100lb) plus the weight of the aquarium itself and all the other contents besides the water; which adds up to a total which is very heavy! So beware of setting up a 90×30×30cm (36×12×12in) tank, which weighs-in at something like 80Kg (180lb) in your bedroom: the floor may not stand it. Check out the position of supporting joists and the legs of the aquarium stand in your bedroom – which should ideally coincide – before deciding.

Many of today's aquaria are housed in beautifully built and very practical cabinets. Pumps, filters and piping etc. can all be hidden away in various cupboards and drawers.

Full fish tanks are very heavy. Here, I am having a new fireplace built, and the site of the new aquarium is being reinforced to take the considerable weight. Note the double electric socket purposely placed there.

The finished fireplace and aquarium.

Similarly, don't stand a filled tank on flimsy supports, such as bookshelves, coffee tables or DIY projects built out of thin wood or metal. If you do decide on a DIY support – and I've seen some real beauties in my time – then bear in mind the weight of the filled tank and the contents, and remember that the *whole* of the aquarium bottom has to be supported, not just either end, so make it very strong.

Further, *never* stand a filled aquarium next to, or on top of, any electrical or electronic equipment such as televisions and stereos. Drips and condensation from the tank will produce that very expensive electric-blue flash, the smell of burning and lots of smoke, which repair shops are so very fond of, giving you a double shock. In the same manner, the cable which connects your aquarium's power distribution box (*Algarde Power Centre* etc.) to the mains electricity *must* have a drip loop in it. Avoid running the cable directly downhill to the wall socket. Any drips will then fall off at the drip loop and not run directly into the electrical wall socket.

No Weighting

Tanks in display cabinets tend to spread their total weight on the floor more evenly, along the length of the cabinet's 'footprint' area. But the popular skeleton, angle-iron aquarium stands concentrate all the weight of the tank and stand into the four small areas of their metal legs.

It helps in such circumstances either to fit 'feet' to the bottom of these legs, which help spread the load more evenly and also stops them from cutting through carpets, or fit a length of thick wood slightly larger than the length and width of the aquarium stand under the carpet, which will again help to spread the load more evenly. Wooden floors are stronger near the walls than they are towards the centre of the room, so try to position your tank and stand near to a wall. Naturally, if your floor is concrete, then you may position your aquarium anywhere within the room.

Positioning The Aquarium

The ideal situation for an aquarium is a darkish corner of your living room, which just so happens to be a fraction bigger than the size of the tank, an electric powerpoint on one side, and a tap and drain on the other. OK, it's fantasy – but let's start 'trading down' from this ideal.

It's unlikely that you'll have a tap in your living room, so we can forget that, and use buckets or hoses like everyone else. We need a darkish site because we don't want direct sun-light shining into the tank for most of the day, causing overheating and algae problems. Sun-light which shines into the tank for around an hour a day, especially in the mornings, can be very acceptable, though. It often acts as a trigger to the spawning cycle of certain fishes.

The electric socket is a must and, if you find a site that's ideal in all other respects, it's well worth having an electrician fit one at this location. You really don't want an extension cable and flying socket wending its sinuous way across the floor to the aquarium, a potential death trap for all who have to keep stepping over it.

Choose a place which is free from draughts, not in front of a heating radiator, away from

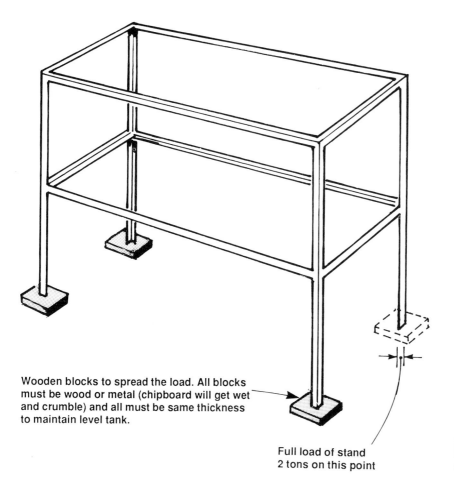

Wooden blocks to spread the load. All blocks must be wood or metal (chipboard will get wet and crumble) and all must be same thickness to maintain level tank.

Full load of stand
2 tons on this point

Figure 5.2 Spreading the load of metal legs on a steel skeletal stand.

people who smoke, and away from doors which may bang into the tank and frighten the fishes, or cause draughts. In my experience, it's rare to find a location which doesn't need some slight modifications. If this is the case with you, then *do* them! Otherwise you'll spend the rest of your fishkeeping career wishing that you had.

Filters

We have our tank. Eventually we will fill it with water. Keeping this water clean is a priority, as it decides whether our fishes live or die. In the closed world of the aquarium, filtration is how we achieve this.

When I first started fishkeeping, I couldn't afford any of the 'new' technology, such as air pumps and perforated pipework for an under-gravel filter system, although I did buy a heater and then made, in retrospect, a rather lethal thermostat! Therefore I, and countless other aquarists, managed without filters of any kind. I simply relied on sensible feeding, lots of plants and plenty of fresh water changes. I didn't know it then, but I had created what aquatic pundits now refer to as a 'balanced biosphere'.

It's ironic that today's younger aquarists are rediscovering the simplicity and effectiveness of the balanced biosphere, and loudly proclaiming it as 'new' and 'revolutionary' – much like the present fuss over trickle filtration, which has been with us since at least the 1940s! It is perfectly possible to maintain an aquarium without any artificial filtration system at all. Some of us have been doing it for the past three decades or more. How to achieve this aquatic Utopia is fully explained later on.

Over-feeding

If it wasn't for the fact that ninety percent of aquarists over-feed their fishes in the first place, there would be no need for any form of extra filtration. The amount of pollution produced by plants, fish and natural chemical reactions in the aquarium is minimal when compared to that introduced by the aquarist, and a well-planted aquarium could easily cope with this level of loading. However, we all love to watch the fishes feeding.

Viva Dirty Water!

During the late 1970s, and throughout the 1980s, there was a steady move towards greater filter efficiency, which culminated in aquarium water which was rather purer than the stuff coming out of most domestic taps! In no way does this situation even come close to imitating nature – have you ever seen the natural habitat of *Colisa lalia* (Dwarf gourami)? It's often a virtual toilet! Certainly, we need a filtration system, but not a water purifying refinery. Many home aquaria are tremendously over-filtered. Real aquarist success depends on giving the fish the water *they* want, not what you think they ought to have.

Before you decide on which type of filtration system you will utilise in your aquarium, let's first consider exactly what it is we're trying to achieve. In my experience, a complete under-standing of the problem usually provides its own solution.

Why Filter?

Why, indeed? As you've already read in Chapter 4, *Aquatic Plants*, filtration in an aquarium is not compulsory. Then why must we filter our aquarium water? Well, not many aquarists are happy keeping a small handful of fishes and masses of plants, as found in the balanced biosphere. Understandably, most aquarists want to utilise the maximum water space available to them, so their aquarium water is usually filtered.

In the natural environments of our fishes, the river or lake water is quite able to cope with the effluent load placed upon it by plants, fishes and other aquatic animals, without recourse to external filtration systems. The sheer volume of water, and the amount of surface area, substrate and aquatic vegetation available, provides a

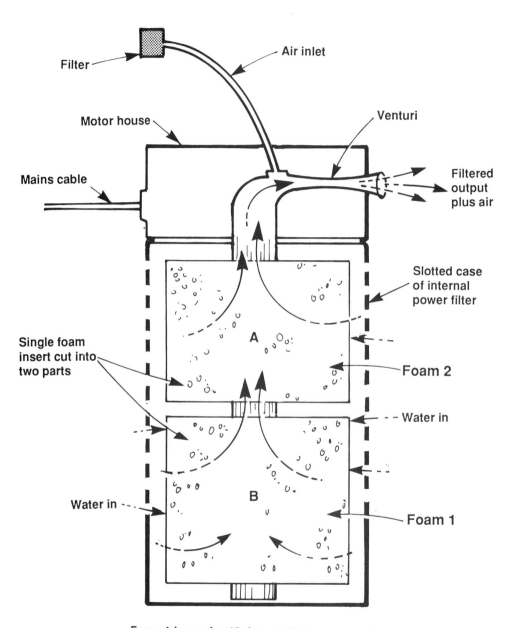

Foam 1 is run for 10 days and then cleaned. Foam 2 is placed in Position 'B' while the newly cleaned Foam 1 is placed in Position 'A'.

After 15 days Foam 2 will contain both aerobic and anaerobic bacteria, which will seed Foam 1, now in Position 'A'. After 20 days, Foam 2 is cleaned and switched with Foam 1.

Figure 5.3   Mechanical filtration. Twin foam power filters – the 10/20 day switch.

buffer against rapid changes in water chemistry, assuming that there is no additional loading on the system, such as man-made pollution. Of course, that's not to say that such waters *never* change their characteristics, I've already explained how freshwater does indeed change markedly, sometimes even within the same lake or river system, in Chapter 2 *Water*. Fishes adapt quite easily to these minor, often seasonal disturbances to their own environment. Indeed, were this not so, they would have become extinct a long time ago.

But all of this doesn't apply within the static confines of the average home aquarium. There is no great volume of water or surface area to provide a buffer between temporary upsets of water chemistry and the fish. And, as we're constantly polluting the water by feeding the fish two to three times a day, we have to do something or conditions quickly become rank. We have to replace that which nature is no longer supplying, and that's why we must filter our aquaria.

More Problems

We have to filter the aquarium water because nature is no longer assisting with the destruction or conversion of toxic waste products, particularly those in the Nitrogen Reduction Cycle. Now we know why we have to filter, how are we going to achieve a working system? Well, we haven't finished with the problem yet. *There is no universal filtration system which can be used in all applications*, so don't bother looking for one. The complete 'Wet and Dry' filtration system is the nearest you'll come to the 'perfect' system, but this is still very much an idea awaiting discovery (rediscovery?).

Each species of fish has its own needs. For example, a fast-swimming torpedo, such as a Zebra danio, would be delighted to find a fast output, such as that from a powerhead or power filter, causing a swift current in the aquarium water. On the other hand, the peace-loving, stately, slow moving members of the *Anabantidae* family, such as Pearl (Lace) and

Dwarf gouramis, would find such a current extremely unsettling, as well as very tiring.

Some fishes are renowned messy eaters, such as large oscars, *Astronotus ocellatus*, and other, large species, so their filtration needs are going to be different to those of the dainty feeders, who leave little refuse afterwards. Any species who enjoy a regular diet of meat in whatever form will have special filtration requirements too. Meat is rich in protein, and this quickly deteriorates in water, causing pollution.

For those aquarists who are maintaining a water chemistry different to their domestic supply, then their filtration requirements will have to reflect this situation and provide for these changes to be made easily and quickly. If you've no means of passing the aquarium water through an ion-exchange or chemical medium, then you won't be all that happy with your chosen system.

The End Of The Problem

So, we filter to clean the water, to remove solid waste products, to either remove or convert toxins into usable substances, such as plant fertilisers and (indirectly) CO_2, and to change the basic chemical nature of the water itself. Direct influences on the eventual filter system chosen are, the species to be kept and their numbers, the size (and often shape) of the tank itself, whether or not good plant growth is required, and any special requirements the aquarist has, such as fundamental changes in the chemical nature of the water, or personal preferences. There are three basic ways we can achieve all of this – chemically, mechanically or biologically. We may choose any one, or even all, of these basic methods of water filtration.

Mechanical Filtration

Aquarium water is drawn through a material – such as synthetic wool-type floss, foam pads, metal or fibrous gauze – which acts like a sieve trapping larger particles of effluent, such as uneaten food, fish faeces etc. The solids are physically removed from the water, and remain within the medium of the mechanical filter until it is cleaned out. Mechanical filtration has no direct effect on dissolved gases, neither does it have any direct influence on the basic chemistry of the water. However, if a mechanical filter is left uncleaned for more than two or three days, then bacteria will form within the filter's medium, and biological filtration (see later) will begin.

It is very rare for a tropical aquarium to rely entirely on mechanical filtration alone, as its effects are limited to removing solids only

(unless it's left deliberately 'dirty', of course). It often forms the first part of a combined system, such as a mechanical and chemical or mechanical/ biological system, acting as a pre-filter, taking out the worst of the particulate waste before the water hits the sensitive biological or chemical media.

There is a type of mechanical filter available which utilises diatomaceous earth as the medium. It takes the form of a power filter (see later) which is filled with the diatomaceous earth. As the water is fed through such a system, particles down to diatomic size (very small

A diatomaceous power filter.

Various filter media. *Top –
man-made filter floss and
activated carbon. Bottom left
– Siporax* sintered glass.
Bottom right – Zeolite.

indeed!) are entrapped within the medium. This type of filter is expensive to run, but it does trap even single-celled algaes and protozoa, removing them from the aquarium water – a kind of super-effective mechanical filter.

Chemical Filtration

This is the usual method chosen by aquarists who require changes in the basic nature of the aquarium water, changes such as water softening/hardening, pH adjustment and nitrate, nitrite, ammonia, and the removal of various metals. Biological filtration can duplicate some of these actions, particularly the reduction of nitrogenous material via the Nitrogen Reduction Cycle. Where chemical filters score over biological is their speed and controllability of bringing about these changes.

It is usual to add the chemicals, which come in many guises, into some form of filter box, whether internal or external; directly into the substrate or sometimes in mini bubble chambers, which sit on the uplift tube of undergravel filters. The more common substances used by aquarists in chemical filters are: activated char-

coal, peat, crushed coral or sea shells, Zeolite*, and Nitrex*.

(* Commercially available resins; see later.)

Chemical filters can have a lowering effect on the dissolved oxygen content of the aquarium water when using certain media. Furthermore, they are sometimes capable of removing any medicaments you may have added to the water to treat an outbreak of disease. For example, adding Methylene Blue solution into a tank to combat an outbreak of *White Spot* will be absorbed by any activated carbon in a chemical filter, and therefore rendered useless. Dosing the whole tank is never a good idea anyway (unless *all* the occupants are infected, of course) but, if you must, then remember to remove the chemical filter before adding the treatment.

Removing the chemical filter when treating disease also prevents the disastrous effects which certain disease remedies can have on the filter's medium. Certain medicaments can affect the chemical medium causing it to suddenly release all of the toxins it has sequestered back into the aquarium water at toxic levels, killing the fishes.

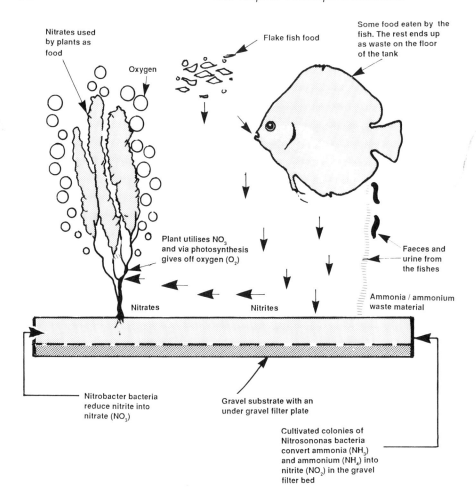

Nitrates used by plants as food

Oxygen

Flake fish food

Some food eaten by the fish. The rest ends up as waste on the floor of the tank

Plant utilises NO₃ and via photosynthesis gives off oxygen (O₂)

Faeces and urine from the fishes

Nitrates

Nitrites

Ammonia / ammonium waste material

Nitrobacter bacteria reduce nitrite into nitrate (NO₃)

Gravel substrate with an under gravel filter plate

Cultivated colonies of Nitrosononas bacteria convert ammonia (NH₃) and ammonium (NH₄) into nitrite (NO₂) in the gravel filter bed

Figure 5.4   Nitrogen Reduction Cycle.

Biological Filtration

Instead of an imposed regime of mechanical or chemical filtration, which imitates nature (although still producing the same desired end result), biological filtration *is* nature. It naturally reduces fish/plant and any other waste in the aquarium water into less harmful substances, via the Nitrogen Reduction Cycle.

Basically, biological filtration makes use of some very handy bacteria which absorb aquarium waste, and modify it into something less toxic. *Nitrosomonas* and *Nitrobacter* are the two forms of aerobic bacteria involved in this

process. All you have to do is provide them with board and lodgings, plus plenty of oxygen and, of course, lots of nitrogenous waste to work on.

Wherever there is nitrogenous material and oxygen, then you'll also find aerobic bacteria. No matter what filter system is chosen there will always be some *Nitrosomonas* and *Nitrobacter* colonies within the aquarium, covering rocks and decorations, and on the surface of the substrate, which will be acting biologically on any waste present. However, biological filtration relies upon the mass creation and cultivation of colonies of these bacteria in a specific area, rather than a haphazard distribution around the tank.

Perhaps the best known example of biological filtration is the undergravel system, or U/G filter, as it is known. Briefly – full details later – a gravel or sand substrate is laid to an average depth of 7.5cm (3in) on top of perforated filter plates. The bacterial colony will then make this gravel substrate their home. Utilising an airlift, the aquarium water is drawn down through the gravel and filter plates, and is returned via the airlift tube. As the water is drawn through the substrate, the aerobic bacteria begin their task of converting ammonia into nitrite (*Nitrosomonas* bacteria), then nitrite into nitrate (*Nitrobacter* bacteria). The constant flow of water through the substrate guarantees the aerobic bacteria colony plenty of nitrogenous waste and oxygen.

Obviously, the larger the area colonised by these helpful bacteria, the greater will be the biological filtering effect. In a U/G filtration system, the whole of the floor area in the aquarium forms a huge colony which, properly maintained, will work for a number of years before any major changes have to be made.

You may have picked up the idea that I don't personally like the undergravel filter system. This isn't strictly true; I'm very much in favour of any system which works with, rather than in spite of nature. Any system which stops the need to dump chemicals into the water is OK with me! It's just that the U/G filter configuration is very prone to giving new aquarists a false sense of security. He or she sees the bubbles, or output from the powerhead leaving the airlift tubes, and assumes that everything is working, when in fact this may not be true.

New Tank Syndrome

There is a phenomenon known as 'New Tank Syndrome' which afflicts numerous beginners

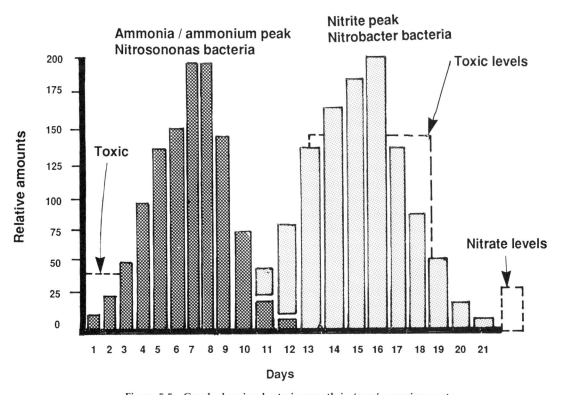

Figure 5.5 Graph showing bacteria growth in 'new' aquarium water.

to fishkeeping, and is often the factor which forces a would-be aquarist to 'pack it all in', regarding fishkeeping as a waste of time and money. Before I explain what new tank syndrome actually is, it's worthwhile following the development of the biological filter bed in a newly commissioned aquarium.

First, and assuming that there's some waste material present, either deliberately introduced, or from some fishes; after a few days the ammonia or ammonium level will begin to rise, stimulating the creation of *Nitrosomonas* bacteria in the filter bed. As the ammonia (NH_3) or ammonium (NH_4) – depending on pH, remember? – level increases, the *Nitrosomonas* bacteria begin to multiply and start absorbing ammonia/ammonium ions into their structure, changing it chemically into energy (heat) and nitrite, which is expelled. Note that the bacteria don't actually chomp on waste products, like we would eat a steak. It's the chemical nature of the water which is modified: bacteria cannot reduce particulate waste, they must wait for it to decompose into ammonia/ammonium first.

Levels of NH_3, which is lethal to fishes at around 5mg/l, and the relatively harmless NH_4 will carry on growing until the slowly increasing colonies of *Nitrosomonas* bacteria can cope with the amount. Finally, as the build up of bacteria gets 'topside' of the waste problem, ammonia/ammonium levels begin to fall rapidly towards zero. The time period, from beginning to end of the NH_3/NH_4 peak, is around ten days.

Only when the ammonia/ammonium levels are very low or non-existent can the *Nitrobacter* colonies begin to form, so, for the first week of a new aquarium, there's likely to be no *Nitrobacter* bacteria present at all. The decreasing NH_3, NH_4 levels and the increasing amount of nitrite (NO_2) triggers the formation of *Nitrobacter* colonies, which absorb nitrite (still a toxic substance to fish) through their cell walls, converting it into heat energy and expelling nitrate. NO_3 (nitrate), is relatively harmless to fishes, although levels above 200mg/l are toxic. It will take around three weeks before *Nitrobacter* reproduction is

capable of reducing the nitrite level to a very low, or even zero level.

Summary

To summarise, then – with a new aquarium filled with fresh water, it will take about a month before the biological filter is working anything like well enough to support the introduction of fishes. New tank syndrome is caused not by any chemical or filtration problems as such, more by the aquarist, whose impatience or ignorance of the mechanics of the biological filtration system leads him/her to introduce fishes well before the bacteria colonies can cope with them. *You* now have no such excuse!

The effects of new tank syndrome are: a new tank is set up complete with heating, lighting and filtration; decorations and plants. Water is added and left to mature for a few days, and then some fishes are added. *Nitrosomonas* and *Nitrobacter* colonies have yet to form, so the tank is effectively without any filtration at all, and the fishes die. More fishes are bought, and then they die too. Gradually the filter bed matures, despite the impatient aquarist. Fish deaths decrease, and everything settles down. It is very significant that new tank syndrome is almost always associated with the undergravel filtration system, although I don't know why. It should also happen when using any form of filter.

New Lamps For Old?

A range of products is available which claim to shorten the time required for the two forms of bacteria involved in biological filtration to form. At least one of them further claims to remove ammonia and nitrite! Now, as *Nitrosomonas* bacteria cannot proliferate *until* there is some ammonia present to start with, how this particular product can claim to boost the formation of the biological filter bed is slightly puzzling. Perhaps someone could explain this paradox to me? To speed things up, 'seeding' a new tank with 'dirty' gravel from an existing tank will quicken the maturation of a new biological filter bed. But, if you're setting up your first aquarium, then you won't have this option.

Some General Thoughts About Filter Types

Newcomers could be forgiven for thinking that undergravel filtration is the *only* system available to them. It seems that, for the past thirty years or so, beginners have traditionally been pushed towards the U/G system as an ideal way to filter their aquarium water – some kind of universal cleansing panacea for all the ills of your tank. In actual fact, the reverse is true – to set one up and maintain it properly requires a fair bit of aquaristic skill. Undergravel filters do have a very useful role to play, but their creation and maintenance is not as simple as some people will have you believe.

The filter methods discussed next are 'primary systems' – that is, they may be used just as described as the only filtration method in an aquarium. After the primary systems come the more exotic ideas which you may care to experiment with in the future. It is not my place to tell you which system to choose. What I intend to do is to demonstrate and explain the various methods, their application to any specific tasks, and their advantages and disadvantages. You must then choose the method which most suits what you're trying to achieve, and your pocket.

K.I.S.S.

Aquarium filtration can become a very complicated subject if you allow it to. In the field of telecommunications there is a philosophy known as KISS. This excellent advice has numerous applications throughout life in general, but particularly to the subject of filtering aquarium water. You'll never go very far wrong in your aquarist career if you abide by the KISS philosophy. And KISS? - Keep It Simple, Stupid!

Filter Types

The Poly Or Foam Filter

Filters don't come any simpler than this! The Polyfilter (also known as a foam filter) consists of an 'L'-shaped, airlift tube with a cylinder of foam on the horizontal arm of the 'L'. It utilises two filtration principles – biological and mechanical. Air from a pump causes water to be drawn through the foam cylinder, and is returned to the aquarium via the airlift tube. Any large waste particles will adhere to the surface of the foam. However, its more useful function is the biological effect of the aerobic bacteria within the cell structure of the foam cylinder.

Its main use is for the smaller aquarium – up to around 60cm (24in) in length, where it may be used as the primary method of filtration. Polyfilters come in various sizes, ranging from small to very large cylinders of foam. Many aquarists use them in breeding tanks, where its gentle action won't suck fry into the system, as could happen with a power filter. One little tip when using this type of filter – don't let the foam cylinder rest on the substrate. This will restrict the surface area of the foam which can be used. Make sure that the bottom of the foam is raised about 25mm (.5in) above the gravel, but it is essential to ensure that the bottom half-inch of the tank below the foam is filtered. However, the output from the airlift tube of the polyfilter, and subsequent water movement, usually prevents any water stratification, providing there's enough air passing through the filter.

Once the outside of the foam cylinder becomes clogged with detritus, it will require cleaning. This has to be done very carefully, or the colony of aerobic bacteria within the foam will be destroyed. Remove the foam, and wash by squeezing it very gently, using water taken from the same aquarium as the filter. Do not use tapwater, as this will injure or kill off the bacteria. Altogether, this is a very cheap and useful filter for the smaller aquarium, but do remember that you also need an air pump to run it.

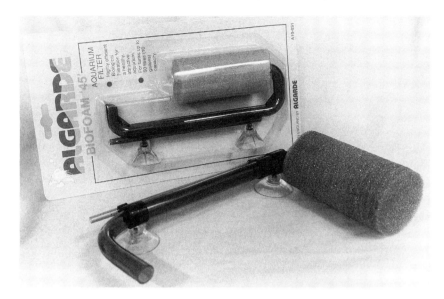

Polyfilter (foam) biological
filter.

Constant Running

As with all forms of biological filtration, the
basic principle of operation requires a constant
supply of oxygen. Therefore, the air pump must
never be switched off. It has to be kept running
all the time, constantly feeding the bacterial
colonies with fresh oxygen. If the air pump is
turned off, then the bacteria will begin to die.
Therefore you should a) have a spare pump
handy, and b) ensure that you have spare parts,
especially the diaphragms (see later) ready for
both airpumps.

The Box Filter

Another simple filter, again for smaller aquaria,
which is also very useful in the breeding tank.
It consists of a square, triangular or sometimes
round plastic box, which has an airlift tube,
often with an airstone in it, through the centre.
Aquarium water is drawn down into the box,
and through the filter media, then returned to
the tank via the airlift tube. The box filter can
operate as a mechanical, chemical or biological
filter, or all three, depending on how the box is
packed.

Figure 5.6 shows a typical box filter kitted out
for mechanical, chemical and biological filtration. Water enters the box filter through the
slats at the top. It first passes through a layer
filter floss, which traps larger, particulate waste,
stopping it before it reaches the sensitive chemical medium. Below the floss is a layer of activated carbon which absorbs gases such as
ammonia. The carbon could just as easily be
Zeolite or peat. Another layer of filter floss keeps
the chemical medium nicely contained. At the
bottom of the box filter, gravel – or one of the
more modern gravel substitutes as a biological
filter bed, such as *Siporax* sintered glass – serves
to add weight, keeping the box filter submerged. Biological filtration utilising aerobic
bacteria occurs here. Finally, the filtered water
is returned via the central airlift tube.

Bigger Boxes

Design-wise, the internal box filter is a good
one, as you can pack it with a variety of media,
which makes the creation of special water conditions – acid/alkaline, hard/soft etc – very
simple. You simply stuff it with the appropriate

materials. However, in larger aquaria, the size of the box required becomes too great to fit internally. Instead, it is removed from the aquarium and hung either on the side or the back of the tank, as an external box filter.

External box filters may be packed with a variety of media, or a single material depending on the effect you want. They can be obtained in a variety of sizes, from quite small to very large; and used in small to medium sized aquaria. One potential drawback to using this system is the modifications you may have to make to the hood assembly of your tank. To accommodate the input and output pipework, it is frequently necessary to chop out sections of the hood's back or sides. This type of filter may be driven by the airpump and airlift principle, which again means you have to add the price of the pump to that of the filter; or have its own electric pump – see external power filters later.

Internal Power Filter

The concept of utilising aquarium grade synthetic foam as a home for bacterial colonies is now very well established. It improves on gravel by offering a larger surface area for greater colonisation by the aerobic bacteria, is lighter and easier to handle, and very much easier to clean. Cousin to the polyfilter, internal power filters do the same job, using the same methods. Where they improve on the polyfilter is the

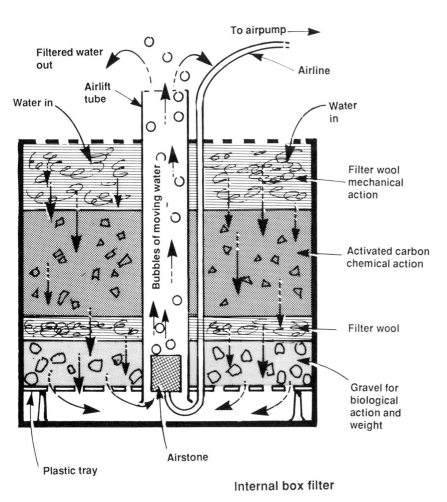

Figure 5.6　Internal box filter. Via the airlift assembly, water is drawn into the top of the filter, passing through filter floss. It then passes through a chemical media, such as activated carbon or Zeolite and then through a biological filter bed, such as gravel.

Internal box filter

An internal box filter
c/w airpump.

amount of water they can treat. Even a small power filter will shift some 300 litres per hour of aquarium water.

Internal power filters have two main parts: the pump assembly, set in a waterproof housing on top, and the canister below, which holds the foam cartridge. The whole assembly is designed to work submerged in the aquarium, and must always be used this way, or damage to the pump will result. Water is drawn through perforations in the canister casing by an impeller in the pump assembly, through the foam insert where the biological action takes place, and is then returned to the aquarium, exiting from the top of the pump housing.

Some internal power filters allow air to be injected into the returning aquarium water, adding aeration as well as filtration. An air intake, usually consisting of a short tail of plastic pipe suspended above the water level, connects to the pump housing. Within the pump, a venturi chamber mixes the air with the exiting water. Again, this type of filter comes in a

variety of sizes and can be used as the primary filtration method for even quite large tanks.

Internal Power Filters; New Concept

The problem with filters which utilise synthetic foam as the biological filter bed has traditionally been cleaning them *without* destroying the bacteria within. Even taking great care usually results in at least some – often around sixty percent – of the bacteria being wiped out. To prevent this situation, various manufacturers of aquatic equipment, such as Interpet, with their *Powerstreem Cartridge* filters, and the Dennerle company, produce internal power filters with twin media compartments, which can accommodate two foam inserts, one above the other.

The advantage of this is that only one foam cartridge at a time is cleaned, leaving the other, complete with its thriving bacteria colony, to carry on the filtration work. The favoured method seems to be the ten – twenty day rule. On the tenth day, the bottom, or first cartridge

Internal foam cartridge
power filters.

is removed and cleaned (method as for the polyfilter). The top, or second foam cell is removed and placed in the bottom compartment, to become the 'new' first cartridge. The just-cleaned foam cell is then replaced at the top of the canister. Now we have a clean foam at the top, and a ten day-old foam cartridge at the bottom.

As water enters the bottom of the power filter, bacteria within the cell structure of the ten day-old foam in the first compartment will seed the next cartridge with some of its own bacteria. This speeds up the maturation of the cleaned foam in the second section. On the twentieth day the cartridge in the first (bottom) compartment is removed, cleaned and swapped with the first (top) foam cartridge.

Twin compartment internal power filters always ensure that there are some bacteria working on the water at all times. If you don't have an internal power filter with two foam inserts, why not simply cut the one insert into two?

Powered External Box Filter

This is simply an improvement on the traditional air-driven external box filter, and shifts considerably more litres per hour. The airlift

assembly is replaced with an electric pump, increasing the throughput of the filter considerably. But do not make the understandable error of mistaking filter throughput – how much of the aquarium water the system will move per

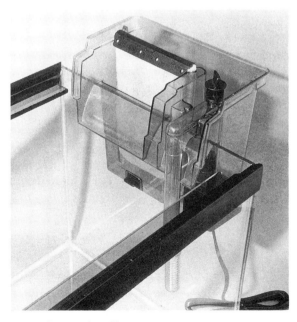

External power box filter.

External canister power
filters are packed with media
in much the same way as the
internal box filter. The only
real difference between them
is the area of the media and
the greater amount of water
treated by the powered
version.

hour – with the volume of the filter media when choosing such a filter for your aquarium.

Powered external box filters obviously move a greater amount of the aquarium water in a given time than their air-powered relations. There is a temptation to purchase a smaller powered box filter, which has a correspondingly lower volume of media storage capability, merely because it moves 'x' number of litres per hour *more* than an air-driven equivalent. Look first to the storage capacity of the external filter. Will it be able to hold enough floss, charcoal etc. to filter that amount of water effectively, without you having to change the media every other day? The larger the amount of the various media used within the filter, then the less time you'll have to spend on maintaining it.

External Power Filter

Big brother to the internal, air driven box filter, power filters come in a range of media capacity and pump turnover ranges. They may be packed with a variety of chemical media, as well as wool floss and biological foams. External power filters act quickly. Ion-exchange resins, or peat, are also easily catered for. This type of filter is ideal when you have a lot of waste material to remove quickly, such as that from heavy feeding species of fishes or, in an emergency, as I had recently, to remove an excess of ammonia from a friend's tank, by using a power filter packed with Zeolite.

Like the external box filters – whether powered or not – the external power filter may require you to chop holes in the aquarium hood assembly, to allow space for the input/output pipework. These filters often return the cleaned aquarium water back to the tank by a spray bar assembly. This may not suit some species of fish, who like a peaceful, undisturbed surface, but the spray bar can be bypassed, and the water returned in a more gentle fashion. Apart from their direct application as a primary method of filtration, external power filters may also form the power source of other water cleaning systems, as we'll see later.

Power Filter Ratings

Before we finish with the subject of electrically-powered filters, there's something you have to understand about them. Their 'power rating' – how much of the aquarium water they will move in a given time, as stated on the box or on the instruction leaflet – *is usually the maximum pump output under no loading conditions!*

This means that, for an empty external power filter located at a certain height *below* (never locate an external power filter above) the water level, the maximum figure quoted will be achieved. BUT! There are a few factors which can cut this maximum throughput figure (which is in practice purely mythical, in my own opinion) by at least half! For example, depending on how you pack the filter, and which media you use, affects the water throughput. A loose, 'spacy' medium, such as *Siporax* sintered glass, used as a 'hotel' for aerobic bacteria, won't cut down the filter flow as much as a denser filter medium, such as *Zeolite*, peat or even filter floss, which can often halve the output value.

The location of the external power filter has an even larger bearing on its eventual output than the media with which it is loaded. A manufacturer will recommend that his filter is located, for example, 1 metre below the water level; and, at this height the filter – even when packed with media – will achieve 500 litres per hour. If you change this 'head-height', as it is called, to 1.5, or even 2 metres below the water level, then again, filter output could be more than halved; from 500 litres per hour down to 200LPH. 'Below' doesn't have to mean exactly vertically displaced beneath the aquarium – it could mean the filter's tucked away eg. remotely mounted in a cabinet. So bear all this in mind when choosing an external power filter.

When buying a power filter, remember that the figures quoted are maxima which are unlikely to be achieved in your aquarium, once the filter is loaded with media and tucked away out of sight. It is usual, when using this type of filter, to aim for a turnover rate of the aquarium water about twice per hour. If you have a 100 litre aquarium, then a power filter with a claimed output of 400 litres per hour is just about right. Filling the filter will cut down its output to 200 litres per hour, which is exactly what you need. Obviously, I've made a complex subject sound very simple. But, if you're in any doubt at all, a) make certain that you *do* know how much water your aquarium holds, and b) ask your dealer's advice.

Undergravel (U/G) Biological Filter – Normal Flow

Traditionally the most popular of all filter systems due to its apparent cheapness to set up, and its low maintenance routine, the normal flow (water is drawn down into the substrate) undergravel filtration system can and does work very well indeed. Many aquarists around the world swear by the system as near perfect for their needs, as it provides them with crystal clear water and luxuriant plant growth. However, please do note my words of caution – especially when allowing the biological bed to mature. And don't forget the rules regarding the air pump – *never switch it off*. Have another pump available in case of a breakdown, and carry spares for both pumps.

A plastic sheet, known as a filter plate, perforated with either holes or slits, is laid across the entire floor area of the empty tank. At the back right- or left-hand corner of the filter plate is an access hole for the airlift tube, which has to be firmly connected before laying the gravel. Incidentally, it is often a good idea to glue the airlift tube into its hole with aquarium silicone sealant. Certain rough playing fish species can soon dislodge an airlift tube if it gets in their way. Larger tanks may require two filter plates (or many, depending on whose system you're using), but not normally more than two airlifts.

Once the filter plates and airlifts are in position, the substrate can be laid. Certain fish species, eg. cichlid, have a habit of digging into the gravel and exposing the bare filter plates, which then will not function as they are

A wide variety of undergravel filter plates is available. Some can be used to create special shapes, such as for triangular or hexagonal aquaria.

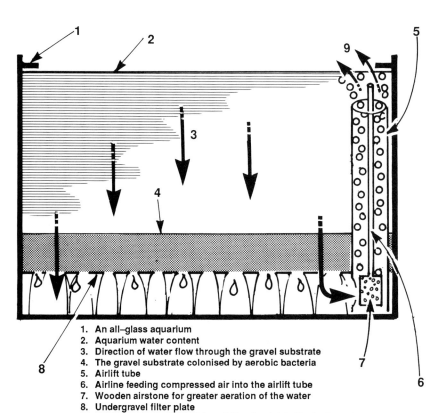

1. An all–glass aquarium
2. Aquarium water content
3. Direction of water flow through the gravel substrate
4. The gravel substrate colonised by aerobic bacteria
5. Airlift tube
6. Airline feeding compressed air into the airlift tube
7. Wooden airstone for greater aeration of the water
8. Undergravel filter plate
9. Exiting water and air mixture falling back into the tank

Figure 5.7   Normal flow undergravel filter.

designed to do. To prevent exposure of the plates, lay around 25mm (1in) of gravel on top of the plate, and cover with a *Gravel Tidy*. This is a plastic net which prevents fish digging into the substrate and exposing the filter plates. However, as they are costly, and can't be cut easily, to allow for the burying of hydroculture pots, nylon, or synthetic net or lace curtaining is a much cheaper alternative, being easier to clean, and cut or shape to any size or layout. Then add the rest of the substrate on top of the netting, not forgetting to position any peat planting mats or substrate additives at this stage, before adding the water.

After the plate(s) and airlift tube(s) are fixed, and the gravel added, you have to arrange the delivery of air into the airlift tube(s). For tanks using two airlifts, it is much better to buy an air pump which has twin outlets, so that each tube receives a fairly equal supply. When using a single outlet pump and a twin feed airline connector, one airlift tube usually receives more air than the other. Instead of simply pushing the open-ended airline into each tube, many aquarists like to add extra aeration to the aquarium water by terminating the airline with an airstone, which then sits inside the uplift tube. But remember to insert the airstone before gluing the airlift tube into place!

A normal flow undergravel filter system will last on average around two years before the biological bed has to be seriously disturbed (never replaced!) Of course this period very much depends on how much waste is being produced and how good your maintenance schedule is.

U/G Filter – Maintenance

Part of the key to success with the undergravel filter system is a regular regime of maintenance. Anything you place into the aquarium (food etc.) will stay there in one form or another. If left, then the accumulation of such detritus will eventually block the filter bed, and exceed its power to reduce this waste. There are various devices available to assist you with regular aquarium maintenance, such as algae scrapers, and substrate hoovers, but they have to be used! But do have a care – disturbing the biological filter bed unnecessarily can cause many problems.

The surface of the substrate should be gently cleaned around every two to three months. As this is bound to raise a fair amount of muck, it must be accompanied by a thirty percent water change, and then reduced feeding of the fishes for a few days, while the filter bed has time to recover from being disturbed. Partial water changes – around twenty percent every twenty days – using dechlorinated and conditioned tapwater will help reduce pollution of the filter bed enormously. There are also various additives which, when mixed with the fresh water, are said to aid the support of the biological bed. For example, *Cycle*, from the Rolf C Hagen company, and *Filter Aid*, made by Interpet, act directly on the biological filter bed, refreshing it and reducing the amount of sludge which accumulates.

After a couple of years, it will become necessary to seriously disturb the biological filter bed, because the bacterial coating of individual gravel particles becomes so thick that it stops the water circulating properly. In this case, you need a friend with an external canister-type power filter. Remove the fishes and plants, leaving the bare substrate. Give the gravel a hard raking over and, borrowing your friend's power filter, run it to remove the worst of the dirt. Change forty percent of the water, and then rebuild your aquascape and reintroduce your fishes. *Do not* add any food to the aquarium for at least three days (don't worry, your fishes won't starve), and then feed at half your normal rate for another three days. By this time, the substrate will have settled down, and things should be pretty well back to normal, and will last for another two years or so.

Normal Flow U/G With A Powerhead

Unless there is a healthy stream of bubbles

Adding a powerhead – a simple pump – increases the turnover rate when using undergravel biological filtration.

erupting from the airlift tube, the throughput of an air-driven undergravel filter is likely to be quite low. In fact, I've seen some which would struggle to move five litres (1 gallon) per day! Oxygen is a basic necessity of the biological filtration principle, so the bacteria colonies need a lot of it. One way to really get a normal flow U/G system moving is to add a powerhead.

The powerhead – simply a submersible pump – sits atop the airlift tube of the undergravel system and, quite literally, pulls the water down through the gravel and up the tube, where it then exits back into the aquarium. Like the various internal power filters, powerheads often have a means of mixing air with the ejected clean water, for aeration purposes. They may be bought in a variety of output ranges, from 180 litres (40 gallons) to 1080 litres (238 gallons) per hour (Interpet *Powerheads*). Although increasing the rate at which water is drawn through the substrate is a good idea for a biological system, we don't want to pin the fish to the gravel floor via suction! So choose a powerhead according to the size of your aquarium, and not purely on its litres-per-hour rating.

A certain amount of modification may have to be done when converting air-driven airlift tubes into a powerhead system. Sometimes a special adaptor is needed to couple the powerhead onto the airlift tube, and you may also have to reduce the height of this tube by cutting it, to ensure that the powerhead remains fully submerged. Adding a powerhead does not mean that you can relax your maintenance routine, however.

Reverse Flow Undergravel Filter

The last of our primary filter systems to be discussed, reverse flow undergravel biological filtration, is a relatively new idea, which also avoids the major problem associated with normal flow U/G filters: accumulated dirt on the substrate. It is a system much favoured by the marine aquarist, whose filtration needs are much greater than ours. Instead of aquarium water being drawn down into the substrate, reverse flow turns this about by pushing water down the airlift tubes, and up through the gravel. Waste particles cannot settle onto the surface of the substrate, as they are continually being washed away by currents generated from the powerhead, which drives this system.

Air pumps cannot be used for reverse flow, neither is it easy to convert an existing normal flow U/G set-up; although it can be done with some manufacturers' plates and airlift tubes. It is really a much better idea to set up the aquarium from the start as reverse flow; that way you'll get a much more efficient system as you'll only acquire the proper parts. It is also much cheaper too. Changing from normal flow to reverse flow when the first system has been in use for some time isn't such a good idea either. All the accumulated mulm in the substrate will suddenly be liberated into the aquarium, causing problems.

Many aquarists like to run a smallish internal power filter when using reverse flow U/G. The waste products which cannot settle onto the substrate have to go somewhere. Of course you get the added bonus of biological filtration taking place within the internal power filter as well as in the actual substrate itself.

Choose A System

These then are the primary filtration systems used by aquarists around the world. They are all tried and trusted systems which, while not representing cutting edge technology, all work well when used within their limitations. Choose your system bearing in mind the advice detailed earlier, and the depth of your pocket.

But we're not yet finished with the subject of filtration. There are a number of new innovations which, while not forming a primary method of their own, certainly make very useful additions to existing systems. For example, in the Nitrogen Reduction Cycle employing aerobic bacteria, the end product is nitrate, a relatively harmless (in small amounts) substance to the fish. However, larger concentrations of nitrate can be dangerous, and over 200mg/l is often lethal. Unless specific action is taken to either further reduce nitrate into nitrogen gas, utilising anaerobic bacteria, or simply dilute it by a regime of partial water changing, then the nitrate will eventually become a problem. What follows next is an explanation of various devices and combinations of equipment which represent the current thinking of many of the world's leading aquarists and state-of-the-art filtration systems.

Reverse Flow U/G With Power Filtration

This is a combination of two primary methods, but this time the power filter replaces the airpump. Water is drawn into the power filter input pipe and through the canister containing, in this case, wool floss. Instead of the water being returned via the usual spray bar assembly, the output pipe from the canister is connected into the airlift tube, which then forces water down the tube and up through the substrate, which provides the biological filtering action.

This is one of the easiest systems to maintain, although the actual setting up has to be handled with care. It is a good system for heavy feeding fishes, or aquaria with a lot of specimens. Large particulate waste, the bane of normal flow undergravel filtration, is trapped by the floss in the power filter, which, just like any mechanical filter which hasn't been cleaned for more than a few days, will begin working biologically on the water. The pre-filtered and biologically cleaned water then passes through the bacteria bed of the substrate, for a final, low-level biological polishing.

Trickle (Wet and Dry) Filters

They do say that there's nothing new under the sun. Although it is only fairly recently that 'trickle' or 'Wet and Dry' filters as they are often called, have come to prominence (albeit more in the marine branch of fishkeeping), the technology has been around since the 1940s, and has been used by water companies for the treatment of sewerage for many years.

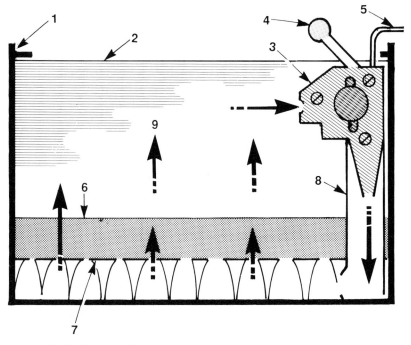

1. All–glass aquarium
2. Aquarium water
3. Powerhead submersible pump pushing water down the airlift tube
4. Air input to powerhead, complete with fibre filter
5. Mains electricity supply lead
6. Gravel substrate colonised by aerobic bacteria
7. Undergravel filter plate
8. Airlift tube assembly
9. Arrows indicating direction of water flow up through the substrate

Figure 5.8 Reverse flow undergravel filter.

Trickle filters are actually cousins of two separate, but not exclusive, methods – biological ('Wet') and gas exchange ('Dry'). Even though the medium required for each system is different, it is not difficult to build trickle filters which combine both methods. Of course, and should you want to, you can easily build either a 'wet' or a 'dry' element as a separate system. In fact you may have to because, apart from the makers of Complete Biosphere Aquaria, very few manufacturers actually produce add-on dry filters. However, at least one British company, *King British*, makes a separate wet trickle filter, the OTP (Overhead Trickle Purification) system, which fits inside the aquarium's hood, but by the time you read this there will be several companies producing them.

They are called trickle filters because the flow of water through them is restricted to a dribble. This keeps the water in contact with either the biological effect of the 'wet' medium, or the air/medium gas exchange interface within the 'dry' filter for the longest possible time, without remaining static. On their own, and as their processing speed is very slow (compared to the primary filtration methods already discussed), they can't really be used as primary systems without additional support. But, as a final 'polisher', or conditioner of aquarium water, both systems are without equal. However, a

Commercial trickle filters at work – Swallownest sewerage treatment plant near Sheffield.

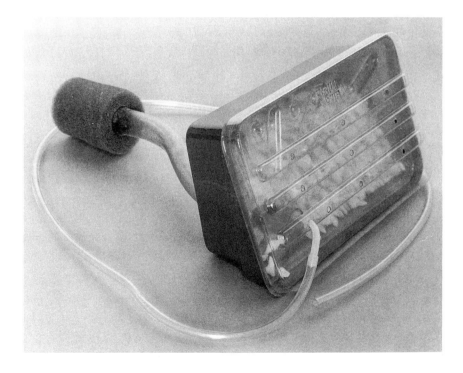

King British OTP (Overhed Trickle Purification) filter is designed to work in the aquarium's hood. It is airlift driven and adds a final polish to the water after previous filtration treatment.

combined system can be used as a very efficient primary filtration method, as demonstrated by the various systemised aquaria, (see *Complete Biosphere Aquaria* p115.) Unfortunately, such systems are very large.

Dry Trickle Filter

The 'dry' bit is a little misleading, as the filter does not work dry at all. But then, it's not completely wet either! Dry trickle filters work on the gas exchange principle, where substances such as ammonia are removed from the aquarium water and are replaced with oxygen.

The basic idea is that aquarium water is fed into the dry trickle filter via either a spray bar assembly, or allowed to drip onto a pierced meniscus-shaped cover. A wool floss or foam mat, sitting on top of the special medium (more of which in a moment), captures any solid, particulate waste. Having passed through the floss or foam, the water then drips down onto the specially shaped medium, where the gas exchanges occur.

The medium – which is the antithesis of that required for biological action – is usually an open, low surface area material with large spacing, or void areas between each piece. Specially shaped plastic balls, such as those produced by the Rolf C Hagen (UK) company, are an ideal design to facilitate the maximum time of water-to-air contact, which aids rapid gas exchange. But ladies' plastic hair rollers do the same job far cheaper!

An arrangement is made to feed air from a pump into the 'dry' filter, so that, as the water trickles down through the medium it is met by a strong updraft of compressed air. As the water meets the uprising air draught, ammonia is given up and oxygen absorbed by the water on its way down through the filter medium.

Unless the dry filter is forming just the first part of a dual, wet and dry system, the de-gased and aerated water collects in a sump at the bottom of the filter arrangement, and is then pumped back into the aquarium. If the dry trickle filter is just the first stage of a combined

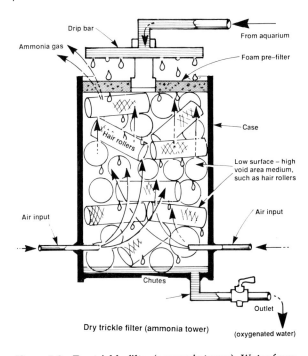

Figure 5.9 Dry trickle filter (ammonia tower). Water from the aquarium is fed into a drip bar which ensures even distribution of the water through the medium. A foam pre-filter traps larger particulate waste. The steady trickle of water is allowed over the medium, which is the exact opposite of that required for biological filtration, being of low surface area with large spaces between.
Air from an airpump creates a strong up-draught against the flow of water and causes it to exchange ammonia products with oxygen.
Special medium, such as the plastic balls manufactured by Rolf C. Hagen (UK) Ltd, can be used as the media; however, hair rollers work just as effectively.
For a 90×30×30 cm (36×12×12 in) aquarium, the dry trickle filter will need to be around one metre tall and approximately 15 cm (6 in) in diameter. Drainpiping makes an excellent housing for an ammonia tower. One problem with dry trickle filters is the high heat losses due to evaporation. Some method of heating the returned water is highly recommended. The ammonia tower may be used as a stand-alone unit, or as the first part of a wet and dry trickle filtration system.

wet and dry system, then instead of the water collecting in the sump, it passes onto the next, wet stage.

Wet Trickle Filter

Being a biological filter, the wet trickle filter medium has to support colonies of aerobic bacteria, and therefore has to be dense, with high surface area, and low void space, such as gravel, or one of gravel's newer replacements. The medium is fully submerged, so is 'wet' all of the time. The input to this type of filter is reduced to a slow trickle, so that it remains in contact with the medium and aerobic bacteria for an extended time, maximising biological activity.

Some wet trickle filters are used *anaerobically*, ie. the medium used is oxygen starved, as the water is reduced to the slowest of trickles only (see *Denitrification*, p. 92).

Problems With Trickle Filters

I know of only one commercially available wet trickle filter, so the chances are that you're going to have to build your own dry, or com-

bined, system. Evaporation losses from trickle filters are high, which means very high humidity in the area where such a filter is located. If this is a cabinet or cupboard, then the wood may begin to rot. High evaporation losses means that the water level will be constantly reduced, and the temperature lowered; so some method, such as automatic water changers, and installing a heater within the system somewhere, will have to be given serious thought.

Furthermore, evaporation losses may also mean that any metal pollution in the domestic water supply could begin to concentrate in the aquarium. Bearing in mind how synergistic metals can be in their effects on fishes, some method of controlling this has to be incorporated into the system too. However, once these slight problems have been overcome, trickle filters work, and go on working very well

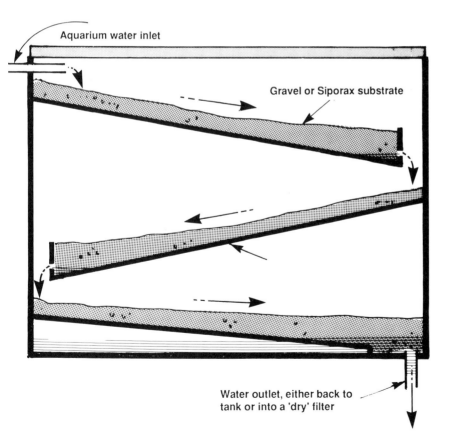

Aquarium water inlet

Gravel or Siporax substrate

Water outlet, either back to tank or into a 'dry' filter

Figure 5.10 Wet trickle filter system. A plastic tank around 60×60×60 cm (2×2 in) should be big enough to hold enough substrate to 'polish' the water in a 90×30×30 cm (3×1×1 in) tank. The inlet is reduced to the merest dribble, enough to keep the substrate damp. As the water dribbles down through the chutes it is kept in contact with the bacteria for a very long time. *Note* Without additional filtration equipment, the 'Wet' filter *cannot* be used as a primary filter method: it doesn't have the capacity.

indeed. They are ideal for species who're very sensitive to water chemistry, such as *Symphysodon discus*, the beautiful and shy Discus fish.

Denitrification

In some areas of Britain, the domestic water supply can have a high nitrate content. For people living in these parts, a regime of partial water changes isn't going to solve their nitrate-level problem. For those aquarists who're not using any form of undergravel filtration, their substrate will already be acting upon any nitrate present. In the absence (or very low levels) of oxygen, where there is nitrogenous material, anaerobic bacteria will develop. Substrates which are not being utilised biologically for filtration will have a high proportion of anaerobic bacteria living within. This will act upon any nitrate present, and decompose it to nitrogen gas, which will then dissipate into the atmosphere at the water surface/air interface.

I've already mentioned twin-celled, internal power filters, holding two foam cartridges and the ten/twenty day switch. One of the reasons for this is so that the twenty day-old foam cartridge is allowed to become really dirty and blocked. When this happens, anaerobic bacteria will begin to colonise the foam structure, and start reducing nitrate into nitrogen gas. (Berti Gesting, *Practical Fishkeeping* April 1991.) Of course, the same thing applies to any mechanical or biological filter type which is allowed to become very dirty, and is also why the bed in an undergravel filter system shouldn't be disturbed.

A final method of denitrifying aquarium water is to use a proprietary product, such as a *Nitrex Box*, manufactured by the Interpet company. This is a slim box filled with Nitrex resin, which is buried in the substrate of the aquarium (whether using U/G filters or not). The Nitrex polymer resin provides a home for bacteria and a source of carbon. Initially, aerobic bacteria must colonise the Nitrex resin, and time has to be allowed for this to occur (leave it hanging in your aquarium, inside some nylon stocking, for

around four weeks). At the end of this time, the resin is inserted in the *Nitrex Box*, which is then buried beneath the substrate.

Now comes the interesting part. Because there isn't any oxygen-rich water to pass through the *Nitrex Box*, and because the resin is colonised by bacteria which are normally found in aerobic conditions, they are now deprived of oxygen. To survive, the aerobic bacteria are forced into an anaerobic condition. It extracts the oxygen it needs to live from the three oxygen atoms present in the nitrate ion (NO_3), and the carbon polymer coating of the Nitrex resin provides 'food' in the form of carbohydrates. The net result is nitrate reduced into gases of nitrogen, which then dissipate harmlessly at the surface/air interface.

Aeration

We have to ensure that there aren't any hot or cold spots in the aquarium water, remove CO_2 and maintain a sufficient level of dissolved oxygen. Aeration is how we achieve all of this.

From the part of this book which dealt with the subject of fish tanks, you'll understand the crucial role played by the surface area of water in an aquarium. Apart from dictating just how many fish can be safely kept in a given sized tank, the surface/air interface is also the place which the aquarium uses to vent unwanted and absorb fresh gases. The daily 'respiration' cycle of the aquarium water dispelling CO_2, nitrogenous gases etc. and absorbing fresh O_2 is what keeps our fishes alive. Note that this has nothing directly to do with any form of artificial filtration process

What Is Aeration?

Thanks to throwaway phrases such as 'aeration increases the amount of dissolved oxygen in the water', many new aquarists make the understandable mistake of believing that bubbles arising from an airstone are somehow directly injecting oxygen, O_2, into the water. This is true

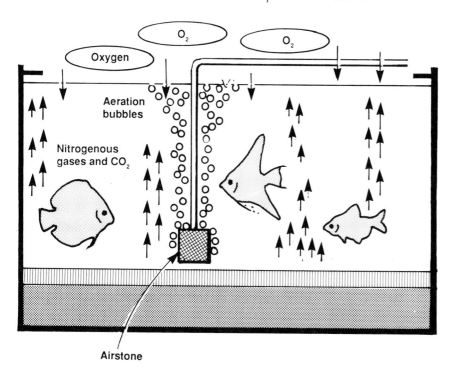

Figure 5.11 Aquarium surface/gas interchanges. Due to movement of the aquarium water, toxic gases are released at the water surface/air interface. Fresh oxygen (O₂) is absorbed into the aquarium water.

to a very minor degree only, and is not the reason for the bubbles. They have but one purpose: to break up any water stratification – layers of water in the aquarium where the temperature or the amount of dissolved gases vary, sometimes considerably.

Bubbles from an airstone cause turbulence in the aquarium, creating currents which ensure that water around the bottom of the tank is swirled up towards the surface, where the interchange of various gases can take place. The more violent or numerous the bubbles, then the more thorough will be the agitation effect, and the more complete will be the gas exchange. An air pump/airstone combination, while the most recognised method of providing aeration, is not the only method available to the aquarist. There are others which are discussed later.

Is Aeration A Good Thing?

Whether or not you require aeration in your tank depends on a number of variables. In certain situations – such as hatching the eggs from a spawning, using normal flow under-gravel filters, keeping Rift Valley cichlids or maintaining a high stock level – you may not have any choice in the matter at all, and be forced into using some form of aeration. In this case, aeration is definitely a good thing. But, then again, for those aquarists who want to maximise the growth potential of their plants, additional aeration may be the last thing they need!

Some aquarists believe that bubbles from an airstone have a decorative effect in the aquarium, as well as their primary function as an aeration device. Therefore you have to distinguish between these two areas: do you want a fancy tank decoration, which certain species of fish will find delightful (conversely: others will hate it!), or do you really *need* aeration, rather than merely want it?

The stocking formula previously described assumes that there will be no aeration used. Therefore, if the number of fishes in your aquarium is at, or below, this recommended level, then you won't need any additional aeration. Despite what you may hear to the contrary, aeration is not compulsory: you really don't have to have it if you don't want it. The exception is, of course, those species which demand high levels of dissolved oxygen, such as Rift Valley cichlids. Having said that, there will almost certainly be some aquarists who are keeping to the stocking formula but still would like to have a nice fizz of bubbles in the foreground, or maybe even a bubble curtain in the background of their aquarium. Then go ahead. Do it.

Whether or not you need, rather than would like, aeration depends on the type and numbers of fishes kept, the range and species of plants, the filtration system in use, and your aquarium maintenance routine. For example, certain fish love to swim against a current in fresh, oxygen-rich water: others would find this most uncomfortable. Some plants thrive in a low CO_2 environment, while others don't. An internal or external power filter will already be providing

An airstone operating. The bubbles keep the water moving which avoids water stratification.

some aeration anyway. While in the balanced biosphere, extra aeration could disturb the delicate balance. The needs of individual fish and plant species are fully explained in the relevant *Databases*, Chapters 10 and 11.

Providing Aeration

Having decided that you need or want some form of additional aeration, how do you provide it, and in what form? Bear in mind that you may already have some sort of device in your aquarium which is providing an aerating effect without you being aware of it. A normal flow undergravel filter system will be providing aeration all the time. First, the bubbles exiting from the uplift tube; and then there's the water flow down into the substrate. Moving water is the basis of all aeration, irrespective of the method used to actually get the water moving.

Power filters have an aerating effect whether or not they are equipped with an external air feed into a venturi chamber within the pump housing. The strength of their exiting water is enough to create currents which prevent stratification of the aquarium water. Even thermal currents from a heater or combined heater/thermostat will provide a little water movement. Aquarium water returning to the tank via a spray bar, or cascade output from an external side or back-hung box filter, will provide aeration. Now you know what aeration you may already have, do you still need more?

The most easily recognised method of providing additional aquarium aeration is to use an air pump, airline and airstone assembly. Compressed air from an air pump is fed along a plastic pipe, known as an *airline*, which in turn is terminated with a porous stone or wooden block known as an airstone (even if it is made from wood!). The airstone is placed somewhere on the bottom of the aquarium, the air pump started, and *voilà*! pretty bubbles and aeration.

Air Pumps

If you choose to use the airstone method to provide aeration within the aquarium, then you'll need an air pump. What follows applies equally to those aquarists who plan to set up a normal flow, air-driven undergravel filter system, or an internal/external box filter, driven by air.

Is Capacity Important?

The capacity of the air pump you will need depends on two things: what you are going to run from it, and the depth of your tank. Water pressure increases with depth, and makes it harder to pump air. Therefore, the pump needed for a 60cm (24in) long by 20cm (8in) deep aquarium running a single airstone would be around 40 litres (13 gallons) per hour. The pump required for an aquarium 60cm (24in) long by 45cm (18in) deep, still running a single airstone would have to pump around 90 litres (20 gallons) of air per hour to deliver the same amount of air to the airstone as the 20cm deep aquarium's pump. But if you also wanted to power an U/G, or box filter system from the same pump, then you might be struggling.

Types Of Aquarium Pump

There are basically two types of air pump available to the hobby aquarist and both have their advantages and disadvantages. The first type is the vibrating diaphragm, which has been around since the earliest days of electrical aquarium hardware, and the second is the piston air pump.

Diaphragm Air Pump

A mains voltage, alternating current (AC) electro-magnet attracts and repels an armature, which is connected to a rubber diaphragm stretched over a small cylinder, known as the valve block. As the armature oscillates, first the rubber diaphragm is pulled away from the cylinder, and a vacuum is created which pulls in the surrounding air. Then the diaphragm is pushed towards the valve block, creating pressure which forces the air out via the outlet valve in the valve block and thence into the aquarium.

Such pumps are very cheap, work well and, given adequate soundproofing, run quietly. They may be purchased in a range of sizes and output configurations, such as single, double or sometimes even quadruple air outlets, and they're relatively cheap to buy.

The Interpet Company's *Whisper* range of eleven diaphragm pumps cover very small to quite large aquaria, with pumps ranging between the model W100, rated at 60 litres (13 gallons) per minute up to the W1000, which generates 630 litres (138 gallons) of air per hour. More expensive diaphragm air pumps come with a rheostat control, which allows the current reaching the electro-magnet to be reduced, slowing the whole pump down, thereby reducing the amount of air being produced.

Disadvantages

The disadvantages of diaphragm pumps centre

around the noise they can make if not suitably soundproofed, and the durability of the rubber diaphragm itself. To restrict the air flow on diaphragm air pumps without a rheostat control, many aquarists use a small plastic clamp which pinches the airline when attached to it. This creates a back-pressure in the cylinder, and can weaken the diaphragm, causing it to split. Replacing a diaphragm is relatively easy, though, and won't need doing all that often. Just ensure that, if you buy this type of pump, you can also get spares for it. Most reputable manufacturers offer a full range of spares for their pumps. As your fishes' lives often depend on an airpump, such as when using undergravel (U/G) filters, it's only sensible to have a spare pump for emergencies, and a spare diaphragm for *both* pumps.

Piston Operated Air Pumps

With this type of air pump, a piston or pistons, connected via a cam to an electrically driven flywheel, are used to compress the air. Again,

Part of the Whisper range of diaphragm airpumps.

Hy-Flo Junior piston-operated airpump.

like their diaphragm-operated brothers, piston air pumps come in a range of sizes and number of outlets. For example, the world famous *Hy-Flo* piston air pump, made by the engineering Medcalf Brothers company in Britain, comes in a range from the *Junior*, at 42 litres per hour (9 gallons) with single piston/twin outlets; up to the *Hy-Flo Model C* – 240 litres (52 gallon) per hour, double piston, four outlet version. Although their output isn't what you could describe as excessive compared to their physical size, I can sit and watch one working all day. Mechanically, they're wonderful to watch!

Disadvantages

Piston air pumps tend to be very quiet in operation, and mechanically very sturdy, working well for many years before any maintenance is needed. Their only real disadvantage is that, on average, they tend to cost a good bit more than an equivalent diaphragm pump (someone

has to pay for all that superb engineering). Spares are a little costlier too. Regular maintenance can be a bit of a problem: they work so well that many aquarists simply forget they're there at all!

Accessories

No matter which type of pump you eventually purchase, you're going to need some bits and bobs to connect it to your filters, airstones or air-operated tank ornaments. The most obvious accessory you'll need is a length of tube known as an *airline* by aquarists, which delivers the air from the pump into the tank.

Airline tubing is a funny subject. Murphy's Law dictates that wherever you need 30cm (12in) of airline, you'll only have thirty assorted lengths handy, all of which are just 1cm (.4in) short! So buy as much airline as you can, then cut what you need, when you need it. The traditional, clear plastic tubing, which is often difficult to work with, and doesn't bend easily, now has a competitor in silicone rubber tubing. This green-coloured airline is very easy to cut, bend and shape, and push onto spigots. Of course, it costs more than the other stuff, but the extra is really worth it.

If your air pump has but the one outlet, and you want to feed air to two, three or even four different devices within the aquarium, then you have to arrange for the pump outlet to be suitably, and equally, split between each feed. A three-way plastic connector can receive the input from a pump, and give two outputs. They cost only pennies. Fastening a plastic airline clamp onto each output line gives an amount of control over the air flow, but remember this may damage the rubber diaphragm when using that type of pump. You may want more than two outputs, and require individual control over each feed as well. For this you'll need airline control valves.

Airline control valves can be bought in a variety of 'gangings', from single right up to six, still only requiring a single input. Each valve has its own tap, which closes or opens, restricting or increasing the air flow through it. They are usually made from plastic - but, for the more affluent, or for marine fishkeepers, some companies make brass versions. For those aquarists who have more than one aquarium, control valves offer a way to make maximum use of a single pump to supply all the tanks with compressed air. However, remember that anything which reduces the output from your air pump, such as 'G' clamps or control valves, will inevitably create back-pressure in the pump, putting extra strain on the rubber diaphragm.

Finally, there is one essential accessory which, while costing only pennies itself, could ultimately save you many hundreds, maybe even thousands of pounds! Many aquarists position their air pump below the level of the aquarium water. Some protection has to be provided to guard against the air pump failing and water syphoning down through the airline tubing, through the pump (naturally blowing out all the electrics in the house) and then flooding the home. It's happened to me: so be

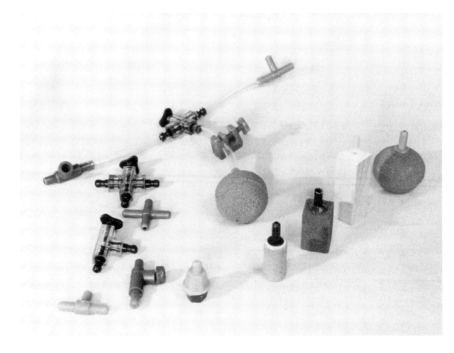

Range of essential airline and airpump connectors, valves, 'G' clamps and airstones.

warned! You can either make an anti-syphon loop in the airline as it leaves the aquarium, or fit an anti-syphon, one-way valve in the airline, between the pump outlet and where it enters the aquarium. Although there are some aquarists who will say that fitting an anti-syphon valve restricts the amount of air flowing through it, if you're using an air pump which is only just up to the job, well . . .

Lighting

You may have noticed: all tropical aquaria are lit. There is a very good reason for this. For millions of years, life on earth has revolved around the daily rising and setting of the sun. When it's dark, we sleep. Come the light, we rise. Except for a few species, fishes need and must have a daily cycle of light and dark – day and night. The diurnal cycle tells them when it's safe to explore for food, when to rest and in some species, when it's time to start thinking about reproduction.

Without any light, whether from the sun or an artificial source, plants wouldn't be able to photosynthesise – their basic life principle. During the day, plants utilise sunlight to form starches and sugars. At night, they switch to their respiration mode, using the absence of light so that they can consume these sugars, which promote healthy growth and strength. Remove the light and there's no photosynthesis, just constant respiration until all the sugars and starches are exhausted. Then the plants die. So, all in all, light is a vital aspect of the aquarium biosphere. We cannot manage our ecosystems without it, nor see our fishes clearly, which is after all the reason why we're keeping them. We could rig up any old sort of lighting system, and it would work after a fashion, but wouldn't be much like the lighting found in the fishes' natural environment.

At tropical latitudes the duration of maximum exposure to sunlight (the *Photoperiod*) is around twelve hours. The sunlight is intense. With the sun almost overhead, its light passes through a minimum amount of earth's atmosphere and therefore retains much of its power. This is the period aquarists have to imitate, so the aquarium lighting should be left on for this time.

As you may remember from Chapter 4, plants respond best to the violet/blue and orange/red areas of visible light in the electromagnetic spectrum. If we're going to create a natural environment for our fishes and plants, one in which they will feel comfortable and secure so that they may thrive, we have to imitate the type and duration of light found in their home surroundings.

Lighting The Way

We could simply use the free sunlight available to everyone. After all, it's what plants and fish have been successfully using for millennia. The problem is we have no control over its duration, intensity or quality, and even if we had, it still wouldn't be much good. Fishes are used to their daily supply of sunlight arriving on the surface of the water, and percolating downwards. Some fishes have even evolved a basic colour scheme to take advantage of this. Dark colours on their backs camouflage them against the dark river or lake bed when viewed from above, while a light coloured abdomen helps them blend with the water surface when viewed from below. If we were to use natural sunlight, it would enter the aquarium not only at the surface, but also through the aquarium's glass sides and back, which is thoroughly unnatural, and very uncomfortable for the fish. But daylight does have a use in the aquarium, as we'll see later.

Synthetic Sunlight

Most aquarists turn to some form of artificial lighting to provide the necessary illumination within the aquarium. The advantages are that the light is coming from the right direction, ie. above, and we can control duration, quality and intensity. In the early days, when I first started keeping fish, I used ordinary, domestic light bulbs. These incandescent lamps produce most of their output as pure heat and an apparently white light, which is actually biased towards the yellow/orange end of the spectrum. They produce very little light output at blue/violet wavelengths, so for photosynthesis purposes they are lacking in what we need. But, make no mistake, many aquarists around the world still use and get excellent results from ordinary domestic incandescent light bulbs, much to the chagrin of the specialist aquatic fluorescent tube manufacturers! I even use them myself for specific purposes.

Incandescent bulbs aren't used as much as they used to be because of their high running cost, short life due to splashes etc. and lack of the right type of output. But they do have a use, such as in fish breeding.

Fluorescent Lighting

Although initially more expensive to buy than domestic light bulbs, fluorescent lights – or 'tube lighting' as it is also known – meet all the criteria set down by aquarists for lighting the aquarium. These units produce their output much more efficiently than incandescent bulbs, they are cool running, use relatively little electrical power, and produce some useful output in the violet/blue area of the spectrum. As an example of their efficiency, in a tank 60×30× 30cm (24×12×12in) the recommended amount of fluorescent lighting is 2×15W tubes, a total of 30 watts. If using ordinary light bulbs, you would need 2×40W, a total of 80 watts. Thirty watts of cool light against eighty of hot, red light.

Unlike domestic light bulbs, where you simply purchase one, and slip it into the holder, fluorescent lighting needs special equipment. So you can't just go out and buy a tube, slip it into the tank's hood and use it. A complete fluorescent lighting system comprises a combined starter and choke unit, from which cables emerge which are terminated with waterproof end caps, which hold the tube(s). Then there is the actual tube itself, which doesn't usually come with the starter/choke assembly. You have to purchase it separately, ensuring that it is the right diameter to fit the end caps, and the right wattage for that type of choke and starter unit:

Incandescent light source. Hot, red light for the plants. (Safety glass cover removed for clarity.)

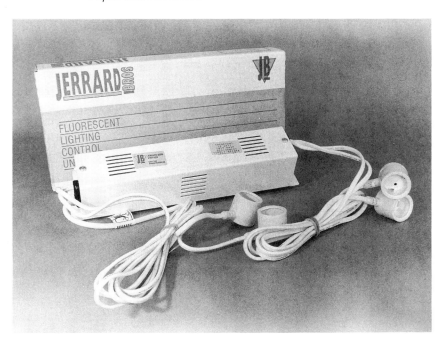

Twin-choke, fluorescent lighting kit. Cheaper than buying two singles.

you can't use a 30 watt tube in a 15 watt choke/starter. The waterproof end caps are then pushed onto each end of the tube, the mains cable wired to a suitable supply and fuse, and that's it.

Special Tubes

When aquarists first started making use of fluorescent lighting, they mainly used ordinary white tubes, as found in offices and homes. These worked well, as they had an output, albeit limited, in the blue/violet end of the spectrum. Research into the basic nature of sunlight, into the absorption spectrum of plants, and the various effects of polychromatic and monochromatic light on fishes and plants, has led to a range of fluorescent tubes whose spectral output has been specially modified for use in aquaria. The first of these 'spectrally modified tubes' was the *Grolux*, which was actually developed not directly for aquarists but for horticulturists.

The *Grolux* tube, still very popular today, produces a pinkish light which has strong output at red and blue wavelengths, so is ideal for promoting healthy plant growth. However, it has little output at yellow/green or violet/blue; which makes the aquarium appear dim, and may give a strange colour cast to fishes and plants. This lack of the right output can be balanced by including an ordinary, white fluorescent tube alongside the *Grolux* in the hood. This gives what is known as 'Balanced Lighting' – all the necessary (and useful) wavelengths of the electromagnetic spectrum of visible light.

Most manufacturers now make their own version of the ideal fluorescent tube for the aquarium. Brand-name tubes, such as *Northlight*, *Sun-Glo*, *Power-Glo* and *Tru-Lite*, all closely match the spectral range of natural daylight. In the Western world, subjected as we are to a constant bombardment of advertising hyperbole, we can and do become somewhat jaundiced, even quite cynical, concerning advertiser's claims for their products. It was my own cynicism which nearly caused me to miss out on a new innovation in aquarium lighting; the *Triton* tube, from the Interpet company.

The Triton Fluorescent Tube

A collaboration between Thorn EMI and Interpet resulted in the first aquarium tube which does *not* try to imitate natural daylight. The basic principle is so simple that I can't think why no one else thought of it before. When sunlight passes through water, the individual wavelengths of the polychromatic light are absorbed and scattered at different depths. The *Triton* tube is balanced so that the most helpful wavelengths are boosted to ensure that they penetrate deep down to the very bottom of the tank, neatly bypassing the problem of absorption.

Furthermore, the *Triton* tube maintains a uniform output up to the end of its useful life, whereas, in other types, the output can often begin to fade from initial switch-on. This results in a higher effective light output for a given tube size, *where the light is most needed* eg. amongst the plants. The result is a tube which promotes very healthy plant growth, enhances the natural colours of the fishes and is cheaper to run. But

Gro-lux and Triton tubes.

it is the *Triton's* effect on the perceived colours of the fishes and plants which really impresses me. I recently installed two 20 watt *Triton* tubes in a friend's tank. She really couldn't believe the difference it made. Blues and reds were really, well. . blue and red; and not the pale, bleached colours which some types of lighting promote. When using a specialist fluorescent tube to light your aquarium, it will gradually start wearing down. With time, the special coatings become less efficient, until a stage is reached where the quality of light is but a fraction of its original output. You won't notice this visually, unless you have exceptional colour vision, of course. But it is a fact that, after around six months of continuous use, the tube will have lost around 60 percent of its efficiency, and will need replacing. So bear this in mind. Adding silver foil inside the hood, or cutting 'U'-shaped aluminium reflectors for the backs of fluorescent tubes, can double the total light output, simply by directing it in the right direction.

Other Lighting Systems

Although I've only discussed incandescent and fluorescent lighting so far, there are other systems available, such as Mercury Vapour and Halide lights. One of the disadvantages of fluorescent lighting is the very even, shadowless light it produces, which is not natural. In the tropics the sunlight is often blocked by trees etc. producing areas of intense light and deep shadow in rivers, pools and lakes. These specialist lamps go a long way towards recreating this natural, dappling effect of light in the water. They provide a very intense light, much stronger and more directional than fluorescent tubes, recreating those areas of intense light and shade.

Mercury Vapour Lamps

When using this type of lighting, you have to dispense with the aquarium hood. The usual arrangement is to suspend each lamp over the aquarium, hanging from either a ceiling or wall mounted fitting, at an average height of 45–60cm (18–24in). As they run hot, cover glasses should be used to keep splashes off. Some aquarists who specialise in aquatic plants use mercury vapour lights suspended over completely open tanks. This allows those types of plants which will grow emerse foliage to flourish, and complete their natural cycle of growing, flowering, pollination (done by the aquarist) and seeding. The Wotan company sell a mercury vapour lighting kit known as the *Flora-SET*, which comes complete with reflectors (wall or ceiling mounted) and the bulb. Cost is around £50 per unit for ceiling, and £45 for wall mounting. Spare bulbs average £14 each. Allow one mercury vapour lamp for every four square feet of aquarium surface area.

Halide Lamps

Used more by marine aquarists who keep light-loving invertebrates and living corals, which tend to occupy the bottom of the aquarium, Halide, also known as Quartz or Tungsten-Halogen lights, use the same system as that used in car headlamps. It is a very expensive option for the tropical fishkeeper. They are used in much the same way as mercury vapour lights, that is, suspended from the ceiling, over a hoodless tank. Halide lamps have tremendous punch, and can cope with deep tanks – over 60cm (24in) in depth – very easily. Each unit, complete with bulb, will cost you around £200, with spare bulbs at around £80 each. Allow one Halide lamp for every three square feet of surface area.

Choosing A System

Just as many hobby aquarists over-filter their aquarium water, many tanks are also either under-illuminated for some species or over-illuminated for others. So know what your fish require by reading-up on them before choosing a suitable lighting system.

The Lighting Myth

Many aquatic books will tell you that a tank up to a certain depth will need so much lighting, while another, deeper tank will need even more lighting. In tropical freshwater fishkeeping *this is nonsense!* This myth (like most myths) has a basis in truth, and began with our marine fishkeeping brothers and sisters, who, keeping such items as invertebrates and living corals, needed a lot of light down at the substrate level. Tropical freshwater fishkeepers *do not need* strong light down at the substrate level. After all, most of their plants will be at least 15cm (6in) above the level of the gravel and, as the only purpose of artificial lighting in a tropical aquarium is to promote photosynthesis of the aquatic plants, why should you want an excessively powerful light to punch its way towards the bottom of the tank when it's the leaves of the plants which need the light?

Most home aquaria – unless specially created – are most unlikely to be deeper than 45cm (18in). The recommended lighting levels, as outlined in this book can be safely followed. Any 'orders' from elsewhere, to increase the lighting level with deeper tanks may be safely ignored.

Balanced Lighting

Most aquarists choose fluorescent lighting to start with. Suppose that the recommended lighting for your size of tank is 20 watts, you could add that quite easily by using a single 20-watt tube. However, it is much better to have two fluorescent tubes rather than just one. This allows you to provide a balanced lighting system, such as a *Grolux* and a *Triton* tube. So, instead of installing a choke/starter for one 20 watt tube, add a double, 15 watt choke/starter and two 15 watt tubes of different spectral characteristics. The extra amount of light won't harm anything. On the subject of choke/starters, if you need two fluorescent tubes, it is much cheaper to buy twin choke/starters than it is to buy two, single choke/starters. It also takes up less space in the hood.

Light Blocking

Having set up your lighting system, you'll be expecting good plant growth and happy fishes. There are a few things which can cause problems within the tank. One of these is scattering and absorption of the light. Suspended particles in the water, usually caused by over-feeding, a tint, such as that given off by a peat filter, which gives the water a slight sepia tone, or dirty cover glasses can all have quite a startling effect on the amount and quality of light reaching the plants. The moral is to keep cover glasses well scrubbed, don't over-feed the fish, and make sure you maintain the water quality. Clean water transmits more light than dirty water.

Heaters

In the Tropics, due to the constant supply of sunshine, water temperatures tend to be fairly stable, averaging from 20–28 degrees Celsius throughout the year. While this isn't exactly hot water, it is certainly warmer than that arriving via the average domestic coldwater supply. Therefore, tropical fishkeepers have to provide some form of heating for their fishes.

A Good Compromise

Many aquarists pin their aquarium temperature at 24 degrees Celsius, although both higher and lower temperatures play a useful role in aquarium management, such as when treating disease, and instigating breeding. However, 24 degrees C is an ideal community tank temperature – a little cool for a few, a little hot for even fewer, but just about right for the majority. Creating and maintaining this temperature is very simple these days, and can be done using a variety of different equipment and techniques,

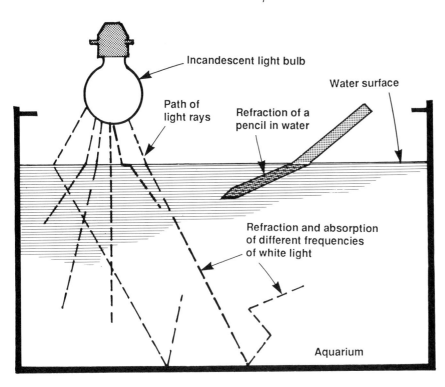

Incandescent light bulb

Water surface

Path of
light rays

Refraction of a
pencil in water

Refraction and absorption
of different frequencies
of white light

Aquarium

Figure 5.12 Light diffraction and absorption in water. The brighter the light, then the deeper the penetration. However, too much light can damage a fish's eyes. A useful alternative is to buy one of the special aquatic fluorescent tubes in which the colour balance is biased to achieve the best results with both fishes and plants.

which allow you to create a range of effects within the aquarium.

Heaters, General

There are now numerous ways to heat the water in your aquarium but, whichever equipment you choose, ensure that it is adequate for the job. Heaters which are too powerful will raise the temperature far too quickly for the fishes. Alternatively, a heater which isn't powerful enough will spend almost all of its time switched on, shortening its potential service life. Once the correct temperature has been achieved, aquarium heaters should be off more often than they are on. Combined heater/thermostats have a neon lamp which lights when the thermostat is passing current to the heating element.

Similarly, external thermostats usually have some visual indication when current is passing to the heater. Keep your eye on this indicator lamp. If it seems to be on all the time, your heater may not be powerful enough or your aquarium is subjected to temperature fluctuations, such as cool draughts, or the actual heater may be broken. A good thermometer has to be used to keep a constant check on the aquarium temperature. Be warned though! There are the few, odd internal 'test-tube' style thermostats where the light goes OFF when it passes current to the heater; therefore, in this case, the light should be ON more than it's OFF.

Combined Heater/Thermostat

This is by far the easiest heating system to use, and one favoured by many aquarists around the world. Once the correct temperature has been set, and normal operation ascertained, it may safely be left well alone to get on with its job. Combined heater/stats comprise a watertight

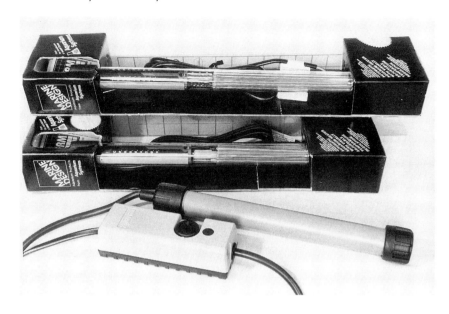

Range of commercial heater/
stats. Note the new Aquarian
heater/stat in the foreground
with the external temperature
setting/control box.

glass, or glass and ceramic tube, at the bottom of which lies the electrical heating element. Above this is the thermostat compartment, which is usually a simple bi-metallic strip. A small knob, which passes through a watertight bulkhead inside the unit and protrudes through the top plate of the heater/stat, allows the temperature to be varied on average by plus or minus 8 degrees either side of 24 degrees Celsius.

Combined heater/stats should be either positioned horizontally in the aquarium, so that the thermostat part isn't directly receiving the heat from the heating element, or with the thermostat section (top part) slightly lower in the water than the heater. This gives a more accurate reading of the ambient tank temperature. Even so, a thermometer should be used to check various locations around the tank, and especially around the site of the heater/stat, for any hot or cold spots.

The heater part of the combined heater/stat should not touch the substrate however, neither should plants be placed where they will grow around the heating element, or tank decorations

placed in contact with it, or sited in such a position that they may fall onto and shatter the glass tube. This has been the direct cause of at least one aquarist's death. With some species, such as large, boisterous cichlids, it is often a good idea to glue the rubber suckers which grip and hold the heater/stat to the aquarium back glass using silicone sealant, which then prevents the heater/stat from being dislodged and possibly damaged.

Although relatively cheap and very simple to install, combined heater/thermostats do have one or two little problems. The bi-metallic strip can begin to corrode after a while, due to the ingress of tiny amounts of water. This corrosion can become so bad, that when the electrical contact is made to pass current to the heater, the contacts can fuse together, keeping the heater permanently on, and which (if not spotted quickly) will eventually boil your fishes! As the contacts corrode, they will also start generating radio interference which can seriously harm any relationship you may have with your neighbours, as the hash wipes out their TV and radio reception. Combined heater/stats are also rather inaccurate, allowing temperature swings of plus or minus anything up to four or five degrees of the required temperature.

Combined heater/thermostats are available in a range of wattages and physical sizes, running from 50 watt, little units for small aquaria, up to 300 watt, huge devices for larger, or deeper aquaria. However, a single heater/thermostat should not really be used in tanks greater than 90cm (36in) length. For larger aquaria there are much better, and more efficient (and cheaper!) ways to heat the water.

Safety Of Combined Heater/Thermostats

The other major problem with combined heater/stats is that time and time again, later in this book, the advice is to not only switch off *all* power to the aquarium before plunging your hands into the water, but also *remove* the wall plug as well. Adjusting a combined heater/thermostat is something which has to be done *with the power switched on*! You have to adjust the thermostat temperature control knob while your hands are underwater, and wait for the neon lamp light to go out, thus telling you that you have successfully changed the setting.

While I've never yet heard of an aquarist being electrocuted when performing this adjustment, the potential is there. The Aquarian company has done something about this situation (see p111) and has also caused me to rethink my own personal prejudice against combined heater/stats.

Heaters And A Thermostat

Aquarium heaters can be bought without the thermostat part attached. They consist of a glass or ceramic tube which contains the electrical heating element only. Of course, they cannot be used just on their own: once switched on they would stay on until the power is removed. You could use a single heater and an external thermostat as your main aquarium heating, but combined heater/stats do a much cheaper, more

efficient job. Where separate heaters really score is when used as pairs in larger aquaria.

Getting an even distribution of heat around a large tank is difficult with a single heater, such as a combined heater/stat. Aquarists mainly prefer to use two heaters, positioned at either end of the aquarium, connected to a separate thermostat, located somewhere in the centre of the tank. Such a system will cost more than a single heater/thermostat, and is more complicated to set up. However, there are advantages over and above those of even heat distribution around the tank.

Because the choice of thermostat now rests with you, and there are many very advanced models to choose from, you're free to take advantage of the application of new technology, such as microelectronics, to aquarium management.

Thermostats

Separate thermostats operate in various ways. There is the simple bi-metallic strip type, as used in the combined heater/stats, which may fit either internally or externally. Where two heating elements are required, the internal, submerged bi-metallic strip thermostat is usually positioned in between the heaters, attached to the middle of the back glass. Of course, the comments made earlier about contact corrosion and accuracy still apply. I use a fairly sophisticated electronic thermometer, which has the handy feature of recording both the highest and lowest temperatures measured during any time period. Using a separate *Ultratherm* heating mat and an internal bi-metallic thermostat, my digital thermometer recorded a lowest temperature of 18 degrees C and a highest of 29 C during a 24 hour period. The thermostat was set for 24 degrees C.

External bi-metallic strip thermostats often take the form of a small plastic box with a metal sensing plate on the back. The unit is clipped onto the outside of the aquarium wall, therefore allowing easy temperature adjustments, with the metal sensing plate in contact with the aquarium glass. And all without getting your hands wet!

Electronic thermostats again fit externally, and vary greatly in sophistication. Price is a good guide. They sense temperature either from a metal plate on the back of the box, which is pressed against the aquarium glass, or from a separate, small probe which is submerged in the water. The facilities they offer are now very advanced indeed. At their most basic they will keep the water temperature to within 1 degree F of that required. More advanced units can measure the water and the ambient room temperatures, have over/under temperature alarms, a memory facility to record the maximum and minimum temperatures over a set period of time; provision for a back-up heating element – which may be battery powered in case of mains

failure – and clear, usually digital Liquid Crystal Displays (LCDs) of all this information.

External Mat Heaters

For those aquarists who're looking for luxuriant plant growth, and don't want a bulky combined heater/thermostat intruding into their aquascape, heating mats provide the answer. A heating mat is an electrical heating element sandwiched between a thermocoating of rubberised material. They come in a range of physical sizes and power ratings to suit different size aquaria, from 60×30 cm (24×12in) @ 120 watts; right up to 183×45cm (72×18in) @ 475 watts.

Fitting An Ultratherm Mat

The heating mat, which has a plastic terminal

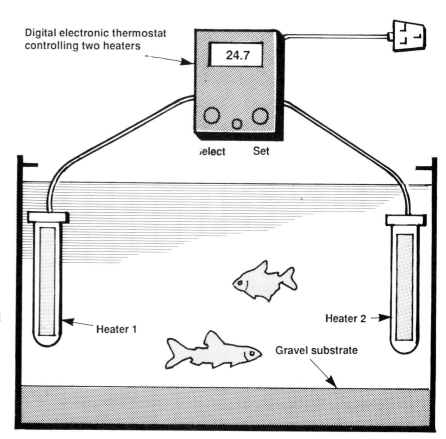

Figure 5.13   Two heaters and one thermostat. In fish tanks over 3 feet (90 cm), it's better to use two heaters, one at each end of the tank, controlled by one thermostat. Do ensure that the combined wattage of *both* heaters does not exceed the switch rating of the thermostat.

Digital electronic thermostat controlling two heaters

24.7

select   Set

Heater 1

Heater 2

Gravel substrate

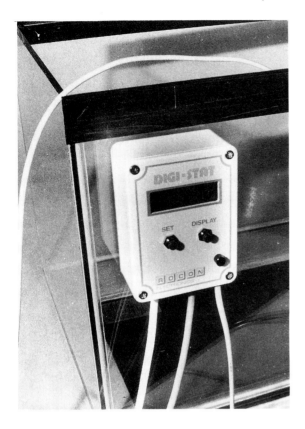

Rocon Digi-Stat.

beneath the heating mat, *never* put another one on top – this will cause the device to overheat, and maybe even catch fire. The heating mat is just a heating element, with no means of temperature sensing or power switching, so it has to be used in conjunction with a separate thermostat.

The advantage of the heating mat is that, as the mat covers the whole of the aquarium floor, it ensures even heat distribution without having to resort to aeration techniques. The heat passes

block protruding around 5 millimetres above the level of the actual mat surface, *must* be stood on a sheet of 10mm (minimum) expanded polystyrene. A cut-out of 40mm square has to be made in the sheet of polystyrene to accommodate the terminal block, which then stops it pressing against the bottom of the aquarium glass. It's a good idea to stick some aluminium foil on the bottom of the polystyrene as this will reflect the heat upwards, into the aquarium. Ultratherm recommend that you do not exceed a total substrate depth of more than 8 inches when using their mats.

However, the thickness of the base glass is unimportant, as the devices are designed to work effectively through 6–25 millimetres. Having placed a sheet of polystyrene plastic

Polystyrene mat, 10 mm thick, with cut-out and cable channel for the Ultratherm heating mat (foreground).

into the aquarium through the bottom glass, and then percolates upwards, warming the roots of the plants, and creating thermal currents which ensure a constant oxygen supply to their root systems – very useful in tanks which don't use undergravel filters. Aesthetically, they are more pleasing to the eye because they remove the heating apparatus from within the aquarium, allowing the aquarist to create a more natural aquascape. However, the heat they produce may well be too much for some plants. But we can still apply the basic concept by using a substrate heater. Heating mats should *never* be used for tanks smaller than the mat was intended for, and *never* on plastic aquaria.

The only real disadvantage of heater mats is if, and when, they pack up working. You have a choice: either strip the tank and replace the mat, or disconnect the broken mat and replace it with an alternative heating method, such as a combined heater/stat or separate heaters and a thermostat.

External/Internal Substrate Heaters

A straightforward external mat heater may be too powerful for the root systems of many aquatic plants, but for those aquarists who approve of the basic concept, you can get external heating mats in a low wattage range. For example, 90×30cm (36×12in) @ 42 watts, up to 183×45cm (72×18in) @ 240 watts. These low wattage mat heaters are not powerful enough to be the main source of heat in the aquarium, so they have to be backed up with an internal heater. Both the low wattage heating mat and the internal heating element are easily connected to a suitable thermostat, which will then control the aquarium temperature by switching both devices. But do ensure that the 'rating' of your thermostat is up to the job.

For example, you couldn't use a 150 watt auxiliary heating mat *and* a 200 watt internal heater with a thermostat rated as switching 300 watts. You'd need a thermostat which was capable of switching at least a 400 watt load. When working out what size mat and internal

heater you will need for your size of tank, simply subtract the wattage of the heater mat from the relevant column in Figure 5.1 and then make up the difference with an internally fitting heater, rounding up to the nearest commercially available size. But don't forget the thermostat rating. This situation also applies when using two heaters and a thermostat. If the combined wattage of the heaters is greater than the switching rating of the thermostat, then there will be problems. Thermostats are usually labelled with their maximum switching rating.

Substrate Heater Cables

Yet another method of providing some heat within the substrate is to use a ribbon cable heater, although these are becoming quite rare nowadays. They are actually strips of low wattage heater mat material in a waterproof casing. Like the low wattage mat heaters, they are not powerful enough to be the only heating element in the aquarium, and so need to be backed up with an additional, internal heater or heaters. They connect into the heater/thermostat system in exactly the same way as a low wattage mat heater/internal heater system. The cable is buried in the substrate, and gently warms plant root systems, while also producing a slow thermocurrent, promoting the flow of water.

Other Heating Methods

Aquarists who're using either mercury vapour or metal Halide lamps will already be putting a fair amount of heat into the aquarium water, as will those who are using incandescent light bulbs, so this has to be borne in mind. An aquarium exposed to direct sunlight for more than an hour per day, or positioned near a central heating radiator, will also acquire a fair amount of additional heat; hence the importance of sensible aquarium location, and the need for an accurate thermometer. Head off these problems before they occur by not siting your aquarium badly in the first place.

Ignore any outside influence on the aquarium temperature, and base your heater requirements purely on tank size and volume. During the day, when the lights are on, the thermostat will ensure that the heater doesn't receive any power. However, at night, when the lights are off, the thermostat then maintains the overnight temperature at the correct level by switching the heater on. When using this type of lighting, daytime overheating of the aquarium water is likely to be the greater problem. A balance has to be struck when positioning these specialised lamps, to ensure that overheating doesn't occur.

Thermofilters

Increasingly popular these days, especially in complete biosphere aquaria (where all the heating, lighting and filtration is already supplied and hidden) is the thermofilter, which is simply a heating element combined with a filtration system, such as certain power or wet and dry filters. The advantage of this heating system is an almost perfect distribution of heat around the aquarium. The water is warmed immediately prior to its return from the filter into the aquarium, so the exiting stream from the filtration system ensures good mixing. Again, this aids aquascaping as the heater is hidden from sight.

Aquarian Combined Heater/Thermostats

To meet the new EEC electrical safety regulations (at least; this week's version) the Aquarian company has brought out a new range of combined heater/thermostats which completely break with tradition by placing the thermostatic adjustment section *outside* of the aquarium, while keeping the temperature sensing probe inside the tank. Further, the actual thermostat control 'box' is a solid-state (electronic) device which guarantees accuracy to .25 degrees C!

A grey tube, sealed at each end with a black rubber bung, contains the heater. A power lead from this tube exits the aquarium water, passes through the temperature control box, and then to the mains electricity. No-one is saying how they've done it, but obviously the tip of the grey tube contains the temperature sensing probe separated from the heater by a thermally opaque bulkhead. Information regarding temperature is then passed along the mains cable, back to the box of electronics.

The one I borrowed for a week worked perfectly, and was a sheer joy to use. Temperature adjustments were made quickly and simply – and with dry hands! The one thing which did bother me a little, though, was the way that the heater 'on' lamp kept chattering on and off as the temperature varied slightly in the aquarium, during the night. However, an FM radio I keep close by my wordprocessor (to stop me nodding-off in the wee small hours) didn't pick up any radio interference at all. Perhaps the setting is a little too accurate, Aquarian. I can't see it being too long before other aquatic manufacturers copy this very sensible and highly usable idea.

Accessories

So far I've discussed filters, aeration, heating, lighting and the actual aquarium itself. We're almost ready to begin creating our community tank. But, before we do that, there's a few accessories to be discussed. Some are necessary, others merely desirable. I'm fully aware that not all fishkeepers are also millionaires so, where I am exhorting you to part with your hard earned cash, you can be assured that it is for a very good reason.

Thermometers

There is a wide range of thermometers available to the aquarist, ranging from the simple, stick-on, multi-coloured LCD (Liquid Crystal Display) strip, which attaches externally to the aquarium glass, right up to electronic thermometers, which may be certified for accuracy, and have prices to match. Whatever type of thermometer you acquire it has to be easy for you to read. Although this does sound obvious, it is actually a little more complicated than appears at first sight.

For example, I've been using a digital wristwatch for something like twenty-five years now. With a single glance at the digits I can abstract all the information I need, such as the time now, the time elapsed since, or the remaining time to a particular event. However, if I have to look at an analogue watch or clock, I have to pause and really think about things, translating the position of the hands into digits first, and then working backwards how long since, now, or to. The point is that I much prefer information in digital form as I find it easier to assimilate, therefore I use digital thermometers. I know that many people find the exact opposite of this, and prefer an analogue thermometer. Whatever you prefer, do ensure that you actually acquire *your* preference!

The thermometer is your continuous guard against chilling your fishes, you will be looking at it every day. (That's why it has to be easy to read.) Any change from the usual should be immediately obvious to you, without you having to perform mental gymnastics. Some aquarists like to have a constant readout of water *and* substrate temperatures, as some heating systems – such as undertank heater mats – can actually make the substrate a little warmer than the tank temperature. This of course requires two thermometers.

Thermometer Types

Most aquarists manage quite well with the stick-on LCD type. You simply peel off the backing paper and stick it onto the front of the aquarium glass, where it is easily viewed. Once stuck on, they cannot be removed and re-positioned without destroying them. They actually measure the temperature of the aquarium glass, which is usually the same as the water inside; *but not always*.

For those who prefer the more traditional mercury or alcohol-type thermometer, there are plenty from which to choose, ranging from the cheap and cheerful up to the certified accurate types, costing quite a lot more. Traditional mercury thermometers are usually fixed inside the aquarium, attached to the front glass by a small rubber sucker. Unfortunately they do display a tendency to want to float upwards! Some types have a weight at the bottom of the tube to counteract this positive buoyancy but, if yours doesn't, then simply wrap a piece of plant lead wire around its base.

It's also a good idea to have some idea of how accurate (or otherwise) your thermometer is: I recently acquired an alcohol-type thermometer which was reading *eight* degrees C too low! One way of calibrating your thermometer is to find a friendly photographic dealer, buy a film for your camera and ask them to check your thermometer's accuracy against one of their certified types. If it's reading too high or low, that doesn't make it useless. Providing that you know by how much it is out, then you can simply allow for that margin when measuring tank temperatures. Mind you, I have six thermometers, including a mercury one certified by the National Geophysical Laboratory for accuracy. Three of my six are digital-electronic. *None of them agree with each other!* There's always at least two tenths of a degree difference between them all somewhere.

Electronic thermometers are simple to use and are very accurate in operation. However, they are not usually fixed in any way to the actual aquarium, but you can arrange this if that's what you want. When a temperature reading is required, the electronic thermometer has to be taken to the aquarium, the probe placed in the water and a reading taken. Although this sounds like a lot of messing about, it's actually not a bad method because it makes you really think about what you're doing.

I Did It My Way

This is the method I use to provide a constant digital read-out of the water and the substrate

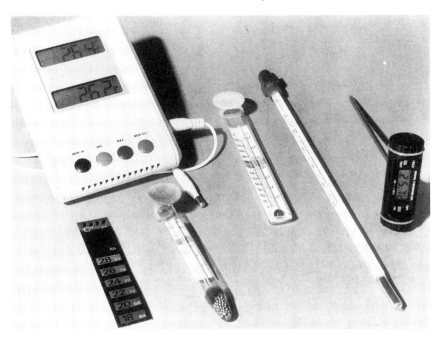

Range of thermometers, traditional and electronic.

temperatures. I use an external heating mat and a thermostat which is one of the newer, high-tech electronic devices, the Rocon *Digi-Stat*. The case of my *Digi-Stat* attaches externally to the aquarium (but only if you want it to, it isn't compulsory), and a small temperature-sensing probe goes into the water. The case has simple controls for adjusting the temperature range (variable from 0 to 159 degrees F), a warning light when the heater is active, and a constant digital read-out of the measured temperature. Accuracy is to 1 degree F (more than adequate for most aquarists). This is backed up with an LCD stick-on strip positioned on the right-hand side wall of the aquarium, at the bottom, where it gives a continuous display of substrate temperature.

Power Distribution

Power for the lights, power for the heater, power for the thermostat, power for the air pump, power for the filter. That's at least five separate mains voltage commitments. You could just simply connect these devices straight to your domestic electricity supply, but that means cables, and multi-outlet adaptors cluttering up the room; and is potentially dangerous.

There are several power distributors available from various manufacturers such as the Interpet's *Cable Tidy And Connector*, or the *Power Centre*, from Algarde. What they all do is take the separate leads from the various electrical aquarium devices and connect them all into a single cable and plug. In many books on tropical fishkeeping, the power distributor, usually a Cable Tidy type, is often shown stuck on the actual glass of the aquarium, close to the top. *This is not a good idea*; any drips, such as from your arms when working in the aquarium, will run straight into the power distributor. Once the electricity is turned back on again – you *never* have your arms in the water with the power still on – a short circuit, caused by water entering the power distribution device, is a real possibility.

Power distribution boxes, no matter whose, all have a maximum wattage rating. In other words, they can only supply so much current, so you have to ensure that you're not trying to take more watts from the distribution box than the recommended maximum. Most electrical aquarium devices do state the wattage of the device. All you need to do is add-up the total of *all* the devices you want to connect, and ensure that it is *below* that recommended for the power distributing box.

Working Tools

There will come a time when you want to remove a fish from the aquarium, but first you have to catch it. Fish nets come in a variety of sizes and styles. Only when you have spent a frustrating half-hour chasing a fish around the aquarium with a circular net do you realise how unsuitable this shape is for a rectangular tank! Two square-shaped, fine and soft meshed nets – one to coax, one to catch, around 10cm (4in) across – will be suitable for a community aquarium. Bigger species require larger nets, of course; smaller aquaria need nets smaller than 10cm.

Algae scrapers come in various forms, and are used for removing any algal bloom from the inside of the aquarium's glass walls. There is the razor blade on a handle type, the plastic blade on a handle, or the magnetic version. This comprises two magnets, one of which has a scouring surface, and goes inside the tank. The other magnet has a felt pad and is positioned outside the tank. Both magnets are lined up, and the outside one is used to guide the scouring magnet around the tank, cleaning the glass. Whichever type of algae scraper you choose, be very careful when using it on acrylic or plastic aquaria as they scratch relatively easily.

Acrylic (Plastic) Aquariums

For plastic aquaria, I've found the best device to be either a rough-woven cloth, such as that used by window cleaners (well, what they used to use before the invention of the squeegee), and known as *Scrim*, net curtaining, or a soft bristled nail brush. Wet the scrim or net curtaining, and gently wipe the inner walls – most of the removed algae ends up in the cloth. During a partial water change, when the water level has been dropped, gently wipe (*do not scrub*) the inner walls with the nail brush, wiping in one direction only, not backwards and forwards.

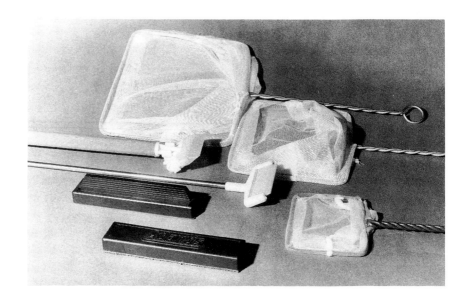

Nets, algae scrapers and planting sticks.

Vacuum Cleaners

Substrate 'hoovers' may be battery, syphon or air-powered. They remove mulm from the surface of the gravel by suction, and deposit it either in a collecting bag connected to the 'hoover' or into the bucket along with the dirty water. Actually, gravel cleaners are a luxury you can manage without as you can get virtually the same effect by using a syphon. When you're due to make a partial water change (see *Aquarium Management*, p129), use a piece of airline tubing as a syphon, and run it over the surface of the substrate. This achieves the dual purpose of removing water, and cleans the gravel at the same time, *without* seriously disturbing the biological bed.

Discus fish.

A 'Shammy'

One final accessory I find essential is a chamois leather – or rather one of today's more environmentally acceptable substitutes – which I use for cleaning the outside of the aquarium. It does seem to give glass that added sparkle, and is great for mopping up the inevitable spillage when doing a partial water change.

Apart from a few simple test kits, such as ammonia and nitrite/nitrate, that's all the basic accessories you need successfully to create and maintain a tropical fish aquarium. Of course, as your aquaristic skills and enthusiasm grow, you'll suddenly find that there's many more accessories you simply cannot manage without, especially once you start reading the aquarists' magazines!

Complete Biosphere Aquaria

A recent innovation which is finding a very ready market amongst modern day fishkeepers, who are often very busy people with little time for trivia or inessentials, is the complete biosphere aquaria. Basically, the concept is a completely self-contained aquatic environment for tropical freshwater, or marine fishes, providing everything they need in terms of aquarium, water treatment and conditioning. Complete biospheres usually comprise a tank, often built into a cabinet, and an in-built, hidden-from-view filtration, aeration, lighting and heating system. I call them *dehydrated* aquariums: all you need do is add water! (Sorry.)

Biosphere aquaria vary in complexity and features. At the top end, technologically and price-wise, are the computer controlled, multi-biofeedback automated systems, which monitor and control water quality using mechanical, chemical, and biological filtration. They feed the fish, change the water, inject CO_2 and medicaments as and when needed, and switch the lighting on and off. At the other end (price-wise not quality) is the *TropiQuarium*, the ideal biosphere starter aquarium, comprising an acrylic tank 50×25×36cm (20×10×14in), and lighting, heating, power filtration, all in-built. You simply add water, decorations and, of course, the fishes. This is the tank I mentioned earlier, whose acrylic construction appears to have better light transmission characteristics than glass. Odd but true.

Advantages

The advantages of complete biosphere aquaria are many. They remove the need to seek, check

The Hockney complete
biosphere aquaria – one of a
range.

for compatibility then purchase separate pieces of equipment, such as a tank, stand and hood, heaters, lights, thermostats and filtration system. All this equipment is already present. You don't have pipes, wires and boxes etc. trailing around the site of the aquarium either. This can often be the cause of discontent between domestic partners, who may object to the piles of 'spaghetti' and gurgling noises which makes their beautifully decorated lounge resemble Doctor Frankenstein's laboratory!

With a biosphere aquarium you have just the one power plug for the whole unit. Everything else is neatly tucked away out of sight, either behind special panels in the aquarium itself, or hidden within cupboards of the cabinet. Each complete biosphere aquaria, no matter who from, represents many hours of designing and testing. Prototype concepts are run, complete with fish for extended trials, ensuring that it works, that plants will grow and the fish are contented. The final product on sale to us represents the present state-of-the-art in modern aquatic technology. They often include high tech trickle, or wet and dry filtration systems. This

exciting new concept will carry the fishkeeping hobby well into the twenty-first century.

Once such systems are correctly set up and running, they require minimum maintenance, freeing the owner to pursue perhaps more interesting aquatic activities. However, like balanced biospheres, they cannot be ignored! Water quality still has to be checked at least monthly. A complete and self-contained biosphere aquarium undoubtedly looks very good, sitting quietly in a corner, humming gently to itself and drawing all eyes towards it. But of course, this level of technological sophistication has a price.

Disadvantages

There aren't that many, but they are important. When you purchase such an aquarium, you're also buying someone else's idea of what constitutes a good heating, lighting and filtration system, and not your own. Even though such systems are usually very advanced technologically, and have been proven to work, you may still think that you could do a better and cheaper job. Maybe you can – you do have the choice and the freedom to find out.

You have to 'stick to the rules' of such aquaria, ie. use them for their intended purpose. If you add too many fishes, never run a water test, use or maintain the equipment badly, or attempt to keep marines in a system designed for fresh-water species, then you can't in all fairness claim that the system doesn't work. Certainly, self-contained biosphere aquaria aren't every-one's idea of aquatic heaven. There wouldn't be much point in buying one to set up a balanced biosphere, for example. And of course, there is the price – they don't come cheap. At the top end they can cost several thousands of pounds, while at the bottom a mere £60 or so. Some-where in between will be one which will suit most people's pockets and needs.

Some aquarists can become very expressive indeed when pronouncing their dislike of com-plete biosphere-type aquaria. They claim that this level of automation removes your direct involvement with the hobby, reducing and debasing the aquarist's role to that of an interested bystander, and the aquarium to the level of an up-market room ornament. I've followed this same discussion through TTL (Through The Lens) metering and autofocus on cameras; vane versus radio control on model racing yachts, and even typewriters v word-processors! My conclusions are that new developments and technology bring into the hobby many new people who would not have bothered otherwise. And that's ignoring any time-saving element they provide for the average aquarist.

Furthermore, more advanced fishkeeping systems, such as biosphere aquaria, do actually encourage the keeping and breeding of the more exotic species of fish. For example, the Discus fish, *Symphysodon discus* – although nowadays nothing like as difficult to keep as some aquarists claim – does have very specific requirements regarding water chemistry and quality. Such conditions are easily met in a complete biosphere aquarium, and an aquarist who has up until now been put off the idea of keeping them because of misleading infor-mation, may decide that he or she now has the ability and equipment to meet their needs.

Love them or hate them, complete biosphere aquaria are a boon to many people and will play an increasing role in the hobby because they're what people are demanding: instant aquaria. And never forget: they are not compulsory! I knocked together a simple survey which I circu-lated amongst family, friends and friends of their friends, some of whom kept fishes while others had no specific interest.

Basically, the survey asked them given the choice, would they prefer to purchase separate components and create their own biosphere, or purchase a ready-made one. Ninety percent of the returned questionnaires said that they much preferred the single-plug, complete biosphere aquarium, rather than create their own. More importantly, *every* survey returned, where the person had said that he did plan to set-up an aquarium at some time in the near future, also said that he would prefer to buy a complete biosphere-type aquarium!

Although this mini survey only involved thirty people in total, twelve of whom said that they planned to set up 'a fish tank' quite soon, there's definitely a message to aquatic manu-facturers here.

Chapter 6
Creating a Community Aquarium

You now have all the basic information needed to construct your first community aquarium. This chapter deals with this subject, using three different systems and approaches.

It is time now to apply the knowledge you have gained from reading earlier chapters of this book, and combine it with your personal preference to create your first community aquarium. You should now have a rough idea of what equipment you'll need, what it does and the various ranges available to you, but to jog your memory, there's a shortlist below. Of course what you purchase is your decision, but remember that your local dealer will want to retain your business, so be guided by him – it'll nearly always work out cheaper for you in the long run.

Equipment Checklist

You will need a tank (buy the biggest you can afford), a hood arrangement and something to stand the tank on. You need some form of filtration, heating and lighting equipment, gravel for the substrate, tapwater and de-chlorination treatments, a thermometer, power distribution box, tank decorations (rocks, bog-wood etc.), some plants and, of course, some water and fishes.

General Or Specific

As already explained elsewhere, beginning with a community tank means that the newcomer doesn't have to become involved with the com-plex subject of water chemistry etc. Community fishes are also very forgiving of the new aquarist's inevitable mistakes. A species-only tank, on the other hand, requires you to know a certain amount about that species' special require-ments, so that you create a biosphere which fulfils all of their specific needs. The usual pattern is for the newcomer to start with a community aquarium, and then, as interest develops, graduate to a species-specific bio-sphere. Like a bacterium multiplying, in no time at all tanks begin to appear all over the house!

A Trio Of Tanks

As a pictorial guide to creating your aquarium, I've taken three conventional set-ups, and photographed each stage. The systems are: 1. An all-glass tank with undergravel biological filter, combined heater and thermostat, and fluorescent lighting in the hood. 2. All-glass aquarium, external power filter, undertank heating mat with external thermostat, and balanced fluorescent lighting. 3. An example of a complete biosphere aquarium, the *TropiQuarium*, by the Rolf C Hagen (UK) company. It is assumed that you require good aquatic plant growth in your aquarium.

For ease of comparison, and clarity of ex-planation; apart from the *TropiQuarium*, the other two demonstration tanks are both the same size, as detailed on p119. If you're not going to use this size of tank you will have to calculate the heating, lighting, planting, stocking and substrate requirements for yourself, using formulae already given elsewhere in the book.

Demonstration Aquariums

Tanks 1 and 2 are:

60cm long, 30cm deep and 30cm wide (24×12×12 inches).

Volume = 54 litres (12 gallons). Surface Area = 1800cm² (288in²)*.

Heater requirements = 100 watts*. Lighting requirement = 30 watts*.

Substrate requirements = 20 litres / 31.75 Kg (70lb) (4.5 gallons)*/+

Plant requirements – around 40 plants of various species.

Maximum stock level – 60cm (24in) of fish length*.

Air pump requirements – 200 litres per hour*.

* calculated using the relevant formulae in the appropriate sections of this book.
+ 1 litre of gravel weighs approximately 1.58Kg (3.5lb)

Common Elements For All Aquaria

Before I start talking specifics, there are some things I recommend you acquire no matter which type of aquarium you intend to create. You will need a tapwater dechlorinator and conditioner, ammonia and nitrite test kits, and a substrate. Whether you choose to use river (not beach) sand or gravel as the substrate (a mixture of both can be very eye-catching, and natural for the fishes), it *must* be thoroughly cleaned, using the method already described in Chapter 3, *Hygiene*.

Amount Of Substrate

It's very much more than you would think! To create a pleasing perspective effect, and depending on whether or not you're going to use undergravel filtration, the gravel should slope from a height of around 10cm (4in) at the back of the tank, down to 5cm (2in) at the front. Arranging the substrate in this fashion means that any detritus in the tank will eventually gather at the front (rolls down the slope), where it is then easily removed. Furthermore, a sloping substrate avoids the rather displeasing optical effect of a very 'thin' aquarium, which happens when the gravel is merely laid flat and not shaped into a slope.

As to how much you will need, the accepted formula is: allow 10 litres of gravel (2.2 gallons – 16Kg [35lb]) for every 900cm² (1ft²) of floor area. In an aquarium 90×30×30cm (36×12×12in), the floor area is some 2700cm² (432in²), so you would need a minimum of 30 litres (6.6 gallons – 47.5Kg [105lb]) of gravel. This formula is just for a normally-laid substrate, which may or may not be used to cover an undergravel filter plate.

If you plan to aquascape the substrate, sculpting it into terraces etc. then you will need even more; so adjust the formula to 15 litres (3.3 gallons – 24Kg [52.5lb]) of gravel per 900cm² (1ft²) of floor area. As gravel is relatively cheap, it is always better to have too much rather than run out half-way through creating your aquascape. I have already covered the subject of substrate colour, but to recap briefly; fishes prefer a dark coloured gravel. They can become stressed when swimming over a very light substrate.

Electrical Safety

Electricity and water do not mix, runs the old adage. In actual fact they do, and rather well too; water is an excellent conductor of electricity. The results of such a mix however, are usually quite lethal, and very permanent! Consequently, the potential for a serious accident in and around the location of the aquarium is very great indeed. Follow these simple rules and you will not have any trouble. Before putting your hands in the aquarium water, switch off the power to the tank *and remove the wall plug*. Then no one can accidentally turn the power back on again. Don't attach *Cable Tidies* or *Power Centre* type mains distribution junction boxes onto the outside walls of the aquarium, where drips or condensation may so easily run down into them, causing a short circuit.

When *not* using a power junction box, ensure that electrical aquarium equipment is fitted with the correct type of plug, *and* a fuse of the appropriate rating. To calculate the correct fuse rating, simply divide the wattage of the device (which is usually stated in the instruction manual) by 125. Then fit a fuse which comes closest to your answer. Most electrical aquarium equipment will require a 3 amp fuse. It is also a very good idea to terminate the lead which connects the junction box to the wall socket, or the power lead from an extension socket block,

with an RCCB – Residual Current Circuit Breaker – which will trip and isolate the electricity supply to the aquarium before an ordinary fuse can even think of blowing.

Finally, to promote safe working practice, once you have acquired all the components for your aquarium, carry out all the electrical installation work *before* getting your hands wet. Fit the lighting into the hood, attach end caps, wire filters, heaters, air pumps and thermostats into the junction box before washing the gravel, cleaning the tank etc. *But don't apply any power to these devices just yet*! If you do they'll blow up, and you'll invalidate any guarantees.

Wiring-up the electrics. Note the mains plug in the foreground, removed from the wall socket and out where the aquarist can see it.

Shopping List

You will need the following items for System 1.

Basic Equipment

1. An all-glass tank, 60×30×30cm
   (24×12× 12in) £15.00
2. Hood assembly (excluding lights)
   for this size tank £15.00
3. Aquarium disinfectant, such as
   Liquisil £3.45
3. 15 watt, twin-choke fluorescent
   lighting starter kit £14.95
4. 1, 45cm (18in)/25mm (1in) diameter,
   15 watt, *Grolux* fluorescent
   lighting tube £4.66
5. Triton fluorescent lighting tube £7.73
6. Interpet UG No. 5 Filter Plate,
   58×28cm (23×11in) £5.39
7. Air pump (200 litres per hour) £10.00
8. Heater/thermostat
   (100 watts, magnetic contacts) £12.00
9. 20 litres of gravel @ .45p per litre £9.00
10. Plastic airline, airstone,
    connecters & valves, etc. £6.00
11. Tapwater conditioner/dechlorinator £3.00
12. Ammonia and nitrite test kits £10.00
13. Nets, scrapers etc. £5.00
14. Mains power junction box £4.50
15. One piece of styrofoam
    60×30cm (24×12in) £0.50
    _____

    Sub-total £126.18

(Optional)

15. Metal aquarium stand for
    this size tank £25.00
    ========

    Basic Equipment total £151.18

Basic Tank Decor

16. Aquatic plants – 40 plant selection* £6.95
17. One piece of *Bogwood* £5.00
18. Aquarium background picture £1.00

19. Substrate additives £3.00
20. Plant food £4.75
    _____

    Basic Tank Decor total £20.07

System 1 Total cost of all items
        (including stand) £171.25

Prices will obviously vary greatly. I've only included these average prices to give you some idea of what it's all going to cost you to set up. However, remember that the setting up cost is a non-recurring expense: once you have the equipment it will work well for a number of years.

* This is an example of an aquarist shop's special plant selection for a particular size aquarium. In this instance the offer is 40 plants, comprising 5 specimens each of: *Cabomba aquatica, Elodea densa, Straight vallis, Water wisteria, pygmy Amazon swords, Bacopa, Amazon sword, and Ludwigia*. It is much better to purchase your plants by this method, rather than buying individual specimens eg. individually 40 plants at an average price of .35p each total some £14!

Many aquarist shops supply complete starter kits, comprising most of the items in the above list, at very advantageous prices. For example; Top-Up Aquatics of Congleton offer everything you need for a 60×30×30cm (24×12×12in) aquarium, including a hood, but *excluding* the actual fish tank itself, for £60.30. While there should be no compatibility problems with a starter kit, you don't actually get any choice of the type of air pump, filter, or heater/thermostat etc. This may not suit some people.

Setting Up System 1

Step 1.

Having arrived safely home with all your purchases, there is now an irresistible urge to get everything connected together and fishes swim-

Part of a special 'forty-plant' offer from Ocean Aquatics own plant nursery. This is the cheapest way to buy aquatic plants for your aquarium.

ming about as quickly as possible. You have been very patient so far, so try not to give in to this temptation. The more care and attention to detail you provide now, then the more certain your chance of aquatic success will be. The main cause of New Tank Syndrome is actually the impatience of the fishkeeper!

Firstly, read all the instruction leaflets supplied with the electrical equipment thoroughly, before attempting to connect it together. When you're satisfied that you know exactly what each piece requires, begin assembling and connecting it. Fit the lighting system into the hood, wire up the filter and heater to the mains junction box etc. But do remember, do not apply any voltage just yet. Items such as heaters / thermostats are designed to work submerged; they will quickly burn themselves out if switched on out of water.

Step 2.

Once you've gone as far as you can with the electrical equipment, start on the cleaning. Using a proprietary aquarium disinfectant, or weak solution of Methylene Blue (2 percent), wash the tank inside and out, rinse thoroughly and drain. Do the same with everything else which will go into the aquarium, including all aquatic plants – especially artificial ones – nets and algae magnets. Pay particular attention to cover glasses or condensation trays. Once everything has been cleaned, position your tank support (stand or cabinet) in the location earmarked as the site for your aquarium. Once your aquarium has been filled *you will not be able to move it.*

Sometimes there are small flaws in the bottom glass of tanks, or the surface of the stand/cupboard may not be perfectly flat. Standing a heavy aquarium on an uneven surface may cause the tank to crack; therefore you have to guard against this. The usual practice is to place polystyrene ceiling tiles, or felt underlay, between the bottom of the aquarium and the supporting surface. This will then cover any bumps etc. and cushion the aquarium. Some new types of all-glass tank have a soft plastic strip running around the tank bottom and top. Such tanks should still be stood on a supporting surface *using polystyrene or felt padding, even though it may look safe not to, due to the plastic strip.*

Step 3.

Unwrap the undergravel filter plate, check that all the parts are present, decide whether you want the airlift tube on the right- or left-hand side of the tank, then fit it into its locating hole on the filter plate, where it should be a tight fit with no excess play. You may or may not care to glue the tube into place using silicone sealant; however, some types of U/G filter require an airstone to be fitted inside the airlift tube before attaching it to the plate. So check the instructions carefully, before gluing the tube into position. Having checked that the tube is perpendicular to the filter plate, and that the underside of the plate's edging is smooth, carefully locate the filter plate/airlift tube assembly into the bottom of the tank. Note that some maker's U/G airlifts are made over-size and may require trimming with a sharp knife or saw so that their tops are below water level. This is especially so if adding a powerhead. Again, check for size before gluing anything!

Now you have to arrange the airline which will feed compressed air from the air pump, and which actually drives the U/G system. Some filter plate/airlift tube arrangements require the airline to be pushed into a spigot on the filter plate, at the side or back of the airlift tube. This of course, becomes impossible if you've already laid the gravel! Cut a suitable length of airline, to reach from the air pump into the airlift tube, not forgetting to leave enough spare to form an anti-syphon loop. Some aquarists push only around 50mm (2in) of airline tubing into a 28cm (11in) tall airlift tube. This is wasteful, as well as severely restricting the effectiveness of the airlift. Make certain that you push the airline all the way down to the bottom of the airlift tube, maximising the airlift effect.

Step 4.

After locating the heater/stat in the recommended position (Chapter 5 *Aquarium Hardware – Heaters*), now is the time to start aquascaping the interior of the aquarium. Although minor alterations to the tank's decor can be made afterwards, this will naturally cause a great deal of disturbance, so it's better to get it right now rather than later. With a single-species aquarium, the usual practice is to try to recreate the natural habitat of the fishes. With a community aquarium, the fish come from many, different locations, so whatever you want is

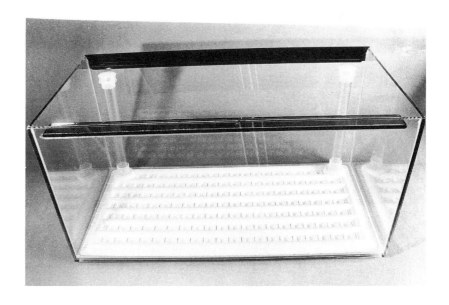

Fitting the undergravel filter plate. Note the twin airlift – this isn't strictly necessary for a tank this size, but it does increase the flow of water through the substrate without resorting to a powerhead.

going to be alright. Even plastic deep-sea divers and an opening/closing treasure chest, if you really must! Try drawing a little plan of how you would like the finished aquascape to look. Place species of similar plants in clumps, and don't forget to leave the fish plenty of free swimming space at the front of the tank, where you can watch them playing.

Tank Decorations

A finished aquascape usually consists of rock-work, tree roots – specially treated or made from concrete, gravel or slate – and of course aquatic plants. When out and about, you may see a particularly attractive piece of rock or an old, gnarled tree root, and think that it's just what you need for your aquarium. Be careful: in a tropical aquarium it is not wise to use calciferous or limestone rocks as these will raise the pH of the water. Granite and slate etc. are fine, just as long as you can distinguish between

them. Rocks, roots, even plants taken from the wild and placed in your aquarium can very often be the direct cause of an outbreak of snail/parasite infestation, or disease.

As for tree roots, I would strongly urge a newcomer not to bother. The roots and *bogwood* you see on sale in aquarists shops have been collected from old peat bogs, where they have survived for many years, becoming completely waterlogged in the process. Digging them out is hard and costly work. However, apart from a cursory spray down to remove the worst of the muck, they're given no further treatment. Therefore the aquarist must ensure that he/she thoroughly washes and disinfects *all* bogwood before putting it into the aquarium. You'll be amazed at the dirt which comes out!

Many companies now make an inert resin imitation casting of tree branches, roots, walls etc. And although they are very convincing, especially when they've acquired a coating of algae, they are expensive.

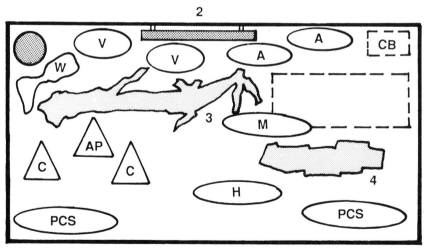

1.	Airlift tube	2.	Heater / stat
3.	Bogwood	4.	Chunk of stone
W.	Water wisteria	V.	Straight vallis
A.	Ambulia	C.	Cryptocorynes
AP.	Aponogetons	PCS.	Pygmy chain sword
H.	Hairgrass	CB.	Cabomba
M.	Myriophyllum		

Figure 6.1 Drawing up an aquascaping plan.

Completing The Aquascape

Cover the U/G filter plate with the washed, sieved and disinfected gravel, taking care to slope it from the back down to the front. If you've elected to use any substrate additives, such as fertiliser pellets, iron-encrusted baked clay or peat mats, this is the only time you'll get to position them in the substrate, so do it now. But remember not to put peat mats directly onto the U/G filter plate, sandwich them between layers of gravel. Neither will you be able to use items like *Aquasoil* or *Aqualit* etc. if using undergravel filters as the soil particles will block the filter plate. Using only non-calciferous rocks, build up your rockwork very carefully. Caves are much appreciated by catfishes and various other species, so you don't want them to collapse, trapping the fishes. Neither do you want to create a rubbish trap, where uneaten food will accumulate and be very difficult to remove.

Don't simply stand rocks on top of the substrate, where they may topple over. Push them firmly down so that they lay on the actual filter plate or bottom of the tank, and then arrange gravel around them. When stacking rock or slate etc. for making caves, it is often a good idea to glue them to each other, and even to the walls of the aquarium, using silicone sealant. This will stop them falling over. Some aquarists prefer to hide items like the heater/stat, airline and airstone, airlift tube(s) and filters etc. behind rocks, roots or plants. If you wish to disguise these items, once you have the basic design laid out, add the equipment in its operating position before creating the camouflage of rocks and plants.

When creating your aquascape, sculpting gravel into terraces, adding rock, tree roots or bogwood, and various plants, always ask yourself: 'Is this aquascape going to be easy to maintain and clean?'.

Step 5.

To complete your aquascape you have to add the plants. We couldn't plant them earlier because, without some water to support their weight, they could be damaged. In any case, it's not until at least half the amount of total water has been added that we can begin to see the final effect of our completed aquascape. Before planting, but after washing/disinfecting, you will have sorted the plants out into species and size. Remember that tall plants go at the back and sides, shorter ones in the midground; specimen, and small plants are positioned in the foreground. Useful accessories to have at hand are a planting stick, hydroculture plant pots, and small amounts of peat or fertiliser pellets. But before planting commences we have to add some water.

Put a small plate on the surface of the gravel, in the centre of the aquarium. This will act as a deflector, cushioning the aquascape from being disturbed by the influx of water. Carefully pour water onto the centre of the plate, stopping when the tank is about half-full. This will be enough to support the stems and foliage of the plants during planting, and stop the aquarium from overflowing when you put your arms into it. Some aquarists like to give the heater and thermostat a helping hand, and use both hot and cold water, so that the eventual temperature of the filled aquarium is close to the operating range of the heater. There are some potential pitfalls here.

Although the danger of copper contamination, when using both cold and hot water in houses with a copper waterpipe system, are usually exaggerated, hot water taken from the domestic supply is usually stored in copper cylinders. The potential for copper contamination, which is harmful to fishes, is therefore greater. Therefore it is wiser *not* to use the domestic hot water supply at all – even after letting it run to waste for several minutes.

The best way to acquire water which approximates the desired aquarium temperature is to proceed as follows. Turn on the coldwater tap and (in houses with copper piping) allow the first minute to run to waste. Meanwhile boil a kettle of water. Fill a suitably sized bucket

Adding the water. Note the saucer, acting as a deflector and saving the substrate from being disturbed.

(whose capacity you know) with cold water, and add enough of the boiled water to reach approximately the right temperature. *Never under any circumstances add boiling water directly to a glass aquarium!*

Now, before adding the water to the aquarium, you have to add a dechlorinator to remove any chlorine products. The trouble is, for a two gallon bucket of water you need around 2 millilitres of dechlorinator, and measuring this small amount is a problem. I get around this by using a 10 ml hypodermic syringe (minus the needle of course, which you don't need) which you can buy from any chemist. Simply dip the syringe into the dechlorinator liquid and suck-in the required amount (when the rubber plunger lines up with the 2ml mark).

Plants which require potting should be potted-up now. But beware! The gravel substrate is more than likely to be a good deal cooler than the surrounding water, and some plants object violently to this situation by dying. Species such as *Cryptocorynes* should be weighted and left floating in the water while the substrate reaches tank temperature – anything up to two days later. When planting, ensure that you don't bury the *crown* of the plant below the substrate.

The crown is that part of the plant where all the stems join, and from which the roots sprout. Although burying the crown will undoubtedly kill-off the plant, planting the crown too high will have no ill effect at all. All that will happen is that the roots will grow and 'pull' the plant down into the correct position. So, if you've any doubt at all as to what the crown actually looks like, leave plenty of the plant sticking out of the gravel, and don't wrap lead wire too tightly around the stem or you'll strangle the plant!.

For those plants which do not require bright lighting, position them either underneath tall-growing species, so that they are shaded, or among the rockwork. When planting in rows or clumps, remember to leave room for runners from plants which propagate by this method, such as *Vallisneria sp.*

Step 6. The Final Touch

We now have an aquarium, instead of just a

tank. The filter system is in position, as is the heater/stat. The substrate has been laid, impregnated with growth-enhancing materials, allowed to warm up and shaped for ease of maintenance and aesthetics. Various decorations have been added to provide the fish with refuge, territorial 'markers' and a natural background which enhances their colour. Plants have been added and the water topped-up. All we have to do now is switch on the electrics, and prepare the water ready for the fish. Just time to stick the aquarium background picture onto the outside-back wall of the tank. This will form a natural backdrop to your aquascape, and prevent anyone looking straight through the tank, and seeing the wires etc. trailing out of the back.

Turn on the power, check that lights are working, the neon lamp of the heater/stat is lit (or not, as the case may be), and that a healthy stream of bubbles is exiting the airlift tube(s) of the undergravel filter system. Your aquarium won't actually look very good at all at the moment. The water will be cloudy and just about everything will be covered with tiny bubbles of air.

This is perfectly natural, and not something you've done wrong. No matter how many times, or even for how long, you wash gravel, there's always a little stone dust and dirt which won't come out. The only thing you can do for the next couple of days is to leave the aquarium alone. Switch on the lighting daily, for the usual period of ten–twelve hours, and don't forget that you *never* switch off the undergravel filter system (which includes the air pump) at all. You may care to add one of the products which claim to boost the formation of the biological filter bed: on the other hand, bearing in mind my earlier comments about the evident paradox such items create, you may not! At least they won't do any damage.

Speeding Things Up

You must let the water and the biological filter

Planting System 1 aquarium.

bed mature before any fishes are added, or suffer the consequences of New Tank Syndrome. Unaided, this would normally take at least a month. The temptation to give in and fill the newly-established aquarium with various fishes will be almost overwhelming, but you must resist! Patience is now the name of the game. All your previous hard work, thoughtful purchases and careful aquascaping can be ruined in minutes by filling your newly set-up tank with fishes just a few days later.

Feeding The Bacteria

Initially, in your new aquarium, there will be little waste for the various forms of bacteria to feed upon, so we have to give them some. For the first week only, add a very small pinch of flake fish food every other day. This gives the bacteria something to 'chew' on. For those of you who are interested in water chemistry, doing a weekly test for ammonia/ammonium and nitrite – NH_3, NH_4 and NO_2 respectively – will graphically illustrate when the biological filter starts to mature, and begins converting waste into less harmful substances via the Nitrogen Reduction Cycle (see Chapter 2 *Water*, Chapter 4 *Aquatic Plants* and Chapter 5 *Filters*).

Adding Fish

Assuming that you've been feeding the biological filter bed, and have used one of the commercially available water maturing and conditioning preparations, and after letting the tank run for a week with everything operating, add a couple of hardy fishes, such as a pair of guppies. This will increase the load on the biological filter, so you can stop feeding it directly. Watch these fishes closely to see if they're suffering any stress or breathing difficulties. If they should die, remove them and do not add any more fishes for at least another week.

After a week, and assuming that the fishes are thriving, it will be safe to add another pair. Another week with no losses, so add more fishes. Continue like this until you've reached the maximum stocking level of 60cm (24in) of fish length, or you have the number required. It takes quite a while for a biological filter bed to reach maximum efficiency (around six weeks), and it can't be done without fish, nor any quicker – unless you're using 'dirty' gravel from an existing tank, of course. It's the fishes which will stretch the performance of the filter bed, forcing it to become more and more active as more waste is produced from an increasing fish population, and the extra amounts of feed dumped into the tank by the aquarist. Finally, after around six weeks, maximum activity of the biological bed will have been achieved, and the aquarium will not support the introduction of any more species without serious consequences to the good health of all the stock.

That's It!

That really is all there is to it; you have created your very first aquarium. Although I've gone through the first system in some detail, in future I'll explain only where the other systems differ from this one. Feeding and looking after your fishes is covered in the relevant parts of the book. Finally, all the hard work is now over. You can relax and begin to enjoy your fishes. The more you learn about them then the greater will be your enjoyment. Very soon you'll be wondering why you ever had any doubts at all!

Setting Up System 2.

In this set up, we will be using different filter and heat control equipment. Apart from that, most of what I said about System 1 still applies. Remove items number 6, 7, 8 and 10 from the Shopping List. Replace them with the following:

6. Interpet *Whisper 2*,
   external power box filter   £20.98
7. Interpet *Bio-Bag* filter
   cartridge (4-pack)   £4.00
8. Ultratherm undertank heating mat,
   120 watt (60×30cm tank)   £9.24
8*. Uno Accurist internal thermostat   £6.95
8*. Or – Rocon *Digi-Stat* external,
   electronic thermostat   £35.00

* Choose between these two thermostats.

Sub-total (Uno thermostat)	£41.17
Sub-total (Rocon Digi-Stat)	£69.22
System 1 total (less items 6,7,8 & 10)	£137.86
System 2 total (including Uno stat)	£179.03
System 2 total (including Digi-Stat)	£207.08

System 2 is more expensive than System 1 by £41.17 when using the Uno thermostat. Or by £69.22 when using the Rocon thermostat.

Step 1.

Prepare as for System 1, ie. wire the electrical equipment first, then wash and disinfect everything which is going into the aquarium. When you're ready to site the tank, position the stand or cabinet in the required location. Because we're using an undertank heating mat we still need a minimum base of 10 mm of expanded polystyrene, which has to be specially prepared to house the electrical terminal block of the heating mat, and to protect the standing surface from excessive heat.

Lay the gravel, adding any growth-enhancing substrate additives now, and don't forget to slope the substrate from front to back, even though you're not using an undergravel filter. Organise the aquascaping and planting. When you've done all this, fill the aquarium three-quarters full: you still have to site the thermostat remember, so filling the tank up will cause it to overflow when you insert your arms. Of course there should be *no* power connected at this stage.

Positioning Aquarium 2 on heater mat and polystyrene tiles.

Fitting The Thermostat

Wiring together the *Ultratherm* heating mat and (in this case) the Rocon *Digi-Stat* thermostat *is not the same as mechanical thermostats* when using a mains distribution junction box, which has custom-designed terminals for an external thermostat, such as the Algarde *Power Centre*. The Uno *Accurist* bi-metallic-type thermostat acts as a simple series switch, shunting mains power, derived from the *Power Centre*, to the heater when the bi-metallic contacts close. In the case of the Uno, the neon light is ON when no current is being passed to the heater mat,

and OFF when current is passing: the reverse of the usual, such as a combined heater/stat.

However, the *Digi-Stat* supplies its own power to the heater, and controls it by *switching the negative line, not the positive*. You *cannot* wire the Rocon *Digi-Stat* into the Algarde *Power Centre* in the same way as the Uno *Accurist*. If you do, you may well blow the triac device which does the electrical switching inside the Rocon. Figure 6.2 shows the correct way to wire together an undertank heating mat, or any other type of heater, and a Rocon *Digi-Stat* thermostat into the Algarde *Power Centre*. If you're not using the Algarde distribution box,

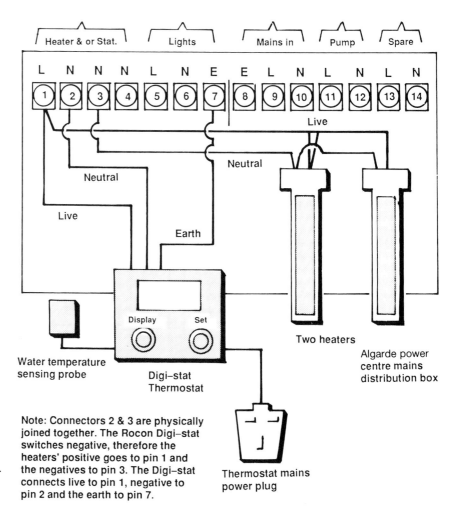

Figure 6.2 Wiring up a Digi-Stat to an Algarde Power Centre.

Note: Connectors 2 & 3 are physically joined together. The Rocon Digi–stat switches negative, therefore the heaters' positive goes to pin 1 and the negatives to pin 3. The Digi–stat connects live to pin 1, negative to pin 2 and the earth to pin 7.

then either remember that the *Digi-Stat* switches the *negative line only*, or, if you're still not happy, telephone Rocon direct (address in Appendix 3). The people at Rocon take great pride (and rightly so) in both their equipment and their service to customers. You will find them very helpful indeed, and a smashing bunch of chaps.

Once the heating mat and thermostat have been correctly connected to the junction box, you have to position the *Digi-Stat's* temperature sensing probe within the aquarium. Place it towards the top of the tank, near to the power filter exit, so that you can measure the temperature of the water entering the tank.

Substrate Temperature

With this form of heating and control, I think it is important to keep an eye not only on the water temperature but also on that of the substrate. So you'll need a thermometer either pushed into the gravel, or an LCD-type stuck at substrate level on the outside of the tank. But you don't have to bother with this if you really don't want to. If the temperature of the substrate is substantially higher than that of the

water, you may have to either start using some form of aeration, to help circulate the water more efficiently, or redirect the output of the power filter straight onto the substrate. This isn't a bad idea, anyway, as the currents generated will sweep up any detritus into the power filter's intake. Using the Rocon's temperature probe, positioned as already described, and a *Thermo Chip* digital, electronic thermometer, I could detect absolutely no temperature differences anywhere in the aquarium, thanks to the excellent design of the *Whisper 2* external box power filter.

External Power Box Filter

From Chapter 5 *Filters*, you know that when using this sort of filter – which is very efficient with this size of tank – you may have to modify

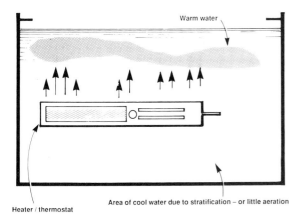

Figure 6.3 **Water stratification and heater currents. A tank with very little water movement is liable to areas of water which are cooler than areas above the water. Adding some aeration moves the water around the tank and ensures that *all* the water is heated equally.**

Warm water

Area of cool water due to stratification – or little aeration

Heater / thermostat

Fitting the Whisper 2 filter to the tank.

Some aquarium hoods may have to be hacked about so they can accommodate the power filter's input/output features. Here the entire right-hand side wall of the hood was cut away.

the aquarium hood assembly. You'll have to make space for the filter's input pipe and (in this case) the cascade return of the cleaned water. Powered box filters may be hung either on the back wall or the side of the aquarium. However, don't use the back wall unless you have clear access to it, without having to stretch over the tank. Aquariums which are situated up against a wall allow only very restricted access to the back. If you can't reach the filter easily then you won't maintain it properly because it will be too much bother.

Filter Media

Any of the various filter media already discussed may be used to fill your power box filter. However, the *Whisper 2* does come equipped with its own, special filter media cartridge, more of which in a moment. Briefly, your filter has to remove solid particulate waste, and dissolved toxic gases, such as ammonia and nitrite.

Remember that you don't have an U/G system now to do this job for you. Synthetic filter floss (never cotton wool: the fibres can separate and clog the gills of fishes) takes care of solid waste, *Zeolite* or activated carbon takes care of ammonia and other nasties, while the anaerobic bacteria, dwelling within the now warm but oxygen deficient substrate, will convert a fair percentage of the nitrate present into harmless nitrogen gas. The odd bubbles rising from the substrate will be proof of this chemical conversion of nitrate into nitrogen gas.

Regular water changes should see off any remaining nitrate, so it should never become a problem, unless of course, you live in an area where the domestic water supply already contains a large amount of nitrate. In this case you'll either have to use a reverse osmosis filter (very expensive) or a denitrifying device, such as Interpet's *Nitrex Box* (see Chapter 5, *Filters*).

Instant Media

Of course, and as ever in the Impatient Nineties, many aquarists don't like the chore of filling and cleaning out a box filter. For such people many companies now manufacture 'containerised' filter media. For example, Interpet produce *Bio-Bags*. This is a fabric bag, which acts as a mechanical filter in its own right, trapping particulate waste on the outer surface. The bag has a cleverly-designed cell structure woven into the material which promotes the proliferation of aerobic bacteria, and so provides a biological filtering action on the water passing through it. Finally, inside the bag is an amount of activated carbon which acts chemically on the water.

Interpet *Bio-Bags* simply slot straight into the media compartment of the *Whisper* series box filters, taking just a few seconds to install, and provide mechanical, chemical and biological filtration all in the one, easily-fitted bag. This award-winning idea means that replacing/cleaning the filter media now takes only a few minutes. The dirty *Bio-Bag* is removed, washed very gently under running water to remove excess muck from the surface of the bag, and is then replaced. For the ultra-cautious aquarists amongst us, *Bio-Bags* are so cheap that you could throw one away every two weeks and replace with a new one, although this would be a waste of the aerobic bacteria colonising the *Bio-Bag* fabric. Other similar products are available from many companies. Activated charcoal, *Zeolite*, *Nitrex* etc. may also be bought in bag or container form, to make changing filters a much more simpler process.

Running The System In

Having completed the aquascape (planting, rock positioning etc), installed all the electrical equipment and wired it up, charged the power filter with the appropriate mechanical and chemical media, and topped-up the tank, all you have to do now is switch on the lighting and heating, and prime the power filter. With the *Whisper 2*, all you need do is scoop up either a handful of water, or use a small cup to drop a little water into the media chamber, and the filter will do the rest. Within a few seconds

there should be a healthy cascade of water pouring out of the filter. Once everything is working, leave the tank alone for two to three days, except for the daily switching on and off of the lighting system, of course.

The power filter is left running permanently, by the way. The addition of so-called filter 'maturing' and feeding agents, such as Interpet's *Filter Aid* or Rolf C Hagen's *Cycle*, are said to help keep down the organic sludge which accumulates, and help the filter media and the aquarium water 'mature'. I must admit that I do use Hagen's *Cycle* in my TropiQuarium, and since using it the *Fluval 2* power filter doesn't appear to accumulate as much sludge as it did before.

Bio-Bags utilise biological as well as mechanical and chemical filtration modes, so you still have to wait for the biological filter bed in the weave structure of the *Bio-Bag* to mature before you can safely add some fishes. This means that, as for System 1, you must let the water mature for at least a week before adding two hardy fishes. You must ensure that the water

Close-up of the Whisper 2 power filter in operation. Note the self-contained and easily-fitted Bio-Bag filter media container.

has been dechlorinated, and conditioned, and the temperature stabilised – and a nitrite and ammonia test should be done *before* adding any fishes.

System 3. The TropiQuarium

If you elect to use this type of aquarium, the first thing you can do is throw away the Shopping List! One of the big advantages of complete biosphere aquaria is that you no longer have to buy all the components separately. So what do you get for around £80?

For your money you get a 50×25×36cm (20× 10×14in) acrylic plastic tank complete with *Fluval 2* internal power filter, 50 watt combined heater and thermostat, and a 15 watt fluorescent lighting system. The only things you have to add are gravel, decorations, water and the fishes. For example:

1.	TropiQuarium Biosphere aquarium	£80.00
2.	10 litres (35lb) of gravel @ .45p per litre	£4.50
3.	Aquatic plants – 40 plant selection	£5.95
4.	One piece of *Bogwood*	£5.00
5.	Aquarium background picture	£1.00
6.	Ammonia & Nitrite test kit	£10.00
7.	1 piece 60×30cm (24×12in) Styrofoam sheet	£0.50
	System total	£106.95

Systems Compared

Note that, with the TropiQuarium, a stand isn't normally used as it is small and light enough to sit on small tables or cabinets.

System 1. Total	£171.25
System 2. Total	£179.03 * Uno stat.
System 2. Total	£207.08 * Rocon stat.
System 3. Total	£106.95

NOTE!

Although at first sight the TropiQuarium would seem to offer the best value for money, you have to bear in mind that it is a smaller tank than the others. Consequently, its maximum stocking level is 40cm (16in) of fish length (excluding the tail) compared to 60cm (24in) for the other two tanks.

Also, there have been some complaints from a few aquarists who own a TropiQuarium that the *Fluval 2* filter, as fitted, won't really cope with anything like 40cm (16in) of fish length without the filter medium being cleaned at least weekly and replaced entirely every two weeks. Around two days in every fourteen I hang a bag of either activated carbon, or *Zeolite* in my TropiQuarium. I have been keeping fourteen fishes for the past six months within it without any problems at all. However, there are a few things you have to beware of. Firstly, the bulkhead separating the heater/filter from the main tank seems to be a magnetic attraction to the fishes, who're always swimming behind it. I used to spend ages fishing them out. But then I suddenly realised that, if they could get themselves in there, they could also find their own way out again. And indeed this has proved the case.

Furthermore, because the TropiQuarium is built entirely from acrylic plastic, only plastic glues are used, and *not* the usual aquarists' silicone sealant. My TropiQuarium has been moved twice (empty of course) but, even so, due to the brittle nature of the glue, it has sprung two leaks. Of course, fixing these leaks was the work of a moment, using silicone sealant. I mention this just in case the same thing happens to you.

Setting Up The TropiQuarium

Having collected the box containing your TropiQuarium, bought the gravel, any tank decorations and plants, and arrived safely home again; unpack the TropiQuarium and put it to one side. You're looking for the superb TropiQuarium instruction manual, so sit down for a very interesting read.

Following the instruction manual to the letter,

there is only one electrical connection to be made, so the first thing to do is attach a 13 amp plug to the mains cable, and *change* the fuse for one of 3 amp rating. But don't be tempted to apply power to see if the light works. Once power is applied, the heater and filter are switched on, which could ruin everything if there's no water in the tank. Wash and disinfect the aquarium, not forgetting the hood assembly. Having already washed and disinfected the substrate, you can now lay it. Remember to slope the gravel from the back to the front of the aquarium. Keep the substrate clear of the filter intake, though. Fill the tank half-full with dechlorinated and conditioned tapwater, and start on the aquascaping.

The *Fluval 2* internal power filter, as fitted to the TropiQuarium, has a sponge insert which operates mechanically and biologically. And, just as with the biological filter bed in an undergravel filtration system, the filter sponge needs time for the bacteria to develop. Add a little flake food every other day for the first week only, to give the developing bacteria something to work on. Assuming that you've used one of the proprietary water conditioners, leave the tank running for around ten days before adding any fishes. Again, an ammonia/nitrite test kit will illustrate the progress of the filter system, telling you when it has matured sufficiently for you to add fishes.

Add fishes as detailed in Systems 1 and 2. First a couple of hardy fishes. Assuming no problems, carry on adding fish until you have what you need. By the way, although I keep on saying 'add fish', there is in fact much more to introducing fish into an aquarium than simply tipping them in! Chapter 7 *Aquarium Management* explains in detail how fishes should be added to your aquarium.

Used within its limitations, the TropiQuarium is a fine introduction to the hobby for many young, and not so young, aquarists. It is cheap to buy and maintain, simple to set up and just the one plug for the power. You can, of course, change the installed tube for another specialist

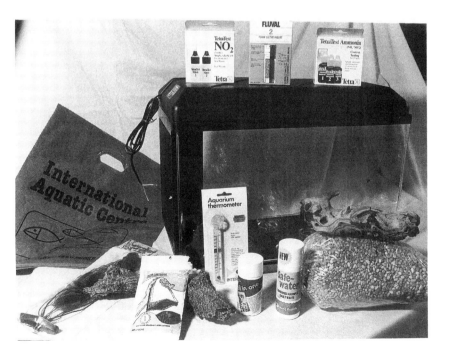

System 3 in our three demonstration aquaria. The TropiQuarium complete biosphere and everything you need to make a start in fishkeeping.

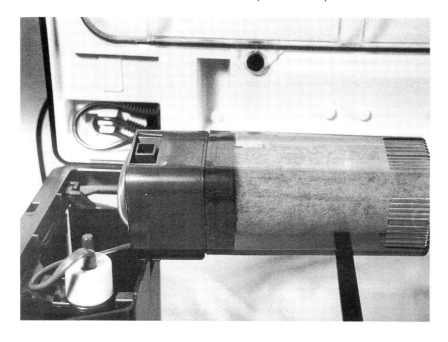

The TropiQuarium's
electrics. Top is the self-
contained hood and 15 watt
fluorescent light. The Fluval
2 power filter removed for
cleaning. Bottom left is the 50
watt combined heater/stat.

one, such as a *Grolux*, or *Triton*. It must, of
course, be the same wattage and size!

Cleaning The TropiQuarium

Eventually, the dreaded algae will appear, and
removing it from acrylic plastic is much harder
than from glass. With plastic you cannot just
scrub away at the algae until it's gone. After
much experimentation with plastic algae scrapers
(useless!) – apart from net curtaining (rather
messy!) – I've found the most efficient method,
which doesn't scratch the plastic walls, is to use
a fairly soft fingernail brush which is kept just
for this job. Gently but firmly, wipe the bristles
along the walls etc. Move the brush in one
direction only, all the time, lifting the brush
back to the beginning for the next 'sweep'.
Don't use a scrubbing action or a backwards and
forwards sweeping method. This will cause
minute scratches to appear which get worse
over time. The filter and integrated cover glass/
hood assembly should be cleaned as the instruction manual recommends, with a soft chamois
(or a more humane alternative) leather.

Summary

I have outlined the creation of one conventional
aquarium system, using rather traditional
equipment which would be easily recognised by
an aquarist from the 1960s. The undergravel
filtration system is used by many aquarists
around the world with no apparent problems. I
just happen to think that you can achieve all the
benefits of U/G filters without any of the problems, by choosing a different route – which in
this case is represented by System 2 – the
undertank heater and external powered box
filter. The thing about external power filters is
that you can actually see them working and
when they need cleaning, something you can't
do with the U/G system.

System 3, the complete biosphere aquarium
is, I am personally convinced, the way forwards
for the fishkeeping hobby. It could well be argued
that I might have chosen a better example to
demonstrate this principle. However, the Tropi-
Quarium contains all the basic elements of the
complete biosphere aquaria concept, while still
remaining eminently affordable, even to chil-

dren via birthday or Christmas presents. And, of course, its price does vary greatly: I've seen it advertised quite recently at both £96 and £60 in aquatic magazines.

There are endless possibilities for variation on this basic aquarium theme, such as adding a powerhead to a U/G filter, or external canister power filters, ammonia towers, trickle tray filters etc. No doubt there are many new filtration methods, or even complete systems on various drawing boards, or about to come into production. In this book, I've tried to collect as much current information as I can, but research and development is constant. If I included everything I wanted to talk about, then this book would run to several volumes!

Armed with the knowledge you now have, you are in an excellent position to make an informed choice when it comes to buying aquatic equipment. You now know what there is, what it does, roughly what it will cost you, and its special advantages and disadvantages. Setting up your own aquarium should now be a simple matter, and success guaranteed. So go to it!

Chapter 7
Aquarium Management

Managing the aquarium successfully requires you to develop a regular routine. At the moment, your interest and thirst for knowledge is at a maximum, therefore your maintenance routine is more than likely to be excessive rather than insufficient, with you checking the pH and water quality every day! After a while you'll begin to realise that, except in the very smallest aquaria, changes don't take place that quickly. Once the new aquarium has stabilised, the conditions within will maintain themselves for quite a while without any interference from the aquarist. And it is at this point that the greatest danger lies: *familiarity does indeed generate contempt*. The twin overriding principles of successful aquarium/biosphere management are:

1. Constant vigilance.
2. Never change anything at all unless it really has to be changed.

That may sound fatuous, and need a little explaining. If your aquarium is running well, plants actively growing, fish thriving – maybe even breeding – then you don't want to disturb things. So why bother trying to make things any better? If your biosphere is performing as outlined above, then how could it be any better? As a highly motivated newcomer, you may want to adjust the pH or the hardness content of the water, maybe just to see how easily (or otherwise!) these changes can be effected. Resist! If you must practise, then please do it in a spare tank with no fishes. The only time that the hardness or pH of the water should be adjusted is when these things have been positively identified as the direct cause of fish or plant problems. The objective of aquarium management is to maintain a stable biosphere for the occupants of the aquarium, so that they may live out their natural life cycles without undue stress. Management can be broken down into the following areas, each of which is discussed. 1. Water management. 2. Tank and filter maintenance. 3. Introducing and caring for species. 4. Correct feeding.

Water Management

In larger volumes of water, changes occur more slowly than in smaller amounts. This has drawbacks as well as advantages. For example, raising the temperature in an emergency can seem to take for ever! A good daily routine will head off any potential water problems, as well as regularly reminding you of the commitment you've made to the lives of the fishes and plants.

Daily

Check the temperature – and I do mean *read* the thermometer, not glance to see whether it's 'something like'. Regular shifts of temperature could mean your aquarium is located badly, in a draught for example, or your heater may be faulty. Count the fishes: are they all present? If one's missing try to find it (not so easy with catfishes!). Having now watched your fishes for hours and hours, you'll be familiar with their normal behaviour patterns, their respiratory rate, swimming posture and 'cruising range'.

Any variation from this norm must be investigated immediately. With disease, the earlier a (successful) diagnosis is made, then the quicker treatment can begin, and the more chance the fish has of complete recovery. Don't forget to check the plants as well.

Also check that everything is working correctly, that a healthy stream of bubbles is exiting the airlift tubes in an undergravel filter system, and ensure that inlet/outlet pipes of power filters aren't blocked with detritus. Inspect all airlines for cracks and splits, especially where they're pushed onto spigots.

Weekly

If you've had to make any adjustments to the basic water chemistry, then check these each week. Weekly is also a good time to concentrate on your underwater garden. Lop off any dead leaves or stems. Plants which are growing too tall may be cut back, and the cuttings either thrown away (what a waste!) or replanted. If you have no more room for any cuttings, there will be many of your aquarist friends who would welcome some free plants.

Checking the aquarium temperature with an electronic thermometer. This model will record both the highest and lowest temperatures recorded over a set time.

Monthly

Nitrate may become excessive in the aquarium water. Assuming that you're not performing a monthly NO_3 test, another way to spot excessive nitrate build-up is the colour of the water, which turns yellow when large amounts of nitrate are present. The quickest way to deal with NO_3 build-up is to perform a twenty percent partial water change.

Before water can be added to the aquarium, you have to remove some first. This is a good time to give the substrate a clean. As disturbing the gravel will naturally create rather a mess in the aquarium, it is best done before a water change, and before cleaning any filters (see later). There are various substrate 'hoovers' available which, working either on the syphon principle, or electrically powered, clean the surface of the gravel, trapping the mulm in a cleanable bag. But be gentle! In an undergravel filtration system, the last thing you want to do is seriously disturb the filter bed by raking it. Once the gravel has been cleaned, remove around twenty percent of the now very dirty aquarium water.

By the way, don't throw this water away. It is very rich in nitrate, phosphates etc. and represents a very fine, natural fertiliser which you can use around the house or garden to water your plants.

Top-up water must, of course, be dechlorinated and conditioned. Don't worry if the temperature is a little lower than the ambient aquarium level; fishes often appreciate a little 'freshness' in their watery world. As to how much water should be changed – around 20 percent every fourteen days or so. I vary the exact times, so that, if there are any parasites in the water, their life cycle can be interrupted. Of course, for those aquarists who're maintaining a water chemistry different to that coming out of their home water supply, then top-up water has to be prepared in advance of any water changes, and stored until needed.

Finally, to avoid complacency, do an ammonia and a nitrite (NO_2) check, to reassure yourself that everything is as it should be, rather than what you hope it will be. If money is a problem, as it will be for younger fishkeepers, then a monthly NO_2 check is the minimum you can get away with while still retaining control over the biosphere. But, at the first sign of trouble in the aquarium, do both an ammonia and nitrite test immediately. Spotting problems before they turn into something really nasty is the art of aquarium management, and a quick test can often show you immediately where the problem lies.

Aquarium/Filter Maintenance

Some manufacturers advocate cleaning their filters at certain times. But, as these often err on the side of caution, experiment for yourself. For example, the instructions for one power filter I use dictate that the foam media is replaced *entirely* every two weeks. As this medium is very expensive, and at two weeks is just beginning to generate a fair sized aerobic bacteria colony, I clean and replace it every week, and throw it away every three months.

Monthly

Excessive algal growth on tank decorations, heating/filtration equipment and on the front glass of the aquarium should be removed, and preferably *before* cleaning out the filter system. The algae you remove from wherever it's growing has to go somewhere: better it goes into a power filter which is about to be cleaned, rather than dirty a freshly cleaned one.

It is not a good idea to remove all of the algal growth in the aquarium. Algae which adheres to the sides and back of the tank should be left there, where it looks quite natural, will provide a browsing area for many species of fishes, and will assist in the removal of nitrate from the aquarium water via photosynthesis and respiration. However, for clarity, the front glass should be kept clean.

Undergravel filters need the substrate cleaning, removing dead leaves, uneaten food etc., as previously explained. Again inspect the airline, making sure that there's no water inside it, which may indicate cracks. Check that the air pump isn't making any strange noises which could indicate water inside, or a split rubber diaphragm. With power filters, check the media. Dirty wool floss should be removed, washed carefully in aquarium water and replaced. This will retain the aerobic bacteria content. Remove activated charcoal and replace with fresh. Once cleaned you may be pleasantly surprised at the increased flow rate of your power filter!

The 'old' charcoal can be reactivated by baking in a hot oven (200 degrees C) for fifteen minutes. Its effectiveness can then be checked by making up a beaker containing a two percent solution of Methylene Blue. Add a sample of the newly reactivated charcoal, which should sink to the bottom of the beaker and completely absorb the Methylene Blue solution within thirty minutes, leaving the water clear. If the charcoal floats, or fails to clear the water, then throw it away and buy some more. *Zeolite* should be removed and reactivated by soaking overnight in a strong salt solution, as per the manufacturer's instructions.

Introducing And Caring For Species

Buying Fish

Having selected examples of the species you want to keep, either from the *Database of Community Fishes* (Chapter 10) or from what you've already read about or seen on display at a pet or aquarist shop, now is the time to go out and buy them. I really do wish that life was as simple as just walking into an aquarist shop, which would have all the species I wanted to buy, and in first class condition, and then going home again happy, with no future calamities lurking within the plastic bags.

Buying fishes is a difficult thing for a newcomer to do, even though nothing appears simpler at first sight. Having spent a great deal of time and money creating the ideal biosphere for your fishes, one careless purchase now could well wreck everything you've done so far by filling your aquarium with disease.

The first thing to look at when you enter a pet or aquarist shop is not the display tanks but the actual premises and the staff. The care (or otherwise) which the store owner expends on his or her shop will be reflected in the way the fishes for sale are selected and kept. Next check out the display aquaria – is the water clean and the tanks (where appropriate), well lit? Don't worry about any lack of tank decorations, such as plants, rocks and roots. Such items only get in the way when the store owner is trying to capture a certain specimen for a customer, and are best left out.

A good aquarist store will mostly keep different species in separate aquaria, although smaller shops with space limitations often place compatible species (read community fish) together in the same tank. Having satisfied yourself that this is indeed a good place to buy your fishes, it's time for a closer inspection. Look first at *all* the specimens in the same tank, not only so that you can choose the best remaining example, and of the right sex, but to ensure that none is carrying any obvious sign of disease or is dead. If just one specimen in a tank of twenty shows any sign of disease, it's a good bet that all the others will shortly follow suit. I've just had a recent example of this, which just goes to show that even people who're supposed to know what they're doing can be stung just as easily as any newcomer!

To begin stocking a newly-created aquarium, I visited a local garden centre with an aquatic section (no names, of course) and after careful examination (which turned out to be not nearly careful enough), bought an Opaline and a Pearl gourami. The Pearl died overnight: the Opaline the next day. Three guppies I purchased from another store on the same day are doing fine, by the way. On examining the gouramis, both were plastered with White Spot (*Ichthyophthirius multifiliis*).

**Pet shop display aquaria –
International Aquatic Centre,
Sheffield.**

**Aquatic shop display aquaria
– Superpets. Note! Don't
expect *all* general pet shops
to be this well equipped with
fish.**

I should add here that White Spot isn't usually fatal to fishes. They normally respond very successfully to treatment, making a complete recovery. However, constant re-infection can weaken a fish so much that it dies. I went back to the place where I'd bought the fishes the next day, examined the tank from which my two specimens had been taken and found *all* the fish in that aquarium covered in White Spot as well. When I asked for a refund, the owner just shrugged, and refused. Needless to say I won't be buying any more fishes from there. By the way, I cover refunds from aquarist and pet shops later in the book.

No Thank You!

Having already established that you're not yet an expert on fish disease, there's still much you can do to protect your biosphere by simply applying a healthy dose of common sense. You know roughly how a fish should appear in the water so, if your potential purchase is tilted over to one side or the other, or cannot maintain a level without constantly sinking and swimming back up again, or suddenly starts shaking (shimmying), then; No Thank You! There is obviously something wrong with the fish, and there's no way do you want to be the one who has to find out what it is. Although a nipped fin or two is all part of community tank rough-housing, fishes with splits, rends or even completely missing fins should not be bought.

Hollow bellied fishes, crooked backs, growths, protruding eyes (on species which don't normally have them – goldfish, such as *Celestials* actually do); missing or sticking-out scales – these are all No Thank You! fishes, and are to be avoided. Although looking for the most obvious signs of disease won't guarantee that you never buy a sick fish, it will certainly go a long way towards this goal. If you've any doubts at all, and no matter how long you've waited for a particular species to appear in the shop, nor how strong your desire to own an example, don't buy it. Remember, it's not just the death of any suspect fish you have to guard

against, you also have many other fishes in your aquarium to protect as well.

Quarantine Aquaria

Most knowledgeable aquarists, who also tend to acquire a rather expensive collection of fishes, usually have a small tank set aside as a quarantine tank, in which all new purchases are kept for a few weeks, while their health is monitored daily. Now, it is a fact that the average aquarist (if there is such an animal) doesn't use a quarantine tank. He or she simply acclimatises the fish in its bag (see later) and, when equilibrium has been reached, they allow the fish free access into the community tank. It's really up to you. If you have a beautiful aquascape with some superb fishes living quite comfortably in it, do you want to put all that at risk?

A quarantine tank will protect your main aquarium from disease introduced by new additions and, if you've some first class specimens, it only takes one tiny fish carrying some form of parasite to decimate your pride and joy. On the other hand, you have the expense of creating yet another fully-equipped aquarium, and yet another tank to maintain. Whether or not you are prepared to set up and maintain a quarantine tank is, of course, entirely your own decision. But no leading aquarists would dream of putting a new addition into their main aquarium without quarantining it first: neither would I.

It's In The Bag

Having carefully examined your intended purchase, the store owner will now attempt to capture and bag it for you – which is often an hilarious process not to be missed! The dealer will quarter-fill a polythene bag with water from the same aquarium as the fish you're buying, and then pop the (eventually) captured fish into this bag. Finally, the package is then tied, trapping the maximum amount of air inside. You may worry that the fish might a) suffocate through lack of oxygen or b) freeze to death.

In fact fish have been bought and transported many miles in this fashion for decades. In all the time I've been buying fishes neither I, nor anyone I know, has ever lost a single specimen while in transit. The water in the bag will obviously begin to cool just as soon as it's put in but, providing this cooling process takes place slowly (which it will), and that re-heating is done slowly as well, then the fish can manage for around four hours inside a dealer's plastic bag, providing the bag isn't left exposed to cold winds or frosts. Often the dealer will also wrap the polythene bag inside a brown paper bag, for further protection.

If you have to travel a long distance, you can insulate the bag or bags, either in a polystyrene box, or a wooden container stuffed with saw-dust, old newspapers, felt or polystyrene chips, as used to pack electronic equipment. Don't use straw or fibreglass insulation material, both of which may puncture the bag.

Introducing New Fishes

On arriving home, open up the tank hood and simply float the plastic bag in the aquarium water, and leave it there for around four or five minutes to allow the temperatures to equalise. As the bag will naturally displace some of the existing aquarium water, be careful you don't let the tank overflow. After five minutes, open the bag and slide it away from the fish, ensuring that it's free of the bag.

Often, aquarists' books advocate a twenty minute equalising time, and then a gradual introduction of the aquarium water, in an attempt to get the new fish used to your water chemistry. If the chemistry of your water is radically different to that which the fish has been used to, then it will go into shock, and will take weeks, rather than five minutes to adjust, assuming that it survives at all. It is far more sensible, and a lot kinder to the fish, to allow the minimum possible time for temperature stabilisation – a fish being moved into water which is slightly warmer will not harm it at all – than to keep it confined within a polythene bag for half-an-hour, with all the other tank occupants nosing around.

If there are other species already in the aquarium, add a little food just before you open the plastic bag and let the new fish loose. This will take the existing occupants' minds off the newcomer, allowing it to settle in without any aggravation.

Getting A Refund

Some shops have an absolute policy: *no* refund on fish under *any* circumstances. The answer of course is obvious; don't buy any fishes from them. Having said that, there is an established etiquette to be observed when claiming a refund. If you can put your hand on your heart and honestly say that the death of a recently-purchased fish is in no way attributable to anything you may have done, or the conditions within your own aquarium, and therefore must have been a 'faulty' fish from the beginning, then, and only then, do you have a just case for a refund.

As a newcomer, there's no way in the world you can claim this if you suffer any fish deaths. You simply don't have enough subject knowledge yet to decide if the death or deaths were your fault or someone else's. And, as you'll have to convince the aquarist store owner that you do indeed know your subject very thoroughly indeed, he will be most reluctant to give you your money back. So any dead fishes in your early days will have to be chalked-up to experience. Still, at this stage of your aquaristic career, you're hardly likely to be spending more than a few pounds on a single specimen. When a fish dies, the first concern should always be to ascertain the cause of death, so that the other fishes may be protected, and not chase around trying to get your money back.

Aquarist store owners are enthusiasts too, otherwise why would they be in this business? They quickly learn who the knowledgeable hobbyists are amongst their clientele, and respond to them accordingly. That's why it pays to keep patronising the same store. Once the owner gets to know you, he or she will pass on tips and advice, give you advanced warning of new stock due to arrive, or even just the latest trade gossip! And, if you purchase an expensive fish which the owner knows you're perfectly capable of looking after, and then it mysteriously dies, he'll be more inclined to give you either a cash refund, or a credit note against further purchases.

Pet Shop Or Aquatic Dealer?

Should you patronise a regular pet shop, or deal exclusively with an aquatic specialist's store? The choice may be forced upon you because of your location – you may only have access to one or the other. Phillip, the owner of Superpets pet shop in the Dukeries' town of Worksop, North Nottinghamshire, is a fairly typical pet store owner. He has to stock the familiar range of rabbits, budgies, hamsters and, of course, fish. Phil has to be a little bit expert in a whole range of pet care, whereas the specialist aquatic shop owner only needs to know about fish.

Luckily for me, Phillip does specialise some-what in tropical fishes and has some lady (he refuses to name her, even after I poured six bottles of *Grolsch* lager down his throat!) who breeds the best guppies I've ever seen! Expect a pet shop to stock the more common aquatic hardware and software items only, although anything you want they'll be able to order for you. The specialist aquatic dealer will have a more in-depth knowledge of the whole aquatic scene, and will obviously hold more stock, hardware and software.

I personally make a point of visiting any shop which sells fishes wherever I happen to be at the time, although I only purchase from the one place. What they don't have, they will soon order for me. I do know some aquarists who wouldn't be seen dead in a pet shop! More fools, they, for they will never get to see Phil's superb guppies and Discus fishes even though he *only* runs a pet store!

Feeding Your Fish

In their natural environment, what fishes eat depends almost entirely on what serendipity serves them. Food arrives within their bio-sphere from a variety of sources: carried by the wind, fallen from bankside vegetation, swept along by the current, and the flora and fauna of the river or lake bed. Should the Gods of supply not be smiling on them that particular day, then the fishes don't eat. This doesn't worry them unduly – they're quite used to managing with-out for a few days, knowing that in a while there will be plenty again. Some fishes travel to find food as well, often moving great distances to obtain it.

Depending on the time of day and the season of the year, in the wild, fishes eat fruit, small crustacea, insects and their larvae, plants and algae, cereals and seeds, fish eggs and, of course, each other! This represents a very healthy and nutritious diet for the fishes, and is also what we hobby fishkeepers must try to imitate if our stock are to live healthy and productive lives. Thankfully, due to advances in aquatic technology and many years of research and development by the trade, this is now relatively easy to realise.

Flake Food

From the earliest days of manufactured fish foods, aquarists have been searching for the perfect food. They wanted a food which was a nutritious staple diet containing a variety of vitamins, minerals, trace elements, proteins, carbohydrate, oils and fats. Through the evol-ution of the first dry foods, which were mostly cereal-based, the aquatic trade gave hobbyists exactly what they wanted, and in a form which was easily manufactured with a long shelf life once the container had been opened: flaked foods.

Today, almost all tropical fishkeepers use some form of flake food as the basis of their fishes' diet. Once you realise just what's in it it's amazing how cheap it really is. It is perfectly possible to feed your fishes on nothing but flake all of their lives – and they will grow and thrive too; after all, flake fish feed is very concentrated. But imagine having to live on nothing but beans-on-toast for the rest of *your* life?

Research into the dietary requirements of fishes is constant. Once the staple flake food had been developed, the next stage was to make it even better. Basic flake food quickly developed into specific feeds for a particular species or purpose – you can now buy flake feeds for herbivores and carnivores, egg-layers and live-bearers. There are flake feeds which enhance the colours of fishes, condition them for breeding, and to feed both egg-layer and livebearer fry. You can buy flake impregnated with medicaments for certain types of fish disease, and there are cichlid and goldfish, as well as growth, flakes.

Variety Is The Spice Of . . .

Although flake feeds are quite capable of supplying everything fish need in the way of dietary requirements, it is not advisable to restrict them to this. Feeding fishes constantly on a diet of flake food can cause them intestinal problems, such as severe constipation. You can often see when fishes have been fed lots of flake – they have trails of faeces hanging from their anus. Just as in the wild, we should be feeding our fishes a variety of different foods. Not for every meal of course. As a basis of a mixed diet, flake is hard to better, with pellets based on the same recipe for much larger fishes, but it has to be supported with other items, such as fresh, live, freeze-dried or deep-frozen foods.

Live food

Live food plays a major role in the fishes' diet in the wild. Items such as insects and their offspring are very acceptable fare to them. For many years, aquarists have been feeding their fishes with live *Daphnia* (water fleas), blood-worms, and mosquito larvae. *Tubifex*, grindle, white, micro, red, and even earth, worms too. And it's true to say that, for bringing a male/female pair into breeding condition, there's nothing finer or more effective than a diet which relies heavily on live food. However, there are some problems to watch out for.

First Catch Your Tiger!

Live food means just that; the creatures are actually alive, and are placed into the aquarium in this condition, where the fish then hunt them down and eat them. One of the problems the aquarist has to resolve is arranging a suitable supply of such food. *Daphnia*, *Tubifex* and blood-

There is an enormous range of flaked fish food available.

Red-tailed Black Shark.

Penguin fish.

Natural biosphere of many species of tropical fishes.

Artificial re-creation of the natural biosphere.

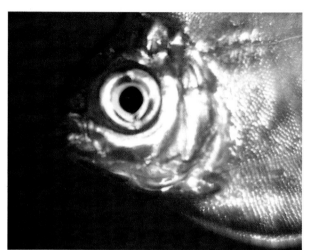

Close-up of the head and mouth of a Silver Dollar fish.

Frisky male Guppy.

Silver Dollar.

Female Platy.

Male Swordtail.

Discus Fish.

Male Dwarf Gourami.

Female Siamese Fighting Fish.

Three-spot Gourami.

School of Kissing Gouramis.

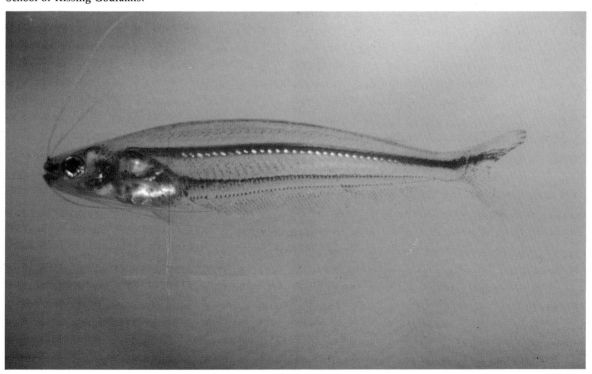

Colour is often used as protection by fishes. Here the absence of colour in the X-Ray, or Glass, Catfish has the same effect by making it virtually invisible in the water.

Lace/Pearl Gourami.

School of Neon Tetras at play.

Female Sailfin Molly.

Male Sailfin Molly.

Female Zebra Danio swollen with eggs.

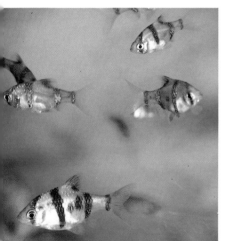

School of Tiger Barbs.

Opaline Gourami.

Male and Female Honey Gouramis – the smallest Gouramis you can get!

Close-up of a Discus fish's head and shoulders.

Close-up of an Oscars' head.

A 'failed mutation' of an Angelfish.

Butterfly fish.

Elephant-nosed Fish.

Armoured Catfish.

worm can all be bought from a pet shop or aquatic dealer, but this is an expensive way if you plan to feed such creatures to your fish on a regular basis. The alternative is to collect your own supply.

Daphnia can be collected from ponds, water butts and ditches. Skimming a fine-mesh net just under the surface of such water will produce a healthy crop of them in the summer months. Bloodworm live in the sludge and mud at the bottom of ponds, rivers, canals, ditches and water butts. To harvest them, you need a long pole with a flat blade of steel attached at a forty-five degree angle to the pole. Lower the pole into the water, and sink the blade just below the mud. Using a scooping movement, lift the blade forwards and upwards – the bloodworms will be sticking to the front edge of the blade. When removing them from the blade be very gentle as they are quite fragile, and it's very easy to pull off their heads.

Tubifex worms are found wherever there is some sewerage, such as outfall pipes, sewerage farms or stagnant pools. They feed by ingesting the raw sewerage, extracting whatever it is they like to eat, and then passing the waste back out again. They are best bought freeze-dried or frozen. Another problem that has to be very carefully handled by the aquarist is the cleaning of any live food collected. You won't know the condition of the water where the creatures have been collected, and to tip any of this into your aquarium is quite literally asking for trouble.

Artemia salina

There is one live food much loved by fishes, which is also a first class fish conditioner as well as being a superb first-food for fry, and which is also completely safe: *Artemia salina*, the brine shrimp. It is safe because you buy the *Artemia* eggs from your local aquatic dealer and hatch them yourself either in a special brine shrimp hatchery, or in a glass tank/bottle. You don't have to use a hatchery – all you need is saltwater, some strong aeration and the eggs, and something to feed them on of course. A hatchery just makes things a little simpler.

Brine shrimp eggs can be bought with or without shells. Without will usually yield more *Artemia* nauplii than eggs with shells, but they do cost more to buy. Assuming that you're using a brine shrimp hatchery, such as the *Hykro* model handled by Interpet, and which comes with full instructions for use, the first

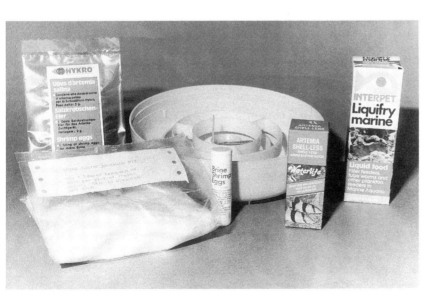

A Brine shrimp hatchery and everything else needed to hatch and rear *Artemia salina.*

nauplius should appear some 24–36 hours after the eggs have been placed in it, and the system activated. Once hatched, and assuming that you're not feeding the nauplii to fish fry, the baby *Artemia* have to be fed so that they can grow into adults, and provide a more substantial meal for your fish. Feeds such as Interpet's *Liquifry Marine* are ideal for growing the nauplii on. Brine shrimp eggs cost around £7.00 for 40 millilitres, which will provide you with a lot of *Artemia salina*.

When feeding *Artemia* you have to be careful that you don't add the salted water into your aquarium. Use a brine shrimp strainer to capture them, give the strainer a quick rinse under cold freshwater, then put the *Artemia* immediately into the aquarium.

Hooray For Freeze-Dry!

For those aquarists who don't want all the hassle of collecting their own live foods, or for those of us who can't get about very well, there is a very creditable second-best option which still fulfils the concept of a varied and balanced diet for the fish, and which guarantees that

you'll not be introducing any parasites or disease into the aquarium water. *Daphnia*, krill, bloodworm, *Tubifex*, mosquito larvae, white and river shrimp may all be bought from your local pet or aquarist shop in pre-packed, freeze dried form.

The freeze-dry process retains most of the original vitamin/protein goodness of the creatures and, as they are often gamma-irradiated too, the integrity of the final product is excellent, leaving no chance of introducing something nasty into your tank. Not quite as good as the real thing, but a very good, easily accessible and relatively cheap (when compared to the same amounts bought live) supply which will be much appreciated by your fishes.

Frozen Food

Many crustacea are traditionally 'wet' frozen, and kept in freezers at aquarist shops. You can buy freshly caught and deep-frozen shrimp, krill, *Tubifex* etc. The pack has to be kept in your freezer, especially once opened, and should be used within the dates specified on the pack. Deep-frozen shrimp, krill etc. are more expen-

Freeze-dried live food.

sive than the freeze-dried counterparts. Usually the warm temperature of the aquarium water will defrost frozen foods, but watch out when feeding larger chunks to big fish.

Other Foods

There are a surprising number of foods in your own larder which fishes find very tasty. For instance, lettuce, peas, lean red meats – both cooked and uncooked – chicken, fish, liver, ox-heart, wheatgerm, shellfish, prawns, spinach, sweetcorn and hard-boiled egg yolks. Lettuce leaves and peas should be blanched with boiling water, which will make them easier for the fish to consume. Blanching breaks down cellulose, a substance most fishes have difficulty digesting. Freeze meat solid, and then grate it on a cheese grater to obtain portions for smaller mouths. But don't forget to count your fingers once you've finished grating!

For really high protein feeds, whether to condition for breeding or simply to grow-on a potential champion, the people to consult are the owners of fishing tackle shops. Carp anglers use a specially prepared bait known as 'The Boilie', which is a rich blend of proteins, carbo-hydrates, oils and fats. Many very large carp have been captured with such baits, proving just how effective they are – only this time we're using them in reverse, to feed, and not capture.

Part of the fun of being an aquarist is designing special concoctions and feeds from your larder, and then going to the aquarist club to boast about how your secret mix has increased the yield from your breeding fishes enormously; and how your fry have put on thirty pounds in weight overnight, thanks entirely to your secret formula!

The Mechanics Of Feeding

Feeding your fishes is one of the highlights of the hobby, and is fascinating to watch, yet it is also one of the hardest things to get right. Over-feeding fishes is the single biggest cause of

Deep-frozen live foods.

'Boilies' – a high protein food cocktail used by carp anglers to capture fish. Boilies make an ideal food for fishes, either broken down for smaller mouths or fed whole to larger fishes such as Cichlids.

trouble within the aquarium; and also the main reason why we have to use filters. *You cannot learn how to feed your fish correctly from a book. Not even this one!*

Authors don't know which fishes you keep or in what numbers, so how can they (I) recommend amounts and times? Only time, experience and your fishes will teach you about correct feeding. If your aquarium water is cloudy, the substrate covered with a dirty coating and your fish look dull, listless and perhaps have spots of grey slime on them, then you're almost certainly massively over-feeding. Especially if you're using a medium size tub of flake every week!

Conversely, if your fish don't appear to be growing at all – bearing in mind that some species are very slow growing anyway – all the plants in the aquarium have been eaten and there are teeth marks on the heater tubes, then you're not feeding your fish either often enough or giving them enough food. Observe how your fishes take and eat their food, how a pecking order has been established, and who the boss is. If you feed your fishes at the same time and in the same place each day, it won't be too long before your fishes are already gathered in the right place waiting to meet you. Some aquarists

have trained their fish to take food from their hand. I used to have a very large and lovely *Osphronemus gourami* (now an inmate at Matlock Aquarium) called 'Ozzy' (original, huh?), who used to just love slurping spaghetti rings from my little finger, where I wore them like jewellery.

In a family situation, where everyone wants to be the one to feed the fishes, it's best to nominate someone in overall charge of feeding. Then make a rule that no one feeds the fishes without his or her say-so first. This prevents the whole family from putting something into the tank during the day.

The Time

When you feed your fishes is really your decision. Some aquarists feed small amounts three times a day, others feed their fishes only once a day. Some feed in the mornings, others during the evenings. There is no hard and fast rule – fishes are used to feeding irregularly, and even going without completely, in the wild. But, if you choose a regular time, the fishes will quickly become accustomed to it and be there waiting for you. Also, choosing a set time each day generates a regular routine which helps jog your memory, so that you won't forget to feed them. I feed my fishes a half-hour after sun-up (tank lights on) and a half-hour before sun-down (lights out) each day. Any remaining food is soon polished off by a suckermouth catfish. My fish live and grow.

How Much?

This is difficult for a newcomer. The usual advice is to put in no more food than will be entirely consumed within two minutes. The problem here, and a common error for beginners, is to mistake the amount of food put into the water with the actual amount eaten by the fishes. You may put a lot in, but only a little may actually be eaten; that's why it is so important to watch your fishes closely at feeding time. Although watching who eats what and when is virtually impossible in practice!

Many books on fishkeeping order the beginner to remove any uneaten food from the aquarium or it will quickly pollute the water. And, if you're feeding them three times a day, this can very soon become a critical problem. The trouble is, once flake hits the substrate it becomes invisible: you can't remove what you can't see.

At first, the best way to work out what's required in the way of food is to put a tiny bit into the aquarium and watch until it's all been eaten. Then keep adding small amounts until further food is ignored. Contrary to popular myth, most fishes will not go on eating until they explode! After a while you'll develop a 'sense' of how much feed is needed, and this will often be the first clue you get should disease strike your aquarium. The fishes will either not eat as much, or may stop feeding altogether.

Take your time with feeding; enjoy it. Far too many fishkeepers simply yank open the hood, dump in a handful of flake, slam the cover back down again and then walk away, disinterested. Watching fishes eat, observing the 'pecking order' in action, as the fish queue up for their share, really shouldn't be missed! And you'll quickly realise if a new addition hasn't yet worked out its place in the pecking order, which recently happened to me on adding a superb male Siamese fighting fish – *Betta splendens* – which took quite a while to find its position in the established tank order.

Match portion to mouth size; there's not much point in tossing a Neon Tetra a bone to chew on, nor offering a mature Tiger Oscar some crumbled flake. Carnivores need meat, herbivores need greenery: you have to ensure they get it. Some fishes are surface feeders, others prefer to take their food around mid-water. Catfishes will look for their food on the aquarium floor. You have to ensure that all your fishes get an adequate supply of food. If no food survives the journey to mid-water, you'll have to get a faster sinking food, so that fishes occupying the middle of the tank get their share. For bottom dwellers, there are food tablets which sink quickly. Some fishes are nocturnal – putting food out for them during the day is a waste of time. Feed such species after putting the aquarium lights out for the night.

In aquaria which have a strong surface move-ment of the water – due to a spray bar, or output from an internal power filter – flake food can be whipped around the tank before the fish can get hold of it. In such circumstances, a plastic feeding ring is very useful. The flake (or any other) food is placed inside the ring, which keeps it in the same place and allows the fish plenty of time to feed, saving them from hurtling around the aquarium in hot pursuit of a tasty morsel, even though the exercise may be good for them!

A similar situation may apply where live foods, such as *Tubifex* worms, are concerned. If they were simply dropped into the tank, they would sink and burrow into the substrate before surface-feeding fishes could get at them. A worm feeder, which is a plastic conical device perforated with minute holes, prevents this happening by forcing the worms to wriggle free of the device, allowing the fish plenty of oppor-tunity to get at them.

Range Of Feeds

Don't forget to add variety to the diet. Have two or three different types of flake food available as staple diet so that you can ring the changes, feeding one type for a week, and then another the following week. Add some freeze-dried or deep-frozen food at least once a week, and preferably more often. Try to feed your fishes with genuine live food, such as *Daphnia*, bought from a shop, at least once a month.

Holiday Feeding

You won't have thought much about this problem until the event is upon you, but at some time you're going to take a holiday, and then suddenly realise there's no one around to feed your fishes. Family or neighbours can help, which also fulfils the dual function of keeping a security check on your home. But, if you are going to use a stand-in to feed your fishes, it's no good saying to him 'Just add a pinch of this, and every other day a pinch of that.' It is more than likely he won't know the first thing about fishkeeping and his idea of a pinch of flake will almost certainly not be the same as your own.

The best way to tackle this situation is to make up an individual parcel of food for each day you're going to be away. Then all your stand-in has to do is to add one parcel of the food to the aquarium each day. Use aluminium foil for the parcels rather than the suspect polythene wrapping known as *Clingfilm*. The plastic canisters in which 35mm films are bought make excellent packages for a day's supply of food, and can also be clearly labelled 'Monday, Tuesday' etc. And, as these canisters are virtually airtight, they keep the food fresh as well.

Vacation Feeder Blocks

Various manufacturers make what's known as Vacation Feeder Blocks, which are simply chunks of fish food encased within plaster of Paris, which slowly dissolve in the water over a

period of days. The fish cannot eat the food all at once because it isn't in a digestible form until the plaster has dissolved.

Automatic Fish Feeders

Again aquatic technology has come to the aid of modern fishkeepers who like their holidays, but

Feeding your fishes while you're away on holiday has never been easier. This automatic dispenser feeds the fishes a mixed diet at pre-set times for up to fourteen days.

don't have useful stand-ins, nor like the idea of Vacation Feeder Blocks in the water. There are several forms of automatic electronic fish feeders currently available which will deliver a pre-arranged amount of food, at a pre-set time, into the aquarium for every day you're away. They consist of a series of chambers around the circumference of a wheel. Each chamber may be charged with a particular type of food, such as flake, freeze-dried etc. An electric motor and time switch drives a chamber over an aperture, and at the pre-set time, allows the contents of the chamber to empty slowly into the aquarium.

And there you have it, everything you need to know for successful aquarium management. Although it does seem a lot to remember, after a while most of the things you have to do become an automatic routine.

Chapter 8
Breeding

Once the community aquarium has been set up for a while, with fishes and plants both thriving, an aquarist's thoughts turn naturally towards attempting to breed the various species of tropical fishes, starting with those already in the community tank.

In a well-established community aquarium, the chances are very good that breeding has already taken place, but has passed unnoticed by the aquarist. Many fishes eat their own and other fishes' eggs and fry. Reproduction is the highest compliment your fish can ever pay you, and is testament to the success of your aquatic management skill; *for fishes will will not breed at all unless conditions are exactly right for them to do so.* However, here we are more concerned with the deliberate attempt to breed certain fishes, rather than haphazard spawning in the community aquarium. I don't have the space to cover all aspects of breeding: what I have done is to explain how to spawn the most common and also what are considered to be two of the easiest species – livebearing guppies, and the prolific egg-laying Zebra danio. But do please note that the breeding techniques discussed here are *not* necessarily directly transferable to other viviparous or oviparous species. Each family of fishes has its own unique method of spawning, so you will have to consult one of the books listed in the Bibliography (Appendix 1) for specific information on other species' requirements.

Egg-Layers And Livebearers

Tropical fishes either give birth to live fry

Zebra danio.

Male Guppy.

(viviparous), which are immediately free swimming, or are egg-layers (oviparous), where the female lays the eggs, the male fertilises them, and the fry go through the egg hatching, yolk-sac consuming stages before they become free swimming. I will explain in a while how to breed guppies (*Poecilia reticulata*) and also Zebra danios (*Brachydanio rerio*), which will give you an insight into the spawning of viviparous and oviparous species.

The Breeding Process – Egg-Layers

In the wild, seasonal fluctuations, such as a sudden influx of cooler, fresher water, a raising of the ambient temperature, the sudden availability of certain foods, plants and algae, or an increase in the illumination level, may act as the trigger which initiates the need for fish to reproduce. In fairly static water conditions – such as those found in the average home aquarium – fish may, and often do, spawn at any time, and repeatedly.

The sudden availability of certain foods, or the deliberate introduction into the aquarium, means that the male and female fishes increase their food intake, causing the female to begin generating eggs. Certain foods do produce an intensification of the fishes' natural colour, but it is their emotional state, especially around breeding time, which causes the colours to become much more vibrant. Around this time, courtship will begin to occur.

Often the male will seek out a particular female, and begin his courtship routine, such as opening his fins wide in an attempt to impress the female. In other species, the female fish will seek out the male. In a shoal situation, where there is a mixture of both sexes, mutual pairing often occurs. With some species the courtship and spawning activities can appear to be very violent, with the newcomer fearing greatly for the ultimate survival of the female. This is why it is important to obtain a good book on fish breeding, so that you know what to expect.

Assuming that a pair of fishes find each other 'compatible', the female will allow the male to press his suit, and will eventually spawn with him. The actual spawning process varies greatly according to species, but basically the mechanics are thus. The female lays her eggs and the male fertilises them with spermatozoa. To give you a few examples, the female angelfish lays her adhesive eggs on a broad leaf of a plant, such as an Amazon sword. The male angelfish then swims over the eggs releasing his milt. Assuming that the angelfish don't actually eat all the eggs (which can happen with a first brood), both the male and female carefully tend the sight of the spawning, fanning water over the fertilised eggs with their pectoral fins, in an attempt to prevent mould from forming on them – or so

Male Lace – or Pearl – gourami in breeding condition.

the theory goes. I've always had to remove the parents, who start scoffing the eggs, and start a gentle aeration under the site of the eggs!

With the Siamese fighting fish (*Betta splendens*), once a pairing has occurred the male will build a bubble nest, in readiness to accept the female's eggs. Both fish swim underneath the bubble nest where they then lock into the typical 'embrace', with the male literally squeezing the eggs out of the female, and releasing his milt at the same time. The lighter-than-water eggs float up through the male's spermatozoa and into the bubble nest, where Mr Splendens then takes good care of them, guarding and returning any eggs or fry which fall out of the bubble nest.

Zebra danios are egg scatterers. That is, the female simply lets go of her heavier-than-water eggs, not caring where they end up. The male danio releases his spermatozoa as a cloud in the water, through which the female's eggs will sink through on their way to the tank bottom. Not all of the female's eggs will pass through the male's cloud of milt, and so will remain infertile. These will have to be removed later, as they will begin to rot and may affect other eggs in close proximity.

Both danios make bad parents, and will eagerly eat any of their own (or anyone else's) they can get hold of.

Apart from the female producing the eggs and the male fertilising them – the basis of all life – how this is actually achieved varies with almost every single species of egg-laying fish. From the haphazard scattering of the eggs around the tank, through careful burying in the substrate up to one or other parent nurturing and brooding eggs in their mouths, or even both. Many aquarists devote their entire time to the really absorbing subject of fish breeding.

The Breeding Process - Livebearers

Guppies are considered the rabbits of the aquatic world. With this species the problem doesn't lay with getting them to breed; it's trying to stop them! You will be very lucky indeed if you buy a female from a shop which isn't already im-

Female Guppy, heavily pregnant. Note the blotching around the anal fin, which are the young fry awaiting birth.

pregnated with sperm from a dozen different males. In the male, the anal fin has evolved into a specially shaped organ known as the *gonopodium*, which is used as a tube to deliver sperm into the female. And, as they sexually mature in just a few weeks, males are very soon looking for some guppy femme fatale to impregnate.

The male guppy swims alongside the female and positions his gonopodium near to her anal fin. Spermatozoa is released and impregnates her. Fertilisation and the growth of the fry all takes place within the female's ovarian cavity, with the free swimming babies being released around four weeks later.

Once fertilised by a male, female guppies retain any unused sperm in their reproductive organs; just one meeting with a male can result in the female producing many broods over an extended period, even though she may have had no further male contact since the first impregnation. This can be a real problem for aquarists who're making a serious attempt at developing a quality strain of guppy. But, as you will see later, there are ways to avoid indiscriminate breeding. Livebearers do not usually make good parents; the female guppy will eat her fry given half a chance.

General Breeding Information

When first starting with fish breeding, many aquarists are quite happy for any results at all, no matter how they are achieved. The quality of any offspring and the suitability of brood stock aren't usually questions the beginner bothers very much about. Yet breeding does endow the aquarist with certain responsibilities regarding the results of a spawning.

The Fish Breeder's Responsibilities

He or she must ensure that all fry are healthy, strong specimens, by choosing and using only good brood stock. Allowing weak, diseased or deformed adult fishes to mate virtually guarantees that the resulting offspring will be very poor specimens, who, if they live at all, will find that they're bullied incessantly, and will probably starve to death.

Similarly, the aquarist must not attempt to breed in any physical characteristics which will cause the fish distress. There is already a good example of this in coldwater fishkeeping with the Celestial Goldfish, whose upwards-facing bubble eyes make it impossible for it to see in any direction other than straight up. This is a case where past aquarists have abused their breeding responsibilities. Of course, this is entirely my own opinion; other fishkeepers may – probably would – argue with this. But I still

The results of in-breeding physical features can often be distressing for the fish. Here this Bubble-Eyed goldfish can only see upwards without standing on its head.

maintain that any bred-in physical features which handicap a fish in any way at all have to be morally indefensible, and downright wrong!

The Breeding Tank

The mechanics of fish breeding can be split into three parts. 1. Sexing and conditioning. 2. Courtship and spawning. 3. Raising the fry. Each stage is of equal importance. The biggest problem when trying to use the community aquarium as a breeding tank is that you just don't have the control over these three stages which you must have if you're to be a successful breeder of fishes.

Using a separate breeding tank means that you can create ideal conditions for whatever species of fish you're attempting to reproduce. You won't have to worry about other fish getting in the way, attacking the spawning couple, breaking up a carefully constructed bubble nest or losing fry/eggs to predation. About the only use for a community aquarium in fish breeding, apart from holding the brood fish, of course, is the growing-on of livebearer fry – although, even here a separate growing-on tank is a better, albeit more expensive, option.

Breeding Guppies (*Poecilia reticulata*) [On The Cheap]

The first problem to be overcome is acquiring a female who hasn't already been impregnated, with sperm. If it is already impregnated then you'll just have to wait for her to spawn and then separate the sexes as soon as they're visible, and raise the females separately from the males, thereby ensuring their virginity. Sexing guppies is quite simple. Females are much larger and less colourful than the male. Although fairly drab, females are slowly beginning to appear with colour in their caudal (tail) fins, due to dedicated breeders deliberately breeding in this feature. And then there's the male's gonopodium – females have a normally developed anal fin. Males also have a very colourful and large caudal fin, which often proves irresistible to other members of the community aquaria, who can't seem to resist nipping a chunk out of it.

Assume that you've been very lucky indeed, and managed to acquire a superbly coloured, virgin, female guppy, and two or three males which have the right shaped fins and the coloration pattern you want, and, of course, *all* specimens are physically perfect and bursting with good health. There's no need to set up a breeding or growing-on tank if all you want to do is to see how a guppy breeds. There's nothing at all wrong with this attitude, by the way. There are thousands of aquarists around the world who're not interested in regular and serious breeding programs, but would just once like to see how fish actually breed.

Breeding Traps

Put the male/female breeding pair into the community aquarium, and simply let nature take its course. Once the female has been impregnated, around three weeks later her belly will take on a swollen look, with dark patches close to the anal fin. You still have to protect the fry from being eaten by their mother and other fishes and, as you're not setting up a purpose-designed breeding tank, you'll be needing a breeding trap. This is a plastic box consisting of two chambers, one above the other, separated by a slatted floor which allows free entry and egress for the tiny fry. When the female gives birth, the fry pass through the slatted floor into the safety of the second chamber, where the mother or other fishes cannot get at them.

The breeding trap is floated in the community tank water, and sometimes clipped to the side to keep it in one place. The floor of the second chamber is often perforated with tiny holes, which allows aquarium water to circulate freely within the trap. Only experience will tell you when to put the female into the breeding trap, but watching the development of fry in her ventral area is a good guide. Leave the female in the trap until several hours have passed since the last baby was born, which can often amount

The fry of livebearers – or even egg-layers – can be reared in the community tank by keeping them inside a fry net which fixes to a wall of the aquarium.

to around 200 fry for a 'virgin' fish, with the numbers decreasing with age to around 50 or so. When this time comes, return the female to the community tank, and move the fry to a fry net rigged within the tank.

The fry net is simply a box-shaped structure covered with a fine mesh which allows the aquarium water to flow freely through, but stops fishes getting at the fry.

Growing-On

An average guppy spawning produces around 100 fry, and these should be fed often on a commercial livebearer fry food, graduating to a normal diet as soon as they can get their mouths around it. During the growing on stage, some fry will develop at a much faster rate than others, and larger specimens will attack the smaller members. Although this may appear cruel, and you may feel honour bound to protect all the fry, this is actually natural selection at work. Only the very strongest fry will (should?) survive, which is what you need. After a couple of weeks, it's safe to let the remaining fry loose from the fry net into a well-planted community aquarium, which will offer the still quite small fry some protection. Although, if you were seriously into breeding quality guppies,

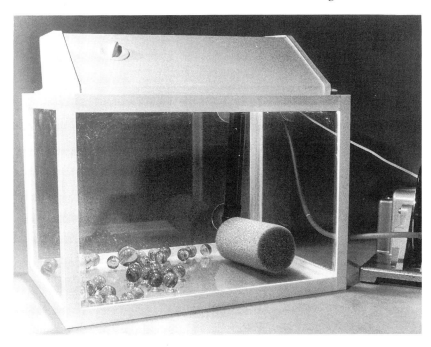

Breeding tank for Zebra danios.

you would separate the sexes as soon as they could be successfully identified, and keep them apart until the next breeding program.

And that's how easy it is to breed guppies. Admittedly there's not much for the aquarist to do when spawning this species, but at least success is virtually guaranteed! However, the aquarist is much more heavily involved when breeding Zebra danios – even if they are generally regarded as the easiest egg-laying species to breed.

Breeding Zebra Danios (*Brachydanio rerio*)

If allowed, Zebra danios will happily spawn as a shoal in the community tank. But if they do, the chances of any eggs hatching and fry developing are virtually zero, due to predation. To have any chance of consistent success you will have to set up a breeding tank. A suitable size is 45×30×30cm (18×12×12in) and, as this is a fairly standard size, you shouldn't have any trouble getting hold of one complete with a hood. Furnish it with a 15 watt fluorescent light, 75 watt heater/thermostat, and an airstone. A

few bunches of plants, such as *Myriophylum*, or *Cabomba* will help make the fish feel at home, but don't overdo it.

While setting up the breeding tank, it's a good idea to start running a Polyfilter foam filter within the community aquarium. You will ultimately need this in the breeding tank, and running it in within the community tank will seed the foam with the vital aerobic bacteria it needs to function correctly. The substrate of the breeding tank needs special attention, however.

My Kingdom For A . . . Marble?

As I previously said, danios make poor parents, with both sexes eager to eat any eggs. You have to stop this happening, and the best way to do it is to put the eggs out of reach of the parents. Traditionally, aquarists have used a substrate of glass marbles to protect the eggs. When the female has let the eggs go and the male has fertilised them, being heavier than water they sink to the bottom of the tank, and fall into the small spaces between the marbles where the parents can't get at them. To ensure that the fish don't scoop-up the eggs as they fall through the water, aquarists limit the water depth in the breeding tank to around 15cm (6in). Be warned! You will need a lot of marbles to cover a floor area of 1350cm² (216in²).

A piece of net curtaining with a fairly open weave makes an excellent barrier between eggs and fish. Stretch the netting across the aquarium, keeping it about 50mm (2in) above the floor area. Fill the breeding tank to a depth of 15cm (6in) with medium-hard water with a pH *no lower than 7*. Zebra danios prefer medium-hard, well oxygenated, slightly alkaline water.

Sexing And Conditioning

Once the breeding tank is set up and running, with some light aeration (be careful when positioning the heater/thermostat as it will have to be laid virtually horizontal in this depth of water), you can begin selecting your brood stock. Sexing danios can be difficult, the only obvious sign is the roundness of the female – especially around the ventral (abdominal) region – when compared to the male. To ensure that you do actually get at least one male, it's best to buy Zebra danios as a shoal of about eight fishes. A good breeding team will consist of three males and two females. Select mature fishes, with no signs of disease or any physical abnormalities.

Before the fishes can be placed in the breeding tank, you have to ensure that they are indeed ready to spawn. Assuming that the fish are actually sexually mature (if not, no amount of conditioning is going to help!), then conditioning with a plentiful supply of live, freeze-dried, deep frozen and fresh foods will bring on the urge to spawn. Actually, aquarists are divided on the best way to condition.

Some fishkeepers prefer to condition the sexes in separate conditioning aquaria, or with a glass partition down the centre of the breeding tank; lifting the partition when they appear ready to spawn. Other aquarists say that separating the sexes for conditioning is unnatural, as it doesn't permit natural pairing, and doesn't happen in the wild. They condition their fish together in the breeding tank, which allows natural selection of partners. As *both* methods are successful, it hardly matters which one you choose, although separation does mean you messing about with the breeding aquarium. On the other hand, conditioning in the breeding tank can create problems with uneaten food, which is difficult to clear away because of the marbles/net curtaining egg barriers.

When conditioning, feed more often than you would normally, taking care to clean away any uneaten food. If your fishes have been kept solely on a flake food diet, conditioning can take a very long time before any noticeable results are seen. But, if you've been feeding them correctly, after two to three weeks you should see the females' bellies beginning to swell with eggs, and the males displaying their courtship routines.

The Spawning

The fishes are near to spawning now. Raise the temperature of the breeding tank to somewhere in the region 27–29 degrees C. and introduce the fish – unless they're already in there, of course. If you're transferring them from a conditioning tank, remember the higher temperature of the breeding tank, and introduce your fishes to the water as you would do for a new purchase. All you can do now is sit back and wait for the spawning to take place.

Everybody wants to see their fish actually spawning; I've sat with camera ready for hours – even days – and never yet seen them spawn. It is said that spawning takes place in the early hours of the morning; as this is the only time I've not watched them closely (I've usually nodded off to sleep!), this is probably true. Check underneath the net, or between the marbles every morning, looking for the small, white eggs. Fairly youngish danios can lay around 60 eggs on their first spawning, with more mature specimens laying anything up to 300. If, after two weeks in the breeding tank (and you're certain that the fishes have been properly conditioned), there's still no signs of any fry or eggs, then return the fishes to the community tank and let them rest a while before trying again. Mind you, on two occasions danios I've returned to the community tank have gone on to spawn within a day of being reintroduced! I did manage to save one lot of eggs.

Success!

You've spotted eggs at the bottom of the breeding tank, or fry attached to the glass walls of the aquarium. If you're going to be using *Artemia salina* (brine shrimp) now is the time to start producing it. The fry will need at least two weeks' supply of this type of food. When you're quite sure that the parents have finished spawning (they can take two or three days), then remove them and put them back into the community tank. Remove the netting, and then wait for the eggs to hatch – which takes around 24 hours. Not all the eggs will hatch at the same time: some will go mouldy, and these infertile eggs should be removed from the tank by the aquarist, or they will pollute the water. Use a plastic straw or pipette for this. Place your thumb over one end, position the bottom of the tube over the mouldy eggs and remove your thumb. The unwanted eggs will be sucked into the tube. Replace your thumb and remove the straw from the tank. Simple! Make sure that the airstone action isn't too violent, or it could damage the fry.

Once hatched, the fry will stay within the substrate, or stuck to the glass aquarium walls, for the next five or six days, while their yolk sacs are consumed. If using some form of netting, remove it once the parents are returned to the community aquarium. Do not add any food at this time: they can't eat it and it will only pollute the water.

In the past, aquarists made use of a substance called *Infusoria* (many still do). This is a conglomeration of minute aquatic life forms, and is made by scalding lettuce and grass with boiling water, allowing the mixture to cool, and feeding the resulting liquid to the fish fry. However, for me, this was always a hit and miss affair, as I was never quite sure what (if anything) was happening. I now prefer to use, and highly recommend the beginner to use, one of the commercial brands of fish fry food, such as Interpet's *Liquifry* for egg-layers.

Remove the now aerobic bacteria cultured Polyfilter from the community aquarium and put it into the bottom of the breeding tank, taking care to keep the air flow level high enough to ensure good circulation of the aquarium water, which avoids stratification and areas of anaerobic bacteria forming around the bottom of the tank – the place where the fry spend most of their early life.

Begin slowly to increase the water level in the breeding tank, taking about two weeks to bring the level to full capacity. At this stage, the fry are very susceptible to poor water quality, so a ten percent partial water change – using treated water of course – should be done every other day, and the Polyfilter kept clean.

Feeding

The fry of livebearers are capable of taking larger portions of food right from the beginning. They do, however, very much appreciate brine shrimp nauplii, and will stuff themselves silly with them. But if messing around with brine shrimp sounds like too much hassle, there are several commercial feeds for both egg-laying and livebearer fish fry, which come in liquid and powder form. Follow the feeding instructions on the packet closely for best results. As the fry grow change their food accordingly, gradually moving on to larger sizes and different types.

Some Final Thoughts On Fish Breeding

Record Keeping

Keep complete records of all your attempts at breeding; this makes success repeatable or, in the event of a failure, you can compare future efforts to find out what went wrong. If you're breeding with a view to selling the resulting fry, then records are essential, as a dealer may want to see them so that he or she can keep a check on quality. When dealing with rare or difficult-to-breed species, then your records could well be the *only* existing information about that species' reproduction process available to Ichthyologists (fish scientists).

BABS

There is a newly established association for fish breeders, called *The British Aquarist Breeders Society* (BABS), which has been set up to promote the captive breeding of aquarium fish. At the moment membership is free but, by the time this book has been published, there will almost certainly be a fee. As they're issuing a newsletter and membership forms, someone will have to pay for this. Their address is on page 194, along with all the other useful addresses.

Number Of Eggs

The number and size of eggs produced in a spawning is a good guide to the parental behaviour of the brood stock. Where thousands of eggs are produced, the species are likely to be egg-eaters and poor parents. On the other hand, where eggs are few, then the parents are more likely to take good care of eggs and fry.

Where numerous eggs are produced in a spawning, the mortality rate is high, therefore nature is ensuring that at least some will survive to grow into adult fish. In the wild, not all the eggs are expected to survive – indeed, if they did then over-population would quickly result. But within the controlled environment of a breeding tank, the potential for survival is very much greater; especially when active steps are taken to avoid disease and egg-predation.

As an example: suppose that, from a spawning of 2000 eggs at least half survive and develop into fry. Of the resulting 1000 fry, around 3 fishes (if you're lucky) will go on to become first-class specimens. Now, the problem is, apart from our 3 prime fishes, what are we going to do with the other 997?

Culling Fish

Deliberately killing fish (for whatever reason) is a very emotive subject, with opinions tending to polarise into 'never under any circumstances' at one end, and 'okay when there's no hope of recovery' at the other. I'm not going to debate the ethics of euthanasia here; I'm far more concerned that, should you find it necessary to kill a fish, you know how to do it in a humane way. Some aquarists advocate a swift, sharp blow to the head (of the fish; *not* other aquarists who disagree with them!), or even separating the fish's head entirely from its body! It's distressing enough to have to dispatch a fish in the first place without having to dismember it as well!

Doctor Neville Carrington in his excellent book *Maintaining A Healthy Aquarium* (see Bibliography, Appendix 1), advocates placing the (doomed) fish onto a bed of ice cubes and then putting the whole funeral pyre into a deep freeze. However, some eminent aquarists disagree with this method. At least one advocates dropping the doomed fish into a pan of boiling water, which is said to kill the fish instantaneously. Severing the spine just behind the head is also said to produces a similar effect. I can't, in all honesty, recommend any particular method. I usually take the coward's way out, and let natural selection cull unwanted fry. At least it adds variety to the diet of the fishes!

At Least Once

Finally, every aquarist should make at least one attempt to breed successfully a species of tropical fish. The learning/education potential from such an exercise will not only teach you much about the lives of fish, it will also hone to perfection your aquatic management skills. As I've already explained, you don't have to spend a lot of money on breeding – there's much you can do using equipment you already possess. Why not give it a go? You could find yourself involved in something totally absorbing.

Chapter 9
The Aquarist

This chapter deals with aquarists as people, the range of their activities and the special organisations and events which they are involved in. Sharing your hobby with others not only adds further dimensions to it, you also get to meet lots of very nice people as well!

No matter how strong your initial motivation, nor how well you're doing with your aquatic hobby, there will come a time when you wish that you had someone to share your interest with. You may have had a resounding success when breeding a particular species, and be dying to tell someone about it. On the other hand you could have a problem which is killing your fishes, and, having tried all the usual methods of treatment, be at a loss as to what to try next.

An Offer You Can't Refuse?

The aquarist club or society could well be the place which fulfils all these needs for you. At 'The Club' you're going to meet people just like you: fishkeepers. People who care for fishes for no other reason than they enjoy what they're doing. But first, let's explode one or two myths about club life. You don't have to be an 'expert' to join one. In fact, clubs were created in the first place for exactly the opposite reason – to bring together people who wanted to learn more about the art of fishkeeping. 'You have to own thousands of pounds' worth of aquatic equipment before they'll let you join.' Ha! If you'd seen some of the 'aquariums' I've seen in use by various club members you'd quickly realise just how silly this is.

Containers ranging from large glass pharmaceutical distilling bottles, lined terracotta plant pots, right up to twelve-foot tanks with their sub-gravel heating pipework plumbed directly into the domestic central heating system – all have been photographed by me at some stage. Some aquarists even have fish tanks! While it's true to say that there are many knowledgeable aquarists within any society or club, in my experience they are only too willing to pass on their expertise, especially to beginners.

Although you can learn a lot from books, especially this one, in the early stages there is absolutely no substitute for real and practical experience. With beginners, what tends to happen is that they are initially interested in almost everything aquatic. Then, once they have solved most of the early problems associated with tropical fishkeeping, especially within the community tank, they begin to explore new areas. Maybe a new breed of fish, setting up a breeding program, creating a single species aquarium, water gardening or even marine fishkeeping. In other words, they feel the urge to specialise. At the local aquatic club you'll find at least one – and probably many more – 'experts' on all these areas. Whatever problem you're currently experiencing, it's a safe bet that some club member has already suffered the same thing, and has a cheap, workable solution.

Not Only But Also

So, apart from meeting like-minded people, what else can the local club offer? Most clubs and societies organise a series of talks – often by members who're expert in a particular aspect of fishkeeping – and lectures, covering items such as the research and development department of an aquatic manufacturer, or the breeding of various specific fishes, given by a nationally acknowledged expert. These talks are often given by a visiting lecturer who sometimes has to travel great distances, and often uses a wide range of opto–electronic presentation devices, such as slide/sound dioramas, videos, 16mm film shows and, of course, many practical demonstrations.

Some aquatic books (not this one, of course) can be very expensive indeed. Another benefit of belonging to a club is that they quite often have an excellent library. Some clubs make a small nominal charge for borrowing, while others are free. Societies also organise many social events, such as friendly (and often hilariously funny) club quizzes, visits to places of interest, such as local dealers, public aquaria – both in this country and in Europe – and, last but by no means least, the famous Fish Shows!

The Fish Show

Just as the local trials riding motorcyclist, or Go-Carting club, is the place where a newcomer learns the rules and the practice of motor racing, where he or she pays her dues; so the tyro fishkeeper learns the requirements of the fish show at club level. You may well think that your 15cm (6in) *Plecostomus* catfish is a mighty impressive specimen. That is, until you 'bench' it next to a 40cm (16in) specimen! Club fish shows are usually of a 'lower' standard than an open or national show. I'm not running down the local club show; it's just that, with open or national shows, people will be bringing fishes from all over the country, rather than from just around the corner, so obviously the standards are going to be that much higher. Often, clubs organise inter-club fish shows with a nearby aquatic society, and many offer some splendid looking trophies for success in the various classes of competition, which tend to look very

Close-up of the head of a Discus fish.

A male Swordtail and male Dwarf gourami swim together in perfect harmony within the community tank.

impressive indeed perched atop the TV set – the trophies that is – not the fishes!

There is a strict set of rules regarding fish shows – both club, open and national – and these are fully explained later. Furthermore, competitions don't just revolve around who's brought the biggest fish to the show. There are many categories of competition, such as aqua-scaping, furnished aquaria, best of a specific breed, best fish in show, breeding teams (fish: *not* man and wife!), aquatic plant displays, and the often controversial tableaux displays.

The Show

The basic idea is that you take along your fish (to the village hall?) and enter it into a specific section, such as guppies, or discus. You arrive, set up your showing tank and put the fish into it (benching), and are given an exhibitor number, which is the only information about you the judges will have. Then you must leave the hall, as must all the other exhibitors while the judging takes place. Now, and for the next three hours or so, you must find something to do. After the judging, exhibitors are allowed back into the hall, where the 'Place Card', showing whether or not your fish has won something, is eagerly looked for. All in all, a pretty boring kind of day! Especially as the bigger the show, the longer the judging will take.

Leader Board

A total of 100 points is awarded in five separate categories, consisting of a maximum of 20 points per category. Each fish starts with the maximum of 100 points. Then, as each category is judged (see below), points are deducted. When all five categories have been judged, the total remaining points are added up which gives your prized exhibit its final score.

Poor fish will score overall around 30–40 points – which in reality means 'why did you bother bringing it?' A top-class fish will score in the high 80s; while the average is around 50–60 points for the 'also-rans'. My personal highest? 77 for second place with an enormous (in my view!) Opaline gourami.

The Scoring System

There is a maximum of 20 points available for the Overall Size of the fish. The nearer to its maximum size (as laid down in the rules for that particular species) the fish is, then the fewer points will be deducted from the initial 20. Growing a fish to a third, or even half, of its full potential is relatively easy to do. But it does take real aquatic skill and good feeding/care to grow the fish on to its full adult size.

Body Shape scores another maximum of 20 points. Your benched fish will be compared to what a perfect example of that species should look like. Any variance from the standard – such as humps, bumps, lumps or even thumps! will lose your fish points. The fins are judged, and this can be a tricky area for a newcomer. Obviously, the fish must have all of the fins it's supposed to have, but fin judging goes deeper than this. The size and shape of the fins are compared to 'The Standard'.

There should be colour or striations (lines) where they should be, and none where they shouldn't. Again, a 'standard perfect model' of the fish in question is used for comparison purposes. Where there is colour in fins, then it has to be clear and vivid, not diffuse and smudgy – unless of course, the 'perfect model' has smudgy colours. And when you've got all that right, the way your fish displays his/her fins to the judges will be very important. Certain fish are expected to hold their fins in a particular position. If they don't, then you lose points. Any male Siamese fighter which opens its dorsal, anal and caudal fins wide, turns to face the judges and gives them a slow, shy smile, followed by a knowing wink will score an easy 20!

Colour is judged by comparing it to 'The Standard' for that species, which does include most known variations and sub-species. It should be evenly distributed and clearly delineated. Where there is more than one colour on the fish, then the separate areas should be clearly defined, without the colours 'bleeding' into each other. Colour should only appear on the correct places, and not where there shouldn't be any. So a fish with a pink dorsal fin which should have either a deep red, or even a clear fin, will lose points. Again, the nearer the fish's colour scheme is to the perfect model, then the less points it will lose.

Unfortunately, there is the a certain 'win-at-all-costs' element within the aquatic hobby. Fish can be fed special colour-enhancing feeds prior to a show, or given hormone drugs which activate the fish's reproductive urge (colours heighten when the fish is ready to spawn). Some fish have even been directly injected with colour dyes in an effort to boost their natural colour! Thankfully, most fish show judges are well aware of these dirty tricks, and have ways and means of discovering them, and disqualifying the exhibitor. Show judges are even immune to bribery and large infusions of alcohol; believe me: I know!

Condition is obviously important. Your fish has to look its best on show day, so conquering the trauma of transportation to the show is vital to success. Never take an obviously sick fish to a show. It is infuriating for another aquarist to see someone's fish in distress, while the owner is oblivious. Your fish should ideally be posing within its show tank when the judges approach it. They should be impressed with your fish, which should look as if it's just completed the whole of the *Charles Atlas* body-building course. It should look *lean, keen and mean*!, and absolutely bursting with good health and vigour, as it bombs around the show tank, flexing its muscles.

Finally, Overall Demeanour – the way your fish presents itself in the show tank on the bench during judging. If it's lying on the bottom of the tank, fins curled and with a sulky expression on its face, then you will lose points heavily. If its fins are held erect, and it swims serenely up and down the show tank smiling benignly at the judges, then you'll lose fewer points.

Totting-Up

To obtain the best possible balance with what is, with all due respect to any show judges reading this, a very subjective opinion of the condition of your fish, more than one judge is usually used at a fish show. Each judge has a scoring sheet and will view all the fishes (or only the categories they've been invited to judge) and record the points awarded. At the end of judging, they all put their heads together, and total up the score cards. Usually, first, second and third places are awarded at smaller shows; while larger ones will have a fourth and fifth, as well as a 'Highly Commended' category.

Transporting Fish To The Show

Just as almost no one loses a fish when transporting it from the dealer to their home, very few manage to lose a fish while taking it to a show; although naturally, special precautions have to be taken. The biggest problem is always heat loss and oxygen deficiency of the water in which the fishes are being transported. Local shows don't present too many problems; it's the national open or county shows where the troubles can start.

The first thing to ensure is that, whatever container is used for transportation, be it a glass toffee-jar, or custom-designed and watertight travelling aquarium, only water taken from the same tank as the fish is used to fill it. Leave an airspace at the top, and then pack the container inside a polystyrene box, to conserve heat. You will also need another container which holds more of the same aquarium water: this will be used to either top up the display aquarium, or even entirely replace that used in travelling, as well as providing water for the journey home. Keep this water several degrees above normal tank temperature.

A 'Hot' Cool Box

'Cool Boxes', used to keep food and drink cool for picnics or freezer shopping etc. work just as effectively in reverse; the same way that a thermos flask keeps liquids either hot or cold (how does it know which is which?). Packing them with heat-retaining parcels (eg. hot water bottles) will keep containers of aquarium water in the 'Cool Box' hot, or at least warm, for a surprisingly long time.

Once at the show, water will be provided for

your use but, as its chemical nature is unknown, it's best avoided. Battery operated air pumps and airstones can be used prior to judging taking place, to give the water some additional aeration. Similarly, 12 volt heating elements can be used to control the temperature of the aquarium water. There are numerous other 'tricks-of-the-trade' which most ardent fish exhibitors know and use. They are not difficult to learn: simply keep your eyes open, and watch closely.

To Show Or Not To Show?

Many aquarists are baffled by this need for aquarists to compete against each other; and I must admit, having tried it first, I'm now one of them. But, just as greyhound dog owners, racing pigeon fanciers, or even horse owners feel the need to find out exactly who has the fastest dog, pigeon or horse, I suppose it's human nature to see who has the best fish. Even if you don't hold with fish shows they are well worth a visit, just to see what goes on there. In any case, don't knock it until you've tried it first.

National Organisations

Once having taken the decision to specialise in a certain aspect or family within fishkeeping, the aquarist can find him/herself rather starved of specific information. There are a some national organisations which support particular species of fish. For example, there are associations and societies which support: catfishes, cichlids, anabantids, livebearers, Killifish and discus. There are also coldwater societies, for goldfish, and Koi carp. In short, there are not many breeds or families of fishes which aren't represented in some way by a specialist organisation. Addresses are listed in Appendix 3.

The Disabled Fishkeeper's Association?

During my research for the writing of this book one glaring omission has come to light. As fishkeeping is a fairly static hobby, with most of the activity taking place in and around the home, it would present an ideal hobby for a disabled or housebound person. Yet there seems to be no specific organisation in existence to take care of their specialised needs. Maybe there's a disabled person living near you who would benefit from becoming a fellow fishkeeper? Surely it is time that this oversight was rectified, and as soon as possible. In does seem a crying shame that the one class of people who are in the best possible position fully to appreciate the soothing beauty of a fully equipped aquarium should be missing out!

For example, I am myself a wheelchair user, although not yet permanently confined to one. I am often 'housebound' for long periods at a time, so consequently, 'nipping down to the shop' is not an option I often have. Neither is going along to a local club, who somehow always seem to meet 'upstairs'! However, when I can, I do! I have to do most of my 'aquatic' shopping (as I do most other shopping) by mail order.

By the way, for anyone in a similar situation, I've found that the range of products, the prices, attention to detail, prompt delivery and extraordinary kindness shown to me by the *Aquamail* company, purely as an ordinary customer, and *not* as a special service for an author writing a book about fishkeeping, of which they were unaware, simply has not (cannot?) be beaten! Send for their free catalogue, which is not just a simple list of items they sell but also has many very informative text sections which explain exactly what a product is and what it does.

Being A Club Member

Even a complete beginner has much to offer any local aquatic society or club. New blood is always welcome and, as the committee is likely to have been *in situ* for many a year, they are always looking for new ideas. As with life in general, the more you contribute then the more you'll get from your membership. You will find your local club by writing directly (enclosing a self-stamped and addressed envelope) to The British Federation Of Aquatic Societies, or the Association of Aquarists – both addresses in Appendix 3.

Finally

If you're a newcomer to fishkeeping, then welcome to a hobby which will grip and hold your attention for the rest of your life. Everyday, some new facet of the hobby opens up, intrigues you and demands further investigation.

I'm no expert: after all, an expert is simply someone who gets to know more and more about less and less until they know everything about nothing! After thirty-odd years as a fishkeeper even now new things, concepts and theories are always being formulated in my mind. I'm always planning the *Ultimate Tank*. Luckily I have a very understanding wife, who doesn't mind my occasional bursts of feverish aquatic activity. Enjoy your fishes – I certainly couldn't contemplate life without mine. One day I hope we can meet and 'talk fish'.

Chapter 10
Database Of Community Fishes

As I said before, when creating a community aquarium it is not simply enough to ensure that the occupants won't actually kill each other. Fishes in the community tank have to get by on a live-and-let-live basis, where the needs of one species do not, and will not, conflict with the others. Each species must pursue their every-day lives without fear or stress. That doesn't mean that if you choose examples from my list you'll never have any problems. Even notoriously peaceful fish can become quite vicious around breeding time! Some fishes should be kept only in small shoals of around four to six: others most definitely on their own. Where this is the case I have clearly said so.

The following fishes, although not represent-ing anything wildly exotic, are all very easy to keep without making any chemical changes (other than dechlorination and conditioning etc.) to your basic tapwater. The species I've detailed here are those which you are most likely to find on sale at your local shop. I know that some aquarists like 'big fish', and I've included a range of sizes and fishes so that there will be activity throughout all levels of the water, from the surface to the substrate. However, big fish need special care, as you will read in the database section.

Some aquarists may raise the odd eyebrow at the exclusion of certain species. This deletion is based on my personal experience and represent fish which have wrecked havoc in my tanks in the past. You may have better luck than I, and may even be able to find your Coolie loach again; or even persuade your Tiger barbs to stop mugging the gouramis!

Cichlids

As almost all cichlids require special aquascaping conditions, and are notoriously territorial, I firmly believe that they have no place within a community aquarium. Ah controversy! By all means construct a species tank, purely for them, where water conditions and tank decor can be so arranged for their specific needs: but this so often directly conflicts with the concept and practice of the community aquarium.

As previously said elsewhere, these are my own views and opinions, at least one cichlid expert has already taken me to task regarding my views on cichlids! But before choosing *any* species of fish, whatever family it belongs to, you must read as much as possible about that fish *before* buying one. The one thing you must never do in fishkeeping is to get this the wrong way around, such as buying a fish, whose name you don't even understand, never mind what type of water it prefers, and what should it be eating.

Due to space restrictions I've had to limit the information about the species listed here to the absolute minimum. What you have to do is learn more about them – such as borrowing from a library, or buying one of the books recommended in the Bibliography (Appendix 1).

An Easy Community Tank

(Plate numbers refer to colour section between pages 50 and 51)

Name: Siamese Fighting Fish – *Betta splendens*
Plates 1 and 2
Family: Anabantidae - Labyrinth Fishes
Country/ies: South/East Asia
Size: 75mm (3″).
Sexual Differences: males are larger and have longer fins and more colour
Water: not critical
Temp: 22-27 C
Position: all levels/surface feeder
Food: not critical
Plants: many soft-to-hard water, acid-to-alkaline, + surface species
Breeding: easy; egg-laying bubble nester, male nest care
Notes: Only one male should be kept per tank or they will fight to the death. Keep with two/three females.

Name: Suckermouth Catfish – *Hypostomus sp.*
Plate 3
Family: Loricariidae
Country/ies: South America
Size: dwarf species (3″) up to giants of 60cm. (24″)
Sexual Differences: none known
Water: not critical
Temp: 22–26 C
Position: firmly attached by the mouth to any part of the aquarium!
Food: has purpose designed under-slung, toothed mouth for algae rasping from rocks etc, when all algae has been cleared will need heavy input of greenery
Plants: has been known to destroy plants by sucking off their algae content
Breeding: not known to have been bred in captivity
Notes: A nocturnal fish which tends to keep the substrate very clean. Even though some grow fairly large they're not known for bothering other fish.

Name: Dwarf Gourami – *Colisa lalia*
Plate 4
Family: Anabantidae
Country/ies: Northern India

Size: 50mm (2″)
Sexual Differences: male much more brightly coloured than female
Water: not critical
Temp: 20–27 C
Position: all levels/surface feeder
Food: not critical
Plants: many soft-to-hard water, acid-to-alkaline, + surface species
Breeding: easy; egg-laying bubble nester, male nest care, high fry mortality rate
Notes: Very shy. Keep as male/two female pair, or male can be aggressive. Iridescent bars of blue/red makes this one of the most beautiful of aquarium fishes.

Name: Pearl/Lace Gourami – *Trichogaster leeri*
Plate 5
Family: Anabantidae
Country/ies: Thailand, Sumatra, Malaysia
Size: 150mm (6″)
Sexual Differences: male has longer, more pointed dorsal fin (female's is more rounded), male develops deep red throat in spawning condition
Water: not critical
Temp: 22–26 C
Position: all levels/surface feeder
Food: not critical
Plants: many soft-to-hard water, acid-to-alkaline + surface species
Breeding: easy; egg-laying bubble nester, male nest care
Notes: Mature males have deep red throat. Takes a while to reach maturity.

Name: Three-spot Gourami – *Trichogaster trichopterus*
Plate 6
Family: Anabantidae
Country/ies: Indo-China, Malaysia, Burma, Indonesia
Size: 130mm (5″)
Sexual Differences: longer, more pointed dorsal fin in male, female more rounded abdomen
Water: not critical
Temp: 20–26 C

Position: all levels/surface feeder
Food: not critical
Plants: many soft-to-hard water, acid-to-alkaline + surface species
Breeding: easy; egg-laying bubble nester, male nest care
Notes: Best kept as male/female pairs with other fish own size. Can bully smaller species. Gets its name from two black spots on flanks with the eye forming the third spot. Needs plenty of plant cover.

Sub-Species: Opaline Gourami – body colour mottled blue/black – no 'three spots'. Conditions as for *Three-Spot*.
Plate 7.

Name: Corydorus Catfish – *Corydorus paleatus*
Plate 8
Family: Callichthyidae
Country/ies: Brazil
Size: 60mm (6") male, female grows larger
Sexual Differences: viewing from above, female is broader than male just behind the pectoral fins, females often larger than males
Water: not critical
Temp: 22–26 C
Position: bottom dwelling catfish
Food: scavenges from bottom of tank, appreciates live foods but don't leave it to eat leftovers, use fast-sinking pellets to reach them
Plants: needs areas of clear substrate to root into, usual aquatic plants
Breeding: easy egg-layer, female collects fertilised eggs and deposits them on glass, rocks or leaves for hatching, raise temperature to 26 C to initiate breeding
Notes: Numerous species of Corydoras catfish, so identification of species difficult for beginner. Usually shy when first introduced. Has endearing habit of rolling its eyes when laying on gravel. A firm favourite with many aquarists.

Name: Beacon, or Head/Tail Light Fish – *Hemigrammus ocellifer*
Plate 9
Family: Characidae

Country/ies: South America
Size: 45mm (1.8")
Sexual Differences: female has the more rounded mid-body shape
Water: not critical
Temp: 20–27 C
Position: top-to mid-water swimmer
Food: usual diet of flake + live etc, (not a fussy eater)
Plants: almost any aquatic plants, but fine-leaved floating varieties give some protection to fry
Breeding: has been successfully bred, but not easy, egg scatterers
Notes: Best bought as a shoal of six, where natural partnerships can form.

Name: Guppy – *Poecilia reticulata*
Plate 10
Family: Poecilidae
Country/ies: Northern South America,
Size: 30mm (1.2")
Sexual Differences: male has modified anal fin (gonopodium), is smaller and more colourful than the larger female
Water: not critical
Temp: 18–28 C
Position: top to mid-water swimmer
Food: usual diet of flake + live etc, (not a fussy eater)
Plants: almost any aquatic plants, but fine-leaved floating varieties give some protection to fry
Breeding: you gotta be kidding! livebearer
Notes: Serious line breeders will have to segregate the sexes as quickly as possible. Makes a colourful shoal display for a kiddies'tank. A very tough and tolerant fish which is usually offered as the *sacrificial* first occupant of a new aquarium.

Name: Black Molly – *Poecilia sphenops*
Plate 11
Family: Poecilidae
Country/ies: North/South America
Size: 70mm (2.8") male – females larger
Sexual Differences: as for all livebearers (male's gonopodium)

Water: not critical, but if kept in a species-only tank they prefer slightly brackish water, add 1 level teaspoon of sea-salt per five gallons *but not* if they're to be kept in a community aquarium
Temp: 20–26 C
Position: top swimmer
Food: all types, likes a lot of greenery
Plants: the more the better – likes to browse upon them
Breeding: easy livebearer, but female *does not like* to be placed within a breeding trap – can cause miscarriages
Notes: Many marbled, albino and coloured varieties now appearing. Lyretail version particularly attractive.

Name: Sailfin Molly – *Poecilia velifera*
Plate 12
Family: Poecilidae
Country/ies: Yucatan (Mexico)
Size: 130mm (5″)
Sexual Differences: usual livebearer gonopodium plus extremely large dorsal fin on the male (from which it gets its common name)
Water: slightly hard and alkaline, although is (can be) adaptable to tolerate soft/acid
Temp: 22–26 C
Position: all levels
Food: all types – prefers some greenery
Plants: medium-to-hard water types
Breeding: easy livebearer
Notes: Keeping more than one male per tank can cause trouble as they will fight over any females present.

Name: Platy & Platy sp. – *Xiphophorus maculatus/var*
Plate 13
Family: Poecilidae
Country/ies: Mexico/Guatemala
Size: 40mm (1.5″)
Sexual Differences: usual livebearer differences, females larger and less well coloured than males
Water: not critical
Temp: 17–27 C
Position: all levels
Food: all types – appreciates live food

Plants: almost any aquatic plants, but fine-leaved floating varieties give some protection to fry
Breeding: easy livebearer
Notes: Likes a well planted aquarium with plenty of free swimming space. Many varieties now, some especially beautiful, such as Gold Dusted var.

Name: Swordtail – *Xiphophorus helleri*
Plate 14
Family: Poecilidae
Country/ies: Mexico
Size: 100mm (4″) male, 110mm (4.3″) female
Sexual Differences: usual livebearer differences, base of male's caudal fin developed into a long sword-like spike, from which species gets its common name, females have normally developed caudal fin
Water: not critical
Temp: 17–26 C
Position: all levels
Food: all types
Plants: almost any aquatic plants, but fine-leaved, tall-growing varieties give some protection to fry
Breeding: easy livebearer
Notes: Usually a peaceful breed, can be aggressive with smaller fishes. Again there are numerous colour versions of this fish around. Interestingly, if there are no males present in a shoal, then one (or more) of the females will change sex to ensure the survival of the species!

Name: White Cloud Mountain Minnow – *Tanichthys albonubes*
Plate 15
Family: Cyprinidae
Country/ies: China, Indonesia
Size: 50mm (2″), female larger
Sexual Differences: males more brightly coloured than females
Water: not critical – not a real tropical species
Temp: 14–22 C
Position: occupies all levels but feeds at the surface
Food: all types

Plants: almost any aquatic plants, but fine-leaved varieties give some protection to fry
Breeding: easy, egg-scatterer
Notes: A nice and easy community fish, especially when kept as a shoal. Prefers cooler temperatures, but a shoal of eight have lived happily in one of my aquaria for around nine months now, at a temperature of 24 degrees C.

Name: Zebra Danio – *Brachydanio rerio*
Plate 16
Family: Cyprinidae
Country/ies: India
Size: 50mm (2″) male, female larger
Sexual Differences: female more rounded around the ventral area
Water: not critical, but prefers medium-hard, slightly alkaline pH
Temp: 18–27 C
Position: surface feeder, will occupy all levels
Food: all food, but likes live foods
Plants: almost any aquatic plants, but must have space to swim around, often at high speed!
Breeding: easy egg-layers
Notes: Best kept as a shoal of six–eight, allowing natural pairing. Likes a current of water to play in, such as the output from a power filter.

Name: Black Widow – *Gymnocorymbus ternetzi*
Plate 17
Family: Characidae
Country/ies: South America
Size: 60mm (2.5″) male, females larger
Sexual Differences: females larger than the males
Water: not critical
Temp: 22–26 C
Position: mid-water swimmer
Food: all types
Plants: almost any aquatic plants
Breeding: easy, egg-scatterer – interesting courtship dance
Notes: Easy community fish. Black coloration fades with age and when stressed

Name: Silver Dollar – *Mylossoma argenteum (Metynnis roosevelti)*
Plate 18
Family: Characidae
Country/ies: South America
Size: 150mm (10″?) male, females even larger!
Sexual Differences: none known
Water: not critical
Temp: 22–28 C
Position: mid-water swimmer
Food: mostly herbivorous, needs lots and lots of greenery in their diet or they'll eat the aquarium plants, especially Amazon swords, Vallis and Sagittaria – can decimate a tank in two days!
Plants: almost any aquatic plants, but try to avoid those they like to eat!
Breeding: nothing known
Notes: Easy shy, and peaceful fish. Although they grow very large – I've personally seen some well over 200mm (8″) – they rarely bother other fish. This is a fish which will grow and grow, so be warned! *do not* keep them (buy them in at least pairs) in a small (less than 90cm (36″) aquarium. I like them because they do grow big but still remain shy and retiring. Lovely, friendly fishes

Name: Bleeding Heart Tetra – *Hyphessobrycon sp.*
Plate 19
Family: Characidae
Country/ies: South America, Guyana
Size: average of 50mm (2″) for most species
Sexual Differences: females usually larger with smaller and duller fin coloration
Water: not critical, unless attempting to breed (see later)
Temp: 22–26 C
Position: middle – to bottom swimmer
Food: all types, prefers live and green foods
Plants: Tetras prefer well planted aquaria
Breeding: moderately easy egg-layers, must have soft, acid water for proper fertilisation of eggs
Notes: Very peaceful and shy community species, best bought as a shoal of six to twelve, depending on tank size.

Community Fish Requiring Greater Care From The Aquarist

Name: Neon Tetra – *Paracheirodon innesi*
Plate 20
Family: Characidae
Country/ies: South America
Size: 40mm (1.5″)
Sexual Differences: females are plumper
Water: soft, acid. pH < 7 ideally – again is, and has been, adapted to medium-hard, neutral-to-alkaline pH water
Temp: 22–25 C
Position: middle – to bottom swimmer
Food: all types, appreciates live food
Plants: Amazon swords, Vallisneria and other, soft-water species
Breeding: difficult egg-layer. water softness and pH must be right
Notes: Best kept as a shoal of a dozen., and preferably not with piscivores (fish eaters).

Name: Angelfish – *Pterophyllum scalare*
Plate 21
Family: Cichlidae (*yes, I know it's a cichlid, but it's the one fish nearly all beginners must have!*)
Country/ies: Amazon River System (South America)
Size: 130mm (6″)+
Sexual Differences: very difficult – sometimes even they don't know! As a guide, the one which lays the eggs is the female! Sometimes a natural pairing occurs, but this is by no means infallible. If you're really interested in breeding Angels seriously, buy a shoal of around a dozen and let them pair-off naturally
Water: not critical, unless attempting to breed them (see later)
Temp: 22–26 C
Position: occupies top to middle layers, avoiding the bottom of the tank

Food: all types but appreciates live foods, such as small fishes!
Plants: usual Amazonian specimens – especially broad-leafed varieties (see breeding)
Breeding: fairly easy, egg depositor with parental care? Lays around 1000 eggs, usually on leaves of Amazon sword plants, aquarium glass or rockwork. Eggs will not hatch if pH > 7. Both notorious egg-eaters, and good parents are rare. Need to remove parents on completion of spawning and provide light aeration around the site of the eggs (in my opinion)
Notes: This has to be the favourite aquarium fish, known the world over. Can be kept in the community tanks when small, but can look decidedly raggy if water chemistry is not to their liking.

Name: Tiger Barb – *Barbus tetrazona*
Plate 22
Family: Cyprinidae
Country/ies: Malaya, Sumatra, Borneo, Thailand, Burma
Size: 50mm (2″) – females larger
Sexual Differences: male more colourful, female larger and duller
Water: adaptable from fairly soft to moderately hard, pH 6.7–7.8
Temp: 19–27 C
Position: middle to bottom swimmer
Food: all types, appreciates live food
Plants: well planted aquaria with free swimming space
Breeding: easy egg scatterer, around 3–500 eggs, fry feed ravenously!
Notes: Best kept in a shoal, where a strong pecking order will quickly develop. Note that this species are inveterate fin-nippers, and can make smaller species' lives a misery! Keeping them in a shoal reduces their attempts at mugging the other fishes in the community aquarium.

Chapter 11
Database of Aquatic Plants

Aquatic Plants – General Information

An aquarium without plants is exactly like a house minus furniture. Of course, there are some types of tank where establishing plants is very difficult (but not impossible), such as certain cichlid aquaria and, in particular, a cold-water goldfish tank. From Chapter Four, *Aquatic Plants*, you'll remember that aquatic plants do so much more than merely look pretty. In a 60× 30×30cm (24×12×12in) aquarium I usually average around fifty specimens. Some aquarists (indeed, many actually do) claim that this is far too many, and can cause CO_2 poisoning of the fishes. In three decades of keeping heavily planted aquaria this has never happened to me yet!

Types Of Plants

Aquatic plants may be broadly separated into two main groups. The *Calcicolous* types, which require water rich in calcium, and therefore need moderate-to-hard water conditions. And the *Calcifugous* types, which prefer water free from, or a very low calcium content, which in practice usually means soft water. Obviously mixing the two types will create problems for the tyro hydroculturist, but remember that plants which consume amounts of calcium will have an eventual softening effect on the hardness of the water. So when such plants begin to suffer, and start looking a little ragged, it may well be due to a calcium deficiency. Dead leaves from *Calcicolous* plants release the calcium they've acquired back into the water, so the more quickly they're removed from the aquarium the better.

Calcicolous plants include: *Vallisneria*, *Elodea*, *Sagittaria* and *Myriophylum*. *Calcifugous* species include: *Cabomba*, the various *Cryptocorynes*, *Echinodorus* species and *Marsilea*. The Aquatic Plant Database includes basic information on: temperature requirements, the eventual fully-grown height, water and lighting conditions, and the best position for each plant within the aquascape. Apart from dealing with a specialist supplier of aquatic plants (details in Appendix 3), your local aquarist shop isn't likely to keep a wide stock range; although they should keep the most common types.

Aquatic Plant Database

(Plate numbers refer to colour section between pages 50 and 51)

Name: *Acorus gramineus* (Japanese Dwarf Rush)
Plate 23
Height: > 25cm (10″)
Lighting: not fussy
Water: not fussy – pH 6–7
Temp-range: 20–25 C
Propagation: divide the rhizome
Position: background and foreground display
Notes: A relatively slow growing marginal species which prefers to grow emerse.

Name: *Aponogeton sp.* (various leaf types)
Plate 24
Height: < 40cm > 70cm (16″–28″)
Lighting: moderate-to-bright
Water: not fussy

Temp-range: 16–24 C
Propagation: seeding, rhizome division (although some varieties haven't yet been successfully propagated in home aquaria)
Position: background or as single specimen in the foreground
Notes: A slow-growing species which may take some time to establish. ALL *Aponogeton* species are 'seasonal' – they have a growing, and then a resting state, before recommencing growth again. Once settled, moving them usually causes the leaves to die. But given time they will grow back again. These plants seem to do very well when planted in pots. Most commonly available species are *Aponogeton crispus* (illustrated), and *Aponogeton undulatus*

Name: *Bacopa var* (Bacopa)
Plate 25
Height: > 30cm (12″)
Lighting: loves bright lights
Water: slightly hard – pH 6.5–8
Temp-range: 15–26 C
Propagation: by cuttings
Position: foreground, in small clumps, or background in larger bunches
Notes: Not a true aquatic plant, but actually grows better submerged. Varieties involve leaf size and colour.

Name: *Cabomba aquatica* (Green Cabomba)
Plate 26
Height: > 2.5 metres (8 feet!) unless regularly pruned back
Lighting: loves bright light, too much makes for truly rampant, but spindly growth
Water: not fussy – pH not fussy
Temp-range: 13–25 C
Propagation: take cuttings around 15cm (6″) up from stem, re-plant as a bunch
Position: superb background camouflage for heater/stats, airlift tubes etc, very fast growing
Notes: Slight problem with the very fine leaves which are prone to collect any floating debris in the tank. However, they do provide excellent cover for the fry of livebearers which will insist on spawning in the community tank.

Name: *Synema triflorum (Hygrophila difformis)* (Water Wisteria)
Plate 27
Height: > 50cm (20″)
Lighting: loves bright light
Water: not fussy – pH not fussy
Temp-range: not < than 20 C
Propagation: cuttings
Position: background and corner filler
Notes: Bear in mind the minimum temperature requirements. Fast growing species which will soon take-over your tank if your domestic water supply contains an amount of calcium.

Name: *Elodea densa* (Canadian Pondweed)
Plate 28
Height: 300cm (10 feet!)
Lighting: bright
Water: medium-hard – pH 6.5–8.5
Temp-range: 10–26 C
Propagation: by cuttings
Position: background, corner filler, or small foreground display
Notes: Needs drastic pruning. Some varieties will need gradual adaptation to coldwater aquaria. Again, too much, or too strong lighting can produce 'forced', spindly growth.

Name: *Myriophyllum* (Water Milfoil)
Plate 29
Height: > 40cm (16″)
Lighting: bright
Water: moderately-hard – pH 6.8–8
Temp-range: 15–25 C
Propagation: by cuttings, strip off lower leaves before re-planting
Position: background and display clumps
Notes: Needs regular pruning to retain shape and curtail excess growth. Fine leaves can collect any floating debris in tank, so water needs to be well mechanically filtered. Provides excellent cover for livebearer fry.

Name: *Eleocharis acicularis* (Hairgrass)
Plate 30
Height: > 15cm (6″)
Lighting: bright
Water: not fussy – pH 6.5–7.3

Temp-range: 18–25 C
Propagation: by runners
Position: foreground – where it will eventually develop a thick, grass coloured carpet
Notes: This beautiful grass-like bog plant, which really does well submerged, is very suitable as a repository for the eggs of certain egg-laying species. Also makes for a very attractive foreground substrate covering. Does particularly well when planted in a substrate additive, such as *Everite*, or *Aquasoil*.

Name: *Limnophila aquatica* (Ambulia)
Plate 31
Height: 50cm (20″)
Lighting: bright
Water: not fussy – pH 6–7.5
Temp-range: 22–26 C
Propagation: by cuttings, leave at least 15cm (6″) of stem with bottom leaves removed
Position: background, and as camouflage for heaters and pipes etc., plant as display bunches at sides of foreground
Notes: Its lovely golden colour makes this plant many aquarists' favourite. Can run riot, so prune regularly. Will grow out of the tank, flower and seed if permitted.

Name: *Ludwigia natans* (Ludwigia var.)
Plate 32
Height: > 40cm (16″)
Lighting: bright
Water: soft-to-hard – pH 6.5–7.5
Temp-range: 16–25 C
Propagation: by cuttings, by seed-pods if allowed to grow emerse
Position: nice mid-ground display in clumps
Notes: Again a marginal plant which some aquarists find difficult as it can soon rot if it doesn't 'take' to your water chemistry/substrate. Many varieties of Ludwigia are now available, with a selection of leaf shape and colouring. Doesn't appreciate too high a temperature.

Name: *Echinodorus sp.* (Amazon Sword Plants)
Plates 33 and 34
Height: *E. cordifolius* 60cm (24″), *E. major* 50cm

(20″), *E. paniculatus* 30cm (29″), *E. tenellus* > 15cm (6″)
Lighting: adaptable, but *not* dim
Water: not fussy – pH 6.5–7.8, although natural habitat is soft, acid waters, and will obviously do best in these conditions
Temp-range: 20–26 C
Propagation: by very prolific runner system, substrate additives help with establishment and propagation, as does a tablet fertiliser pushed into the substrate next to the plant
Position: specimen mid-ground display, nice foreground specimen display- (*E. tenellus* – Pygmy Chain Sword) when planted in small clumps
Notes: Many varieties with prolific leaf shapes, ranging from entire, lanceolate, egg-shaped and linear. *Echinodorus tenellus* in particular quickly establishes a foreground carpet of linear-shaped leaves, acting as an excellent spawning medium for egg-scatterers.

Name: *Sagittaria sp.* (Sagittaria var.)
Plate 35
Height: *S. platyphylla* > 40cm (16″), *S. subulata* > 15cm. (6″)
Lighting: very bright < 1600 lux
Water: not fussy – pH 6.5–7.5
Temp-range: 15–25 C
Propagation: by runners, produces tubers in special circumstances
Position: background or mid-ground specimen display
Notes: This Vallisneria-type species is a very prolific feeder; so *S. platyphilla* specimens are best planted in their own hydroculture pots with an iron or fertiliser enriched compost. *S. subulata*, the smaller species, makes a good mid-ground display, but again does much better with a substrate enriched.

Name: *Vallisneria sp.* (Vallisneria var.)
Plates 36 and 37
Height: *V. spiralis* 20cm (8″), *V. tortifolia* 60cm (24″)
Lighting: bright
Water: not fussy – pH not fussy, but is really a

hard water plant and will do best in this type of water, especially if (like me) you like to make a mini-forest of Vallis at the back of the tank, to cover the hardware

Temp-range: 15–30 C

Propagation: by very prolific runners

Position: *V. tortifolia* makes an ideal back glass cover plant, and is particularly suited to deeper aquaria, where its maximum size can be realised. In smaller aquaria *V. tortifolia* tends to lay flat on the surface. *V. spiralis* more suited to average (30cm / 12″) deep aquaria

Notes: *Vallisneria spiralis* has unusual spiralled linear leaves, and is often more popular than the *V. tortifolia*, or *V. gigantica*; although all have a useful place in any aquarium. It is vital with any *Vallis* species that the crown of the plant is not buried beneath the substrate or the plant will quickly rot away.

Name: *Vesicularia dubyana* (Java Moss)

Plate 38

Height: not applicable – plant is a moss-like growth

Lighting: subdued – shaded positions, however, in brighter light the usual dark brown coloration may change to a much lighter green

Water: not critical – pH 6.5–7

Temp-range: Not < than 24 C

Propagation: pull off small clump from parent plant and relocate

Position: attaches itself to aquarium decorations, such as rockwork, bogwood etc, makes such items look truly aquatic

Notes: Some aquarists find difficulty growing Java Moss due to their aquarium lighting levels. May need some initial help, such as an elastic band to assist it getting a 'foothold'. Once established, the elastic band can be removed.

Name: *Hydrocotyle vulgaris* (Pennywort)

Plate 39

Height: 75mm (3″)

Lighting: bright

Water: not fussy – pH not fussy

Temp-range: 15–26 C

Propagation: by runners

Position: an undemanding foreground plant with multi-branched fine leaves, makes an excellent display in small clumps

Notes: Can often benefit from substrate additives

* Note. All plant specimens for the photographs were supplied by *The Tropical Plantation*

These fifteen plants represent the most common in the hobby. Of course, there are numerous other plants to choose from. There is an excellent book listed in the Bibliography (Appendix 1) *An Interpet Guide to Aquarium Plants* which explains much more about aquatic plants than I've had the space for here, plus a far greater range of specimens.

Choice Of Plants

When thinking of buying aquatic plants from a shop, as many inexperienced (and others, who should know better) often do, be very careful. A good aquatic dealer will have a 'waterfall' arrangement, where a steady stream of clean water is continuously passing over the plants. Other dealers simply dump the various species into trays, where a steady accumulation of dirt, 'foreign bodies' and other contaminents can make these plants very difficult to get started.

Most dedicated aquarists insist on dealing either directly with an aquatic nursery (much cheaper, better quality plants), or with the local aquatic club or society, where the specimens offered are usually of the highest possible quality, and either ridiculously cheap or even free.

Although there aren't any great fortunes to be made by amateur fish breeders, aquatic plant husbandry – especially of the more rarer species – is a different pot of compost altogether! If you approach the subject seriously, you could find yourself supplying many dealers directly, as well as amateur aquarists. As many aquatic nurseries import their plants directly from abroad, they'll be more than a little interested in a *constant and reliable* supply of first-class specimens, even of the most common types.

Chapter 12
Database Of Fish Diseases

An Active Approach To Fish Health

During the past ten years or so, the way aquarists' have been responding to sickness in their fishes has been quite revolutionary. Previously, many fishkeepers merely reacted to disease which they felt sure would soon appear. That is to say, they would wait until symptoms of ill health appeared, and then attempt diagnosis and treatment. As with human disease, this was seen (and has subsequently been proven) to be an entirely negative approach which, far from keeping aquarium stock in good health, actually encourages disease to develop.

Of course this sweeping generalisation fails to take into account the large numbers of dedicated and caring aquarists who have always taken active prevention measures, prior to the 1980s. And so to them: well done, and please accept my profuse apologies. The emphasis today is entirely on health rather than disease: an active rather than a reactive approach. If you can stop your fish (or even yourself) getting ill in the first place then there's nothing to diagnose or cure! This book has continually advocated a policy of heading-off trouble before it appears, by taking into consideration everything which affects the fishes. From the quality of their aquatic environment, the 'goodness' of the air surrounding the location of the aquarium, to the food they eat; each is but a part of a synergistic whole for the fishes.

Fishes – just like us – continually carry around with them a whole range of parasites, bacteria and various other bugs. While they remain in good health, through careful management of their environment and a sensible, balanced diet; their general level of good health ensures that their body's natural immune system will cope and even ignore them.

It is only when the fishes' general health deteriorates (for whatever reason) that any bugs they happen to be carrying around with them can begin to fight, and often overcome the fishes' own immune system, and they fall victim to disease. To reiterate and reinforce this rather vital point: if you can keep your fish healthy, by a regular regime of good aquarium management and correct feeding, then they will have more than enough resistance to fight-off most of the 'weaker' diseases they may be already carrying, or come into contact with. However, no matter how healthy your fishes, there are some parasitic infestations, such as White Spot and other diseases that even a fighting-fit fish may fall victim to.

But?

As a newcomer to the aquatic hobby, good water management, balanced diet etc. are skills you still have to learn. Books help (at least I hope this one does!), but there just isn't any substitute at all for old fashioned, everyday fishkeeping experience. And unfortunately, the only person who can give you this is Old Father Time himself. I really do wish it was otherwise, but it isn't. So, things will go wrong, and at some time in the future your fishes are going to be ill.

Caveat

As you've already accepted complete responsibility for their daily lives by becoming an aquarist in the first place, it is up to you to help the fishes recover from illness. The rest of this chapter explains how to deal with the most common sicknesses and diseases your community fishes are likely to suffer from. Now; I'm no veterinarian, so if you're expecting to find a cure here for anything your fish may fall victim to, then you're going to be disappointed. There are some superb books written by more knowledgeable people than me about fish disease; such as Dr Neville Carrington's excellent book, *Maintaining A Healthy Aquarium*, and the superb (and free) chart of fish diseases from the Interpet, Tetra and the Aquarian companies. There's a list of fish disease and treatment books in the Bibliography, Appendix 1.

What you will find here – and please do remember, this book is entitled *The TROPICAL Fishkeeper's Handbook* – are the symptoms of the more common tropical fish diseases and how to treat them. In almost every case I've recommended various manufacturers' own specific remedies. This isn't a cop-out by me; nor do I receive any commission (I only wish I did!) for mentioning specific products. (Neither is it a lack of subject knowledge!)

British veterinary practitioners have been quite worried about some of the chemicals and antibiotics openly available to aquarists, and have demanded (and are going to get) much tighter control over the dispensing of such items. In effect this is going to remove certain chemicals and medicaments, which many older aquarists' have been using safely and to good effect for eons, from open sale. The only future source of such chemicals (apart from the vets themselves, more of which in a while) is going to be the aquatic manufacturers. And the only form you'll get them in will be as specific aquatic remedies such as Aquarian's No.8 *Whitespot* cure.

Cause Of Illness

Before going on to explain the more common fish ailments it might be a good idea to examine how and where a fish can become diseased. The most obvious place is the aquarium water, and that's why I'm so vehemently opposed to adding any water from 'unknown' sources, such as when buying fish, or bags of live *Daphnia*, *Tubifex* etc. Any single item from the following list can stress a fish, reducing its ability to shrug-off what may initially be a minor irritation. It goes without saying that the more items on the list which are allowed to 'go wrong' then the more certain it will be that your fish will become ill.

Feeding

Vitamin deficiencies caused by a monotonous

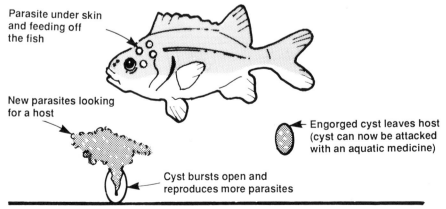

Parasite under skin and feeding off the fish

New parasites looking for a host

Engorged cyst leaves host (cyst can now be attacked with an aquatic medicine)

Cyst bursts open and reproduces more parasites

Figure 12.1   The life cycle of the White Spot parasite.

diet of a single type of food can deplete the fish's natural store of protein, carbohydrate and fats, reducing the effectiveness of its own immunity system. Over-feeding will pollute the water – especially when using certain foods such as live or meat-based products – which encourage the formation of harmful bacteria. Poor feeding may cause: vitamin deficiency, emaciation, and make the fish more susceptible to bacterial infections, such as fin rot, and the highly virulent mouth fungus.

Water Quality

Having already dealt extensively with this subject I'll just recap by listing those things you should guard against. Avoid any rapid changes in: pH, hardness, temperature, O_2, CO_2, $NH_{3/4}$, NO_2 and NO_3 levels. The operative word is *rapid*; gradual changes of these items are taking place all the time within the aquarium, and the fishes respond to them well. But fast changes leave little time for the fishes to adjust. Poor water quality itself doesn't directly cause parasitic or bacterial infestations, but the conditions within such water are ideal for these organisms to proliferate, and render the fish more liable to this type of sickness.

Should any parasite or fungus spore enter your dirty aquarium water – such as through the introduction of a new fish – then this will be exactly just the right conditions for them to replicate themselves, and infect everything in the tank.

Aquatic Management

The importance of a thorough and regular maintenance schedule has been explained. A chemical filter which hasn't had the medium renewed for some time can suddenly dump the accumulated ammonia etc. back into the water with consequently disastrous results to the fishes. Similarly, with an external canister-type power filter, replacing all the biological media at the same time will wipe out all the colonies of

aerobic bacteria, leaving your tank facing the possibility of New Tank Syndrome.

Filter floss should be carefully rinsed and replaced, to preserve the bacteria content, *but not at the same time as any special biological foams!* Apart from replacing the chemical media, external canister power filters, like an undergravel filter bed should be disturbed as little as possible. Remember the rule? *Never change anything unless it really has to be changed!*

Stocking

Over-stocking causes many problems. There's the extra amount of pollution your filtration system probably wasn't designed to cope with, a higher effluent output from the fishes, even larger amounts of food dumped into the water by the aquarist, and possible anti-social behaviour as each species fights for territory. New acquisitions are always a favourite entry point for various fish diseases. Even a specimen which appears perfectly healthy in the dealer's tank may be carrying a latent infection; hence the importance of a quarantine tank.

Diagnosis

How can you tell that a fish is indeed genuinely ill rather than merely 'having a bad day'? The two key elements of successful disease treatment (whether fish or human!) are: correct diagnosis and speed of response. But; a fast response doesn't simply mean that you reach for the nearest bottle of medicine and dump it into the tank! (see *Medication*, later.) Having enjoyed watching your fishes on a daily basis (if not, why are you keeping them?), then you'll have become familiar with their behaviour pattern – the way they take their food, their usual cruising area, their swimming attitude and respiration rate etc. So, your first indication of a possible health problem will be abnormal behaviour, something the fish doesn't usually do, such as not feeding, or an increased respiration rate. This isn't a diagnosis, this is simply a first step which is alerting you to a possible problem.

Having identified that one (or more) of your fishes is behaving abnormally, the next stage is to watch it closely. Is there something it is repeatedly doing, such as rubbing against a rock or side of the tank. Has it refused to eat on more than one occasion. Are there any strange protuberances, blemishes, cotton wool-like growths, spots or any other odd-looking bits attached to the fish which are not usually present. Are the fish's eyes clear? Just like your doctor, begin compiling a list of symptoms; but don't take weeks!

Medication

Each commercially available specific remedy is designed to contain the right 'ingredients' for that particular problem. The remedy will not only contain a dosage chart but also a checklist of symptoms so that you can confirm your own initial diagnosis. In addition, your chosen remedy, in many cases, will also warn you which other types of aquatic medication you should avoid using while the present one is active, and what other steps you should take – such as removing a carbon or biological filter from the aquarium, raising the tank temperature or adding extra aeration. Obviously, the recommended dosage must be strictly adhered to.

Various aquatic medicaments.

Adding an extra amount will not cure the fishes any faster and may well kill them.

Aquarium Capacity

It often amazes me how many aquarists don't know the capacity of their aquaria! Tanks are often bought on a 'Oh yes; that'll just fit into the corner by the fireplace!' basis. And the only clue to its capacity is, 'It takes simply ages to fill it up!'

Before the correct dosage of any aquatic medicament can be safely added to an aquarium, the tank capacity *simply has to be known!* Fortunately this is very simple to work out. Measure the length, depth and width of the aquarium – in centimetres – and then multiply them together. Divide the answer by 1000 to get the volume in litres. If the guide is using UK gallons (they usually use both litres and UK gallons), then further multiply litres by .22 to get the volume in these units. You may prefer to work in gallons anyway. And for American aquarists, multiply UK gallons by 1.2 to obtain the aquarium capacity in US gallons. So our 60× 30×30cm (24×12×12 inch) demonstration tank has a capacity of 54 litres or approximately 12 English gallons, or 14.4 US gallons.

We now have to deduct around ten percent of the water's volume for aquarium decorations, such as roots, plants, sunken pirate ships, rocks and the substrate. Therefore, if we must add 2.5 millilitres of *Whitespot* cure for every 10 litres (2.2 gallons) of aquarium water for a correct dose; we have 54 litres less 10 percent, which gives 54 minus 5.4 = 48.6 litres. Dividing 48.6 by 10 gives 4.86: and 4.86 times 2.5 means that we need to add 12 millilitres of *Whitespot* cure to our 60×30×30 cm aquarium as the correct dose. Easy isn't it? If you found that hard going, then read it again and work it through on paper.

The Hospital Aquarium

I know that I've already landed you with the cost of the main community aquarium and advocated setting up breeding and quarantine

A hospital tank set-up.

Example of a quarantine tank.

aquarian® AQUARIUM FISH

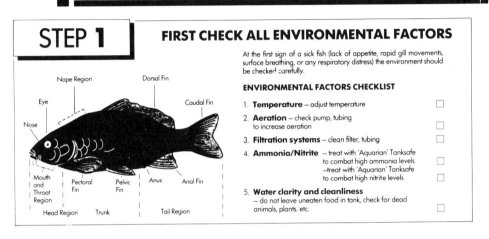

| STEP 1 | FIRST CHECK ALL ENVIRONMENTAL FACTORS |

At the first sign of a sick fish (lack of appetite, rapid gill movements, surface breathing, or any respiratory distress) the environment should be checked carefully.

ENVIRONMENTAL FACTORS CHECKLIST

1. **Temperature** – adjust temperature ☐
2. **Aeration** – check pump, tubing to increase aeration ☐
3. **Filtration systems** – clean filter, tubing ☐
4. **Ammonia/Nitrite** – treat with 'Aquarian' Tanksafe to combat high ammonia levels ☐
   – treat with 'Aquarian' Tanksafe to combat high nitrite levels ☐
5. **Water clarity and cleanliness** – do not leave uneaten food in tank, check for dead animals, plants. etc. ☐

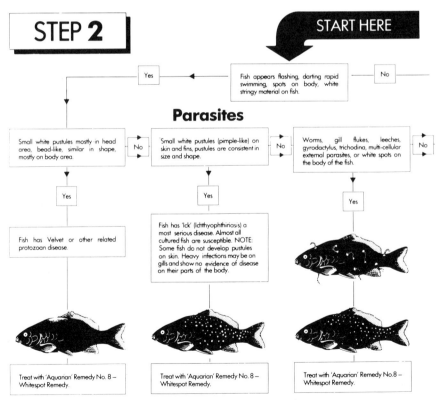

Figure 12.2 Aquarian's disease diagnosis and treatment chart (*reproduced courtesy of Aquarian*).

DISEASE GUIDE

Published by the 'Aquarian' Advisory Service
Thomas's (A Division of Mars GB Ltd.),
Oakwell Way, Birstall, Batley, West Yorkshire WF17 9LU
© Copyright Pedigree Petfoods 1989 'R'. Registered Trade Mark

AQUARIUM WATER CAPACITY CHART

NB: Figures allow 10% for gravel etc. in furnished aquaria.

WIDTH:	12" (30cm)			15"(38cm)			18"(45cm)		
HEIGHT:	12" (30cm)	15" (38cm)	18" (45cm)	12" (30cm)	15" (38cm)	18" (45cm)	12" (30cm)	15" (38cm)	18" (45cm)
12" (30cm)	5.3 galls 24 litres	6.6 galls 30 litres	7.9 galls 36 litres	6.6 galls 30 litres	8.6 galls 39 litres	10.0 galls 46 litres	7.9 galls 36 litres	10.0 galls 46 litres	11.9 galls 54 litres
18" (45cm)	7.9 galls 36 litres	10.0 galls 46 litres	11.9 galls 54 litres	10.0 galls 46 litres	12.8 galls 58 litres	15 galls 68 litres	11.9 galls 54 litres	15 galls 68 litres	18 galls 82 litres
24" (60cm)	10.6 galls 48 litres	13.4 galls 61 litres	16 galls 73 litres	13.4 galls 61 litres	17 galls 77 litres	20 galls 92 litres	16 galls 73 litres	20 galls 92 litres	24 galls 109 litres
30" (76cm)	13.4 galls 61 litres	17.2 galls 78 litres	20 galls 92 litres	17.2 galls 78 litres	21.8 galls 99 litres	25.7 galls 117 litres	20 galls 92 litres	25.7 galls 117 litres	29.5 galls 134 litres
36" (90cm)	16 galls 73 litres	20.5 galls 93 litres	24 galls 109 litres	20.5 galls 93 litres	25.7 galls 117 litres	29.5 galls 134 litres	24 galls 109 litres	29.5 galls 134 litres	36.3 galls 185 litres
48" (122cm)	21.8 galls 99 litres	27.5 galls 125 litres	32.6 galls 148 litres	27.5 galls 125 litres	34.8 galls 158 litres	41 galls 187 litres	32.6 galls 148 litres	41 galls 187 litres	49 galls 222 litres
60" (152cm)	27 galls 123 litres	34.3 galls 156 litres	40.6 galls 185 litres	34.3 galls 156 litres	43.6 galls 198 litres	51.5 galls 234 litres	40.6 galls 185 litres	51.5 galls 234 litres	60.7 galls 276 litres
72" (183cm)	32.6 galls 148 litres	41 galls 187 litres	49 galls 222 litres	41 galls 187 litres	52.4 galls 238 litres	62 galls 282 litres	49 galls 222 litres	62 galls 282 litres	73.3 galls 333 litres

LENGTH OF TANK

ANSWER EACH STATEMENT 'YES' OR 'NO' FOLLOWING
THE ARROWS. WHEN YOUR FISH'S SYMPTOMS MATCH
THOSE ON THE CHART TREAT AS INDICATED.

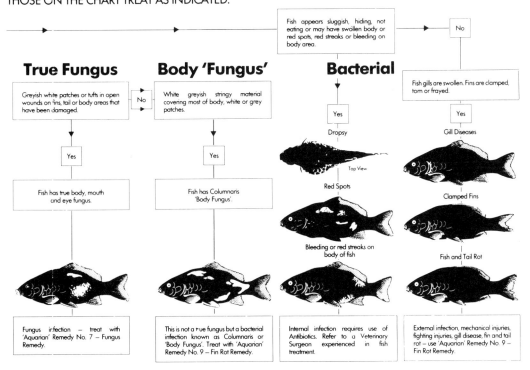

Fish appears sluggish, hiding, not eating or may have swollen body or red spots, red streaks or bleeding on body area.

No

True Fungus

Greyish white patches or tufts in open wounds on fins, tail or body areas that have been damaged.

No

Yes

Fish has true body, mouth and eye fungus.

Fungus infection – treat with 'Aquarian' Remedy No. 7 – Fungus Remedy.

Body 'Fungus'

White greyish stringy material covering most of body, white or grey patches.

Yes

Fish has Columnaris 'Body Fungus'.

This is not a true fungus but a bacterial infection known as Columnaris or 'Body Fungus'. Treat with 'Aquarian' Remedy No. 9 – Fin Rot Remedy.

Bacterial

Yes

Dropsy

Top View

Red Spots

Bleeding or red streaks on body of fish

Internal infection requires use of Antibiotics. Refer to a Veterinary Surgeon experienced in fish treatment.

Fish gills are swollen. Fins are clamped, torn or frayed.

Yes

Gill Diseases

Clamped Fins

Fish and Tail Rot

External infection, mechanical injuries, fighting injuries, gill disease, fin and tail rot – use 'Aquarian' Remedy No. 9 – Fin Rot Remedy.

tanks. So, you can safely reckon that if I'm exhorting you to set up yet another aquarium then it's for a very good reason indeed. In fact, you can sometimes combine the hospital tank with a quarantine tank, just as long as you thoroughly scrub and disinfect each incarnation of tank before switching its usage.

Unless there are special circumstances, it's not a good idea to place aquatic medicaments into the community tank, and treat all the fish irrespective of whether they're ill or not. Exceptions to this are outbreaks of diseases which affect all of the fish, such as *Ichthyophthiriasis* (White Spot).

The hospital tank is simply a stripped-down aquarium which provides the basics, such as heating and filtration (more of which in a moment). Lighting should be quite dim – just enough to allow you to see what's going on – and there should be no substrate, which can act as a hiding place for various flukes, worms, parasites and bacteria. Real plants won't be much good either, as certain types of medicament will only kill them anyway. But the fish will still need somewhere to hide until it begins to feel better, so provide a few plastic plants and some sunken terracotta pots for this purpose. When a fish becomes ill it may also become a target for attack by other species in the community aquarium. Removing the sick fish to a hospital tank – even if you don't actually add anything medicinal to the water – can bring about that fish's recovery.

The type of filter to be used in the hospital tank really depends on what the medication recommends. Certain chemicals, such as Methylene Blue, will destroy the bacteria in a biological filter, as well as being absorbed by an activated carbon chemical filter. In such a case, a small box filter, filled with Zeolite, will remove ammonia, breaking the Nitrogen Reduction Cycle in the first stage. The ideal filter system for a hospital aquarium is a well colonised biological foam filter. If this has to be removed then it's no problem. But if you have to add one – well, you know now that it'll take a week or so for the

bacteria to form, so if you need it now. . . . Chemical filters can be prepared quickly and easily, and swapped for the foam if and when required.

The Vet

A few years ago any thought an aquarist may have had about taking a sick fish to a vet was quickly discarded when fishkeepers, in general, realised that the veterinarian's subject knowledge was more than likely to be no greater than their own. So it was likely to cost them cash to find out what they already knew – their fish was ill!

Now things are a whole lot better. Some vets actually specialise in treating fish disease. And, as very soon you'll only be able to get certain broad spectrum antibiotics through a vet's medicinal prescription anyway, trips to their surgeries are likely to be a much more common occurrence than they used to be. If you need to find a local vet who does deal with fish, contact the British Veterinary Association – address in Appendix 3 – who will provide you with a list of such vets.

The Most Common Tropical Fish Disease

Of course there are numerous diseases a fish may potentially suffer from. Here I've confined myself to the one which will affect almost everyone at some time. Figure 12.2 – reproduced by kind permission of the Aquarian company – lists the most common fish diseases, their symptoms and their (Aquarian's) cures. There is little point in me simply rewriting what has already been superbly covered by people much better qualified than I, on the subject of fish disease, its diagnosis and treatment. And this would add nothing new to the subject. Therefore I direct readers with a further interest in this subject to the Bibliography, Appendix 1.

White Spot – *Ichthyophthirius multifiliis*

Symptoms

Fish is covered with tiny, pin-prick like white spots which first seem to show up on fins before appearing on the rest of the body. Note that this parasitic infection can, and often does attach itself to the fishes' gill system, and can cause severe respiratory distress and even death.

Treatment

Any proprietary White Spot cure. Follow the instructions very closely. As all the fish in the tank are more than likely to become infected, treating the whole aquarium is the best method. From Figure 12.1, you will note that the parasite cannot be killed while attached to the host, only when it reaches the free swimming stage.

Once the white spots have disappeared from their fishes many aquarists' believe that a cure has been effected, and that consequently the problem is at an end. *This is not so*! It is the beginning of the end, for only at this stage can the *Whitespot* cure begin to work effectively. What a shame then, that many aquarists remove the cure from the tank at this time by changing the water, only to be amazed when the white spots reappear a few week's later! Again, simply follow the instructions which come with the cure!

Finally

Most fish illnesses are mainly due to poor water conditions – such as over-feeding – which encourages the formation of harmful bacteria. Imagine being stuck behind an old lorry in a ten-mile traffic jam on the M1 motorway, and having to breathe diesel exhaust fumes for hours! That's just how the fish feel in dirty water. Finally, the other major cause of fish illness is – exactly as in humans – stress. Stress caused by poor water conditions, osmotic shock, poor diet or constantly fluctuating aquarium temperature. Just like us, fishes have 'off days'. Days when they feel grumpy, tired or even fed-up. At this point, the worst possible thing you, as an aquarist, can do is to start dumping chemicals into the water.

Most commercial medicaments are pretty harmless *on their own*! But when you start dumping a little of this, a pinch of that – and just a soupçon of that pretty green liquid; well, just about anything is likely to happen, and sorting out the resulting mess will be impossible. The golden rule with medicaments is: get your diagnosis confirmed (by using any of the books listed in the Bibliography, or use Aquarian's chart) and then add just the appropriate cure *only*, taking great care to use the correct dose and to follow the maker's instructions exactly. Remember: every drug ever made has some form of side effects; even aspirin!

APPENDICES

Appendix 1
Bibliography

Caveat Emptor

Buying books on fishes can be a very expensive business. I can particularly recommend the Salamander and Interpet books for sheer value for money. They are packed with information and cost around £5 each. Beware of books on fish which have been *edited* by someone. You have no idea of who, or even how many authors have been involved, nor how current the information is. It could well have been assembled from books written back in the 1960s.

Freshwater Life by John Clegg, Hon F.L.S. ISBN 0 7232 1762 0. Published by Frederick Warne & CO Ltd. Latest edition 1974.

River Plants by S.M. Haslam. ISBN 0 521 21493 9 (hardback) or ISBN 0 521 29172 0 (softback). Published by Cambridge University Press. Latest edition 1987.

The New York Aquarium Book of the Water World by William Bridges. ISBN 8281 0089 6 (hardback). Published by New York Zoological Society, American Heritage Press, New York. Latest edition 1970.

Freshwater Biology by L.G. Willoughby, D.Sc. ISBN 0 09 125430 2 (hardback) Published by Hutchinson & CO (Publishers) Ltd. Latest edition 1976.

Life in Lakes and Rivers, by T.T. Macan, M.A. PH.D. and E.B. Worthington, M.A. PH.D. ISBN 0 00 219459 7. Published by Collins. Latest edition 1974.

Strasburger's Textbook of Botany (various authors, including Eduard Strasburger). ISBN 0 582 44169 2. Published by Longman Group Ltd. Latest edition 1980, (30th edition).

Plant Mineral Nutrition by E.J. Hewitt, Ph.D., D.Sc., A.K.C., F.I.Biol. and T.A. Smith, Ph.D., M.I.Biol. ISBN 0 340 18498 1 (hardback). Published by The English University Press Ltd. Latest edition 1975.

Biochemistry of Photosynthesis by R.P.F. Gregory. ISBN 0 471 32676 3. Published by John Wiley & Sons – a Wily-Interscience Publication.

How Fishes Live by Dr Peter Whitehead. ISBN 0 86136 895 9 (hardback). Published by Galley Press. Latest edition 1977.

Plant Anatomy by A. Fhan – Professor of Botany, The Hebrew University, Jerusalem, Israel. Last edition 1967! (hardback). Published by Pergamon Press Ltd. 4/5 Fitzroy Square London W1.

Popular Tropical Fish for Your Aquarium edited by Cliff Harrison. ISBN 0 572 01162 8 Published by W. Foulsham & Co. Ltd.

You & Your Aquarium by Dick Mills. ISBN 0 86318 362 X. Published by Dorling Kindersley, London.

The Complete Home Aquarium by Hans J Mayland. ISBN 0 7063 5179 7. (hardback). Published by Ward Lock Limited, London.

Complete Book of Tropical Fish edited by Keith Sagar. ISBN 0 86178 581 9 (hardback). Published in 1989 by Cathay Books, Michelin House, 81 Fulham Road, London. SW3 6RB.

Salamander's *FISHKEEPER'S GUIDE* books

The Tropical Aquarium by Dick Mills. ISBN 0 86101 119 8 (hardback). Published by Salamander Books, London.

Community Fishes by Dick Mills. ISBN 0 86101 124 4 (hardback). Published by Salamander Books, London.

Interpet's *AN INTERPET GUIDE TO* books

Aquarium Plants by Barry James. ISBN 0 86101 207 0 (hardback). Published by Interpet.

Maintaining a Healthy Aquarium by Dr Neville Carrington Ph.D. ISBN 0 86101 235 6 (hardback). Published by Interpet.

Fish Breeding by Dr Chris Andrews Ph.D. ISBN 0 86101 209 7 (hardback). Published by Interpet.

Monthly Magazines

There are currently three magazines dedicated to fishkeepers in the UK which can be bought from any newsagent. These are:
Practical Fishkeeping (PFK).
Aquarist and Pondkeeper.
Aquarium.

Appendix 2
Useful Formulae

Conversion Formula

Centimetres-To-Inches.   Multiply by 0.40
Inches-To-centimetres.   Multiply by 2.54
Litres-To-UK-Gallons.   Multiply by 0.22
UK-Gallons-To-Litres.   Multiply by 4.56
UK Gallons-To-US-Galls.   Multiply by 1.20
Volume = length × breadth × depth / 1000 (answer in Litres).
Surface Area. length × breadth (answers in cm.^{2} or ins.^{2} depending.)
Kilograms-To-Pounds.   Multiply by 2.2
Pounds-To-Kilograms.   Multiply by 0.453.
There are 144 square inches to the square foot.

Aquarium Lighting Requirements

Allow 10 watts of fluorescent lighting per square foot, unplanted aquaria.

Allow 15 watts of fluorescent lighting per square foot, planted aquaria. Ignore tank depth for tropical fishkeeping!

Aquarium Heating

First, calculate VOLUME of aquarium in UK gallons. Then multiply by 7.5 for a tank in a heated room; or multiply by 10 for tanks in an unheated room. For example, a 24×12×12 inch tank holds 12 gallons × 7.5 (heated room) gives a heater requirement of 90 watts – with the nearest in the range being 100 watts. Therefore for this size tanks requires a 100 watt heater.

The same sized tank in an unheated room requires 12×10+120 watts; again with the nearest size in the range being 150 watts.

Substrate Requirements

Allow 10 litres of gravel/sand for every 900 cm^2 (1 ft^2) of floor area. 1 litre of (average) gravel weighs 1.5Kg (3.5lb).

Fish Stocking Formula

Allow 2.5cm (1in) of fish length (excluding the tail fin) for every 75cm^2 (12in^2) of surface area. Ammonia = NH_3 : Ammonium = NH_4 : Nitrite = NO_2 : Nitrate = NO_3 : Oxygen = O_2

Water Hardness

GH 0–4 = Very Soft.
GH 2–15 = Medium-Soft
GH 12> = Hard water.

Calcium Carbonate CaCO$_3$

mg/l of CaCO$_3$/ DH degrees hardness.
0–50   /   3 = soft water.
50–100   /   3–6 = moderately soft.
100–200   /   6–12 = slightly hard.
200–300   /   12–18 = moderately hard.
300–450   /   18–25 = hard.
> 450   /   > 25 = very hard.

Aquarium Capacity

Length × height × width (in inches) × 6.25 = Imperial gallons (less 10% for contents).
Length × height × width (in centimetres) /1000 = Litres (less 10%).

Fahrenheit-To-Celsius

$°F = (°F–32) × 5 / 9$

Celsius-To-Fahrenheit

$°F = (°C × 9 / 5) + 32$

Useful Addresses

Aquarian Advice Service. PO Box 67, Elland, West Yorkshire. HX5 0SJ. Free advice service. Need an SASE.

Aquamail. Tynwald Mills, St. Johns. Isle Of Man. 0624–801849.

Superpets. 203–209 Gateford Road, Worksop, Nottinghamshire. 0602–472967

Ocean Aquatics. 167 Sunbridge Road, Bradford. West Yorkshire. BD1 2HB. 0274–370892. Aquatic plant nursery.

The Tropical Plantation. 1033 Bolton Road, Bradford. West Yorkshire. BD2 4BU. 0274–626315. Specialist aquatic nursery and retail shop.

Seaside Aquatics. 0934–627607. Specialist aquatic nursery.

Rolf C Hagen (UK) Ltd. California Drive, Whitwood Industrial Estate, Castleford. West Yorkshire. WF10 5QH. 0977–556622

JMC Aquatics Ltd. 59 Stubley Lane, Dronfield, Sheffield. S18 6PG. 0246–415275/410412.

Interpet Ltd. Vincent Lane, Dorking, Surrey. RH4 3YX. 0306–881033.

Hockney Engineers Ltd. Unit 7: Mabgate Mills, Mabgate, Leeds. LS9 7DZ. 0532–455061. Manufacturers of Complete Biosphere Aquaria.

International Aquatic Centre. 126–128 West Bar, Sheffield. S3 8PN. 0724–756767.

Medcalf Brothers. Cranbourne Road, Potters Bar, Herts. EN6 3JN. 0707–56925. Makers of 'Hy-Flo' piston air pumps.

King British. Haycliffe Lane, Bradford. West Yorkshire. BD5 9ET. 0274–573551.

NT Laboratories Ltd. Unit 3: Branbrdiges Industrial Estate, East Peckham, Tonbridge, Kent. TN12 5HF. 0622–871387. Chemical test kits etc.

Sera (UK) Ltd. 32 Mermaid Court, London. SE16.

Top Up Aquatics. Elizabeth Street, Congleton, Cheshire. CW12 4DJ. 0260–875144. Retail & mail order shop.

Tetra Information Centre. Lambert Court, Chesnut Avenue, Eastleigh. Hants. SO5 3ZQ. 0703–643339.

British Aquarist Breeders Society (BABS). C/O Peter Muchamore. 16 Grasmere Close, North Watford. Herts. WD2 7JH. (Large SASE needed).

The Catfish Association Of Great Britain. C/O Gina Sandford. 5 Sparrows Mead, Redhill. Surrey. RH1 2EJ.

British Cichlid Association. B.C.A. 5 Winding Shot, Hemel Hempstead. Herts. HP1 3QQ. £2.50p for sample pack of literature.

British Killifish Association. C/O A. Burge (Dept AP), 14 Hubbard Close, Wymondham, Norfolk. NR18 0DU. Send 30p SASE for information.

The Association Of Aquarists. C/O Dave Davis. 2 Telephone Road, Portsmouth. Hants. SASE for information. (Offers individual membership as well as clubs and societies.)

Federation Of British Aquatic Societies. 46 Airthrie Road, Goodmayes, Ilford. Essex. IG3 9QU. SASE for information.

Rocon. 5A Penyrorsedd Industrial Estate, Llangefni, Anglesey, Gwynedd LL77 7JA, 0248–750 134

Anabantoid Association Of Great Britain. (Yorkshire branch) C/O Ms. C.J. Clark. 19 Alder Grove, Balby, Doncaster. South Yorkshire. DN4 8RF. SASE for information.

Appendix 4
Fishes and Plant Index

Fishes and Plant Index

Appendix 5
Miscellaneous Information

After my last book, I was asked by numerous people, who're interested in such things, what equipment I used to write the book. So for all budding authors everywhere, this is what I used to create *The Tropical Fishkeeper's Handbook*. I do not personally endorse any of the equipment mentioned – it's just what I happened to be using at the time. Next time I may use something else.

All the photographic plates where taken using Canon 35mm SLR cameras. Most of the colour transparencies were taken using a T90 and a Tamron 35–80mm F2.8 Macro zoom, with the Speedlight 300TL complete with 'off-the-camera' Sync leads providing the main illumination, and two slave heads (not easy in a shop!). Black and white photographs were taken using a Canon A1 with a Vivitar Series 1 28–200mm F3.5 Macro Superzoom, a series of flashheads and flashmeter.

Monochrome filmstock was Ilford FP4+ rated at 200 ISO and developed for 7.5 minutes in a 1:9 solution of Paterson's *Acutol*. The resulting 10×8″ prints were processed in a Nova Deep Tank Processor, which I found to be superb for my style of working.

Colour transparency film was a little strange to say the least. In the main, 30 metres of Konica transparency film, which was bought outdated in 1986, and kept in cryogenic suspension (deep frozen) until April 1991, was used. The film was allowed to cold thaw for a week, and then allowed to reach room temperature over the next ten days. Its original ISO was 100. A test film indicated that the period of suspended animation had deprived the stock of one third of a stop, meaning that it should have been rated at ISO 64. However, as I always under-expose transparency film by one-third of a stop anyway, for better colour saturation, I exposed the film at ISO 100, and processed via the normal E6 chemistry without any adjustment to the First Developer stage.

The words were crunched using a much modified Amstrad PCW 8256, using *Locoscript 2* version 2.28b and *Locofile*. The manuscript was actually written partly at home, but mostly in hospital. where I used a Cambridge Computers Z88 lap-top computer. Text files were 'modemed' home to the PCW 8256, which uses a WS4000PCW auto-answering modem and some specially written software by me, which captured the incoming *Kermit* 1200 Baud ASCII files from the coupler, and stored them onto disc for later retrieval. In retrospect this was less than ideal as the number of *ABORTS* when using the hospital trolley phone, and the sheer expense often drove me up the wall! I would have been better off waiting until I got home for one of my rest periods, and dumped the contents of the Z88 directly into the 8256. This I was eventually forced to do, as the complaints from other patients regarding the telephone being tied-up for hours soon reached critical levels!

Most of the fish photographs were taken at The International Aquatic Centre, in Sheffield, and in Superpets, of Worksop. This time, *Argus Books* decided that my CAD graphics weren't going to be good enough, so I had to rough out the plan for each illustration and leave the artwork to Peter Holland. A shame really because I couldn't play with my new digitiser and mouse! And that's how TTFH was produced! Easy innit?

GENERAL INDEX

General Index

Notes

Notes

AQUARIUM

A NEW BREED OF MAGAZINE
For fishkeepers everywhere beginners and experts alike

STYLE & QUALITY
From an international team of writers providing exclusive coverage for the growing number of fishkeeping enthusiasts

THE AQUATIC SHOWCASE
Here to fulfil the market's needs

PUBLISHED MONTHLY

AT *ONLY* £1.75

ORDER NOW FROM YOUR NEWSAGENT EVERY MONTH

If you would like to subscribe to Aquarium, your remittance and delivery details should be sent to:

SUBSCRIPTION DEPARTMENT (CG/91), ARGUS SPECIALIST PUBLICATIONS, ARGUS HOUSE, BOUNDARY WAY, HEMEL HEMPSTEAD, HERTS. HP2 7ST

U.K. £21.00 POST FREE	STERLING OVERSEAS £34.50
EUROPE £31.50	US DOLLARS OVERSEAS $63